# Project Cost Control *in Action*

Second edition

# Project Cost Control
## *in Action*

**Second edition**

O. P. Kharbanda
E. A. Stallworthy
L. F. Williams

Gower Technical Press

First published 1980

Second edition published 1987 by Gower Technical Press Limited
Gower House, Croft Road, Aldershot, Hampshire GU11 3HR, England

**British Library Cataloguing in Publication Data**

Kharbanda, O. P.
　　Project cost control in action. — 2nd ed.
　　1. Chemical plants — Design and
　　construction — Cost control 2. Industrial
　　project management
　　I. Title　II. Stallworthy, E. A.
　　III. Williams, L. F.
　　660.2′8′0681　　　TH4524

　　ISBN 0–291–39742–5

Printed in Great Britain by
The University Press, Cambridge

# Contents

# Illustrations

# Foreword

Traditionally, the most significant skills in the whole process which leads to the creation of new process plants have been regarded as those of the design engineers. The complexities of process and plant design require a high level of chemical engineering knowledge and experience, backed up by similar professional competence in the associated civil, mechanical and electrical work. On the other hand, comparable recognition has not been accorded to the other skills needed for the complementary, but no less essential, activities of project management. This situation has been reflected in the education and training deemed adequate for engineers entering the fields of process plant design and construction – indeed it has probably been a significant reason for it.

Various developments and changes have been taking place in recent years which, while not detracting in any way from the necessity to master the increasing complexities of the design and engineering aspects of a project, have led to a better understanding of the need also for a corresponding high level of skills, training, experience and know-how in project management, in order to complete a project successfully. One has only to examine the reasons why some process plant projects have resulted in severe financial losses to realise that poor project management is more often to blame than poor engineering design.

Project cost control is a vital part of project management. Without effective cost control there cannot be effective management. Too often, in paying lip service to cost *control*, all that is actually achieved is cost *monitoring*. It is the difference between an active, forward looking dynamic approach and a passive backward looking one.

The literature on project cost control is growing rapidly and gives the impression that the subject is one of considerable complexity and sophistication, involving extensive computerisation and data processing, but not much else. Many large process plant contractors and owners have developed their own cost control systems and practices, adapted to their particular requirements. To the comparative newcomer, whether an engineer just joining a contractor or owner organisation, or a small owner company itself, only infrequently concerned with new projects, the art of actually *doing* effective cost control, rather than just applying the techniques available, often remains obscure until learned painfully by experience. Project cost control is a prime example of the potential gap between theory and successful practice.

It is here that the real value of this book lies. Effective cost control is so much more than just the application of sophisticated techniques. The authors have broken new ground by concentrating largely on the *practice* of cost control in a most down-to-earth and informative way. In doing so, they have drawn on the wealth of their collective experience and the result is a very readable book packed with useful practical advice. Their general philosophy of 'keeping it simple' is at the heart of effective cost control, and indeed of project management as a whole. Decisions are after all made by people, but the human brain is not very good at weighing up large amounts of often conflicting data and factors of varying relevance and importance. Keeping it simple, by sticking to essentials only, paves the way for clear and timely decisions which are the key to successful project management.

This book should be essential reading for anyone involved directly or indirectly with project cost control. Its know-how and wisdom, distilled from the authors' wide experience, should provide food for thought for even the most experienced cost control engineer and project manager. It is also to be recommended as a textbook for students now that the study of engineering management is becoming a properly established part of engineering courses, as it offers a real insight into this important area of project management.

Professor D. H. Allen, F.I.Chem.E.
Department of Management Science
and Technology Studies
University of Stirling
Stirling
Scotland

# Preface to 2nd edition

This book was first published in 1980 and reprinted in 1983. We and our publishers are very pleased at the splendid response to our very first East-West collaborative effort – it certainly disproves the saying ascribed to Rudyard Kipling:

> East is East and West is West
> And never the twain shall meet

For this second edition we have reviewed and revised the text throughout. Chapter 10, dealing with computers, has been completely rewritten and the necessity for this is a reflection of the very rapid development that has been taking place in this particular field.

We introduce you to project cost control by pointing out that it is as old as history and we doubt whether over the millennia its basic principles have changed that much. Then and now projects have overrun in terms of time and cost, but at the same time many are completed on time and within budget. What we cannot assess, much as we would like to, is the extent to which there has been any improvement in project cost control *as practised* over the years since our book was first published and what contribution it has made.

O. P. Kharbanda
E. A. Stallworthy
L. F. Williams

December 1986

# Preface to 1st edition

This is perhaps the very first book to deal exclusively with the cost control of process plant investment projects. We use the term 'process plant' in the widest sense, seeking to embrace not only the plants we find in the petrochemical, chemical, petroleum and gas industries, but also plants used for the manufacture of cement, glass, plastics, paper, sugar, synthetic fibres, foods and beverages, pharmaceuticals, the production of power (including nuclear plants), and metallurgical plants, such as are used for the refining of steel, copper, aluminium and other metals.

Project cost control is a vital subject, since success in the building of a process plant depends, above all else, upon effective cost control. In fact, the phrase has been coined: 'Cost control *is* project management' (King 1968). Yet, despite its importance, it is still a very neglected subject, project cost control being preached far more than it is practised. So we have aimed at a simple but practical approach to the subject: a 'do it yourself' text.

Project cost can get out of hand very easily indeed. No great effort is needed for that! Cost overruns arising from time overruns and other lapses are commonplace. The overrun can well be so serious as to prove fatal not only to the project, but also to the contractor or owner involved. Two examples, dealt with in some detail in Chapter 5, will suffice. A major British contractor in the petrochemical field, faced with a substantial cost overrun on a petroleum refinery project on *his home ground* had a severe balance sheet problem, which resulted in a major reorganisation of the company. In another case, with a much larger project for LNG (Liquid natural gas) a major American contractor was actually 'wiped out', and that after several decades of profitable construction projects around the world. The crash of giants such as

Lockheed and Rolls-Royce in 1971 can be traced quite simply to a poor cost estimate on a *single* project and even poorer, or perhaps more properly, *no* cost control. This resulted in fantastic overruns of 300 to 400 per cent! So cost control is undoubtedly a subject full of potential, and of real significance to all who propose to own, design or build process plants.

The cost of the projects referred to above was in the multi-million pound range, so their failure had wide publicity, but size has nothing to do with it. Small plants can go just as wildly astray as the one that reaches the headlines, and that is just as tragic for everyone involved.

But let us be positive. Effective and meaningful project cost control must begin even before the design stage and is maintained by proper and scientific cost estimation and data analysis, even though estimating is still as much an art as a science. A project which starts with an incorrect estimate of either time (project duration) or money is doomed. Bad estimating in these areas will negate the most painstaking efforts at cost control during design and construction. Attempts to save money on the estimating and cost control effort in the early stages of a project will only give renewed force to the old adage: 'Penny wise, pound foolish'. In some rare cases a ridiculously low cost estimate may well have been a blessing in disguise. A realistic estimate of cost for the Sydney Opera House or the Concorde plane would without doubt have led to these projects being abandoned before they started, but they *must* remain an exception.

We will say it once again: this subject is vital and yet badly neglected. Why? Project cost control is *not* easy. It calls for conscientious and consistent effort from the very beginning to the bitter end: from the day the project is conceived to the day the last invoice is cleared and paid. Something easier said than done. With most of the so-called cost *control* procedures, the costs that are being incurred are carefully recorded, but *not* controlled. Recording is of course vital to control, but if that is *all* that is being done, those running the project – the project management team – are in fact blind and helpless, although they may have masses of cost information. Effective project cost control involves both reporting project status a few days after the event, and then interpreting the 'trends'. This, if well done, results in what we call 'early warning signals', to which a whole chapter has been devoted. Computers and sophisticated networks can help, but prompt input and simple output, whether manual or mechanised, remains the essence of proper project cost control.

In harmony with this basic concept, we have emphasised

throughout the simple approach: the use of simple means to attain the desired end. To help you remember this basic principle, we exhort you to *kiss* your project – 'keep it *stupid* simple'. Or, if you will not listen, we might well be tempted to say: 'keep it simple, *stupid*'! It is indeed our feeling that too much reliance can be placed on the computerised paper flow, which will bring a high degree of complexity if one is not very careful. Hence our chapter: 'Simple *is* beautiful'.

As we said earlier, our aim has been to provide a simple 'do it yourself' text. It has worked for us, so it can also work for you.

O. P. Kharbanda
E. A. Stallworthy
L. F. Williams

October 1979

# Acknowledgements

The last thing that we must do as authors of this work is to pay tribute to one another, but we have to acknowledge that our spread of interest, background and location, whilst it has added to the difficulties of bringing this book together, has nevertheless added substantially to its scope and flavour and, we hope, to its usefulness.

We must also acknowledge our dependence upon the continuous flow of informative papers, articles and the like that are published in the technical journals and the transactions of the various associations, national and international, who are concerned with the several key aspects of an investment project: project cost estimating, cost control and project management. All this data is copyright, but we read it and then apply it where relevant to improve our technical competence. After all, that is why it was published. For instance, the International Cost Engineering Council (ICEC) has as its declared basic objective the advancement of cost engineering internationally. This they seek to achieve by setting up a forum for the exchange of ideas. But we are left with the fact that some of our ideas about project cost control are not originally our own. Having assimilated them, however, and made them our own, we do not always remember where we first read about it. So if, dear reader, you find that one of your own ideas has been presented by us without an acknowledgement please take it as a great compliment: your concept was so good that it has become a part of the 'cost engineering folklore'!

The first edition of this book included a bibliography, but with this second edition we have chosen to provide only directly relevant references at the end of each chapter. The literature on project management, project cost control and related subjects is expanding so quickly that we thought a bibliography could rapidly become irrelevant. Further, it is now possible to locate relevant books, articles and papers very quickly via the computerised index systems now available at most major libraries, and abstracts can be printed out with ease. Then there are full text on-line information services such as *Nexis*, which stores in its data base the full text of over two hundred daily, weekly and monthly publications, newspapers, magazines, newsletters and the like – worldwide.

We must still count librarians amongst our best friends, particularly those looking after the libraries of the American Library, the British Council, the Industrial Credit and Investment Corporation of India, the Indian Institute of Technology, the National Institute of Bank Management, the Tata Energy Research Institute and the University of Bombay, all at Bombay, together with the librarians at the British Institute of Management, the London Business Library, the Science Reference Library, the Aston University (Birmingham) Library in the UK and last, but not least, the Library of Congress and the US AID Agency Library, both in Washington (DC), the New York Public Library and the Fairleigh Dickinson University Library at Rutherford, NJ, in the USA. Our grateful thanks go to them and their staff for their labour of love in helping us to locate the data we were looking for.

In the old days we used to go to the library 'just for browsing', but no longer. Now you ask the computer to cite references to the specific subject, such as project cost control, scan the printout and then select the desired articles and call them up for a full printout. With the massive and wide-ranging information systems available today, a bibliography seemed to us superfluous. So if our readers wish to follow up any particular aspect of the various subjects we have dealt with, this seems to be the road to follow.

O. P. Kharbanda
E. A. Stallworthy
L. F. Williams

December 1986

# Part One
# FUNDAMENTAL PRINCIPLES

# 1 Basic concepts

We all know that a business can only survive if it makes a profit. There is nothing one can do to *guarantee* that a profit is going to be made, but certain factors can go a long way towards making a profit a near certainty. Foremost among these factors is cost control. Cost control should be exercised whilst a project is being built and whilst it is being operated. We are going to be concerned with the function of cost control whilst a facility is being built, and the contribution good cost control makes to the eventual success of a construction project is all the justification we need for writing this book. We are presenting a well detailed and authenticated text – perhaps the first of its kind – dealing exclusively with the cost control of process plant projects. The principles enunciated, together with the detailed practices and procedures that are outlined as we go along, should however be found to be of general application, and in no way restricted to the building of process plants. It is advantageous to describe the various procedures and practices in specific terms, in order to be intelligible, but what we have set out as a proposed course of action can readily be 'tailored' to satisfy other parallel types of construction work.

**As old as history**

Both project cost estimating and project cost control are as old as history. It could hardly be otherwise. The Bible takes us back 2,000 years in history, mentioning the function of project cost control quite explicitly. We read:

> For which of you, intending to build a tower, sitteth not down first, and counteth the cost, whether he has sufficient to finish it?
>
> *(Luke 14:28, The Holy Bible, King James version)*

3

Notice that not only cost control, but also budgeting and resource planning are implied!

One of the earliest recorded examples of cost control, or cost effectiveness, and patently the result of value analysis, all of which subjects we are going to deal with in their turn, takes us back to the beginning of the eleventh century. The story relates to the rebuilding of a palace which had been destroyed by fire (1). The palace was located in the Chinese capital city Pientu (now Kai Feng, in Honan province), during the Sung dynasty. This rebuilding project was a tremendous task, involving the transport of all the building materials over a considerable distance. It would have required an enormous manpower force over a period of several years. The chief engineer for the project, a certain Ting Wei, devised an ingenious method to reduce his costs: dig a ditch from the worksite along the wide street that led to the Pien river outside the city. Then boats bringing in the building materials could sail right along to berth at the jobsite. As the work neared completion, the ditch was filled in with materials, such as earth, left over from the project, and the ditch or canal became a street once again.

We exercise cost control to avoid cost overruns, and even those are nothing new, if that is any comfort to us in today's context! Shortly after the beginning of the Christian era, the rulers in Rome decided to build an aqueduct for the town of Troas in Asia Minor (now the town of Toras, in Turkey). The budget was about £100,000 (2). The overrun was £100,000, or one hundred per cent. The overrun was covered by the generosity of the wealthy Julius Atticus. Today, it would be the taxpayer who would have to foot the bill! To take an example in our own day, the Sydney Opera House, in Australia, was finally completed some ten years late, at a cost several times the original estimate of $A 7.2 million (3).

Thus, the basic concepts of cost control are nothing new. But cost control today is more vital, more necessary than ever before because of the sheer size and complexity of modern projects and the risks thereby involved. If cost control, led in the first instance by cost monitoring, the prime task of the cost engineer, is not given its proper place in project management, then the owner is likely to be putting not only the project, but perhaps even his whole business at risk. We have now introduced the cost engineer, as the specialist who devotes himself to project cost control. Cost control is now one of the most important aspects of *cost engineering*, a relatively new discipline, but one that is already well rooted and widely recognised. Cost engineering is defined in the Constitution of the *American Association of Cost Engineers* as:

Cost Engineering – That area of engineering principles where engineering judgement and experience are utilised in the application of scientific principles and techniques to problems of cost estimation, cost control, business planning and management science.

So far, cost control and the cost engineer: What is the scope of his interest, so far as this book is concerned? This brings us to the need to answer the question: what is the process plant industry?

**The process plant industry**

The process plant industry covers not only the conventional chemical industry, but also allied process industries such as:

Cement, glass, plastic, paper, sugar, synthetic fibre
    manufacture
Food and beverage industries
Metals manufacture
Petroleum and gas processing
Power generation (from fossil fuels or nuclear power)

The common denominator in all such industry is the fact that the plant and equipment used in the process of manufacture have a substantial degree of similarity. This means that the various techniques used in the design, supply and construction of such plants are also broadly similar. In all cases there is a chemical or a physical change, or both. The operations used to achieve this in these industries can be broadly classified as:

Unit Operations, and Unit Processes

and these are associated respectively with:

Physical change, and Chemical change

This, in fact, was the basis and scope of the then new discipline of chemical engineering when it was first introduced as a separate exercise around the turn of the present century.

The type of equipment that is used in the process industries is generally similar. Apart from what we might call standard items, such as pumps, compressors, pipe and pipe fittings, electrical switchgear and instruments, the rest of the plant is usually 'custom built' for the specific project. Typical plant items in this category are heat exchangers and pressure vessels. These are generally designed and built on a 'one off' basis, designed for the particular service.

Such equipment, except perhaps for the smaller tanks, is rarely 'off the shelf' and is manufactured in a general jobbing engineering workshop with facilities for cutting, rolling, welding and machining of metals. In some cases, additional facilities such as specialised welding equipment and stress relieving ovens are also required. But this specialised process equipment can be categorised and its cost analysed, and the cost analysis of widely differing process plants still has a large degree of similarity. This facilitates the transfer of experience and know-how from one type of plant to another, and provides the basis for the engineering contractor offering his expertise over the whole range of process plants.

The process industry is noted for rapid change. It has been estimated that of the wide range of chemicals manufactured and in common use today, nearly half were not in commercial production less than twenty years ago. In the next five years or so, more than 20 per cent of total chemical sales are likely to come from new products, only now beginning to come on the market. At the same time the basic chemical products, such as sulphuric acid and the chlor-alkalis, still continue to hold their own. In fact, the caustic soda cum chlorine industry is itself, although an 'old timer', a unique example of the rapid change that is possible in the process industries. Initially caustic soda was the main product and chlorine a by-product whose disposal and/or use presented quite serious problems to the manufacturer. Then the requirement for chlorine increased so rapidly that the demand for chlorine far outstripped its supply. Thus, today, chlorine is considered to be the main product and it is caustic soda that is the by-product, presenting problems in disposal.

The process industry in general is also one of the fastest growing industries, worldwide, although this has now slowed down following the 'oil crisis' of 1973. Its annual growth rate has generally been much faster, and often as much as twice as fast, as the growth rate for manufacturing in general.

Another important feature of the process industry is that it is capital intensive, and not therefore a large employer of labour. Relative figures naturally vary from country to country, but typical national relationships for the process industry, as a percentage of the total product cost to the customer, are:

|            |     |
|------------|-----|
| Investment | 10% |
| Sales      | 15% |
| Workforce  | 5%  |

Of the workforce, more than half are engaged in administration, sales, research and other non-production (*not* non-productive) functions. This latter section, called the 'service sector', has been increasing rapidly at the cost (in numbers) of the manufacturing sector. This is part of the so-called transformation from an industrial to an information society. This change, now well on the way, is expected to be as profound as the shift from an agricultural society to an industrial society (4). Let us never forget that the process industry is big business indeed. The annual investment, worldwide, is probably well over £100 billion, of which perhaps a quarter is serviced by some two dozen UK-based international contractors.

On this background, project cost control is a must. In fact, instead of asking whether cost control in such an industry is really necessary, one might better ask: 'Can we afford not to?' As will be shown later, in Chapter 2, the cost control function can save up to five per cent of project cost. And the extra cost of project cost control? Perhaps 0.2 per cent – certainly not more. Isn't it worth it?

## Fixed capital cost

We are concerning ourselves in this book with cost control in relation to the *fixed* capital investment in a manufacturing facility: our project. The total capital investment in a project can well comprise: fixed capital – 85 per cent; working capital – 15 per cent of the total investment, exclusive of any investment in land. The percentages given above are indicative only, and can vary widely from case to case. The major components in the fixed capital cost of a project are:

Hardware:   Process equipment
General equipment
Piping, instrumentation
Electrical equipment
Insulation and painting

Land development and buildings

Software:   Engineering
Construction
Commissioning

The cost of production of the product when the plant is finished will contain a number of components, namely:

Raw material costs
Depreciation

Labour costs, utility costs
Maintenance costs
Overhead costs

Of all these, it is the cost of depreciation that is a direct function of the initial capital cost of the project. Depreciation costs as charged to the cost of a product will vary from case to case, but since all process plants are capital intensive, it will always be a significant proportion of total product cost. The importance of exercising cost control on the initial investment in the project therefore extends far beyond the initial investment as such. It can make or mar the ability to sell the products from the plant at a profit.

However, to be successful, project cost control must start long before construction starts in the field. Decisions taken at the process design and engineering stages can quite possibly 'seal the fate' of a project so far as cost is concerned, for better or for worse. A faulty design results not only in high capital cost, but also in high operating costs. This theme is enlarged upon later in this chapter when we discuss 'the role of the capital estimate'. In such cases a project may well be 'doomed' before it even starts. However, in the present text, we look no further than the fixed capital cost, and when we refer to capital cost from now on that is what it will always mean.

**Where do we begin?**

Management is concerned not only with the operation of existing plant installations, but also with the construction of extensions to those installations, and probably, from time to time, with the setting up of completely new installations. They have to be concerned not only with the economic operation of existing assets, but also with the economic construction of new assets. The purpose of this book is to set out a method of approach whereby all the more common mistakes can be avoided. Further, an approach to cost control is outlined that will ensure, if followed, that the plant is eventually built within the estimate.

There are many firms who have, perhaps, only one major extension in ten years. This could well mean that the managerial staff are confronted with the problem, when it arises, for the very first time. There is then no previous experience to draw upon and such a venture would be, for them, a complete 'leap in the dark'. It needs little imagination to realise how painful *that* could be! The steps they will have to take are illustrated in Figure 1.1, which shows

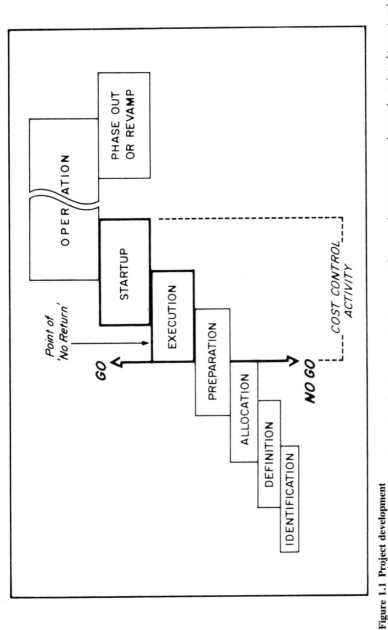

**Figure 1.1  Project development**
This diagram highlights the basic steps in project development. As time passes the commitment grows, and once the point of 'no return' is reached it costs more to cancel than to complete.

the sequence of events involved in the development of a new manufacturing facility, whatever its size. We have experimental work, pilot plant studies and market research leading up to the point in time when the project is approved and the decision is made to build the facility. The plan is laid, the future is forecast, a profit is envisaged. It is at this point, so often, that darkness begins to close in. The plant has to be designed and constructed and the plan can only be a success if the plant is actually built within the estimated cost and time. This is where our story starts. This is where the *action* begins and project cost control, integrated into project management, plays its part. Someone has to play the role, fulfil the function, of the project cost control engineer. He is the one, and really the only one, who can truly 'lighten our darkness'. Dependent upon the size of project, he can be one person or a team. Indeed, since we envisage taking this 'leap in the dark' with someone who, we hope, has a light – the managing contractor – he is likely to provide the cost control team, and the owner will have one engineer or a very small group watching his interests in the cost control sphere.

To see it from another angle, Figure 1.2 gives 'we are here' as our starting point, and the action, which has two key streams, project cost control and project planning, should give us light as we proceed from Chapters 1 to 14 of this book. Figure 1.3 begins from the same point ('we are here') and represents the path we have to follow diagrammatically. It gives some idea as to the relationship between the two major areas of effort and also sets it on a time scale. This is indeed the time scale with which we are involved these days with a project of any substance. It will be a small project indeed that can move from board authorisation to plant commissioning in less than two and a half years.

### The capital budget and cost control

When a project is approved, it will become part of the capital budget of the company concerned, whom we call, throughout this book, the *owner*. The owner's finance director will be responsible for the control of this budget item, together with all the rest of the budget, right from the beginning. The project could be financed in a variety of ways. The funding could be internal or external, but in either event, as costs accrue, it is the finance department who would be responsible for ensuring that adequate funds are available. That department should also take care that allowances and grants are properly processed, so that all the appropriate fiscal benefits to the

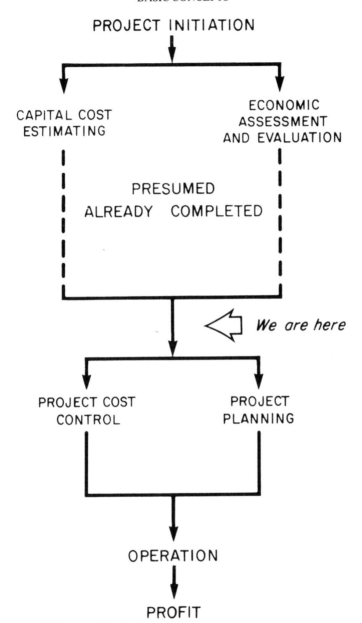

**Figure 1.2 The area of 'action'**
Our work begins when the decision has been taken to proceed. The project cost control and planning work in parallel until the plant is ready for startup. This is discussed in detail in Chapter 9: see Figure 9.1.

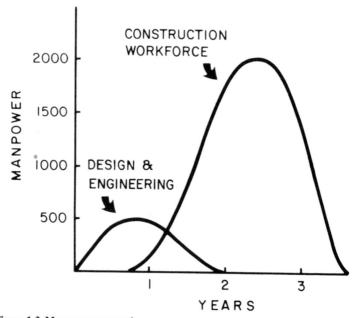

**Figure 1.3 Manpower versus time**
With effective planning, design and engineering should be well in hand when work starts in the field. With a typical project, design and engineering might be a million manhours and direct labour in the field five to six million manhours, but this latter figure is very dependent on productivity in the particular country where the plant is being built.

company are secured. These financial aspects we consider to be outside the province of project cost control as such. Those concerned with project cost control need to be familiar with such matters, since they have to be very clear as to the capital sum they are proposing to monitor, but the detailed administration of those funds in their totality belongs to the financial function.

The scope of project cost control should be limited to the 'gross' direct estimated cost of the investment, exclusive of any interest charges that may be incurred on borrowed money. Similarly, monies recovered by way of development grants and monies paid by way of taxes should all be excluded from the estimate and treated separately. The estimate should, however, be the 'final cost' of the investment, in the sense that escalation should be included, to cover rising costs over the life of the project. The usual technique is to book costs of this nature, as they are incurred, to 'work in progress' (WIP). Then, at a later stage, the value of WIP, or parts thereof, are transferred by the accountant to the capital asset account. In the books of the company, however, the actual outlay may be more or less than this, depending upon the costs for instance of borrowing as compared with the benefits received by way of grants. The cost control engineer, therefore, can look to the finance department for a record of 'defrayed expenditure', and 'work in progress', but for the rest he should have his own records and administrative procedures.

## Cost analysis

The basic concept of cost analysis is well known and the average company will employ cost analysis both in relation to its production activities and its capital assets. The governing factor determining the nature of the analysis made, particularly in relation to capital assets, is usually the requirement of the accountant. This is why the listing of the several groups into which such costs are divided is generally referred as a 'code of account'! However, the ideal system of cost coding will be one that can be used at all stages in the construction of a project. This subject is discussed at length in Chapter 6, and a typical 'code of accounts' is included as Appendix B. However, the underlying principle is that the system adopted in the estimate for the identification of the plant and equipment, is employed on the drawings, used to code the requisitions, incorporated in the order number of the order based on that requisition, and so finally appears on the invoice, to identify the final home of the cost incurred. This integration of the coding system adopted in the estimate at the beginning, and employed in all the various administrative procedures through to final accounting, is not only an estimating 'tool': it is also a basic system for the provision to management of information for the purposes of control.

A variety of systems can be adopted that will achieve this end, and they are, as we have said, discussed in detail later. Meanwhile, let us just emphasise that this is indeed a 'basic concept', fundamental to the ultimate successful completion of the project in terms of cost. It is a tool which both the finance department and the project cost control engineer can use to great effect.

Once the project is authorised, then the project cost control engineer, or whoever assumes that function in the administrative system set up by the owner in order to see the project through, will be involved in reviewing and revising from time to time the estimates of capital cost, particularly with reference to the influence of time on the estimate. He will have to ensure that all the data relevant to project cost flows to him and through him, and a key part of his function is to present management with the analysed cost information to enable them to know the status of the project in terms of cost and then take any necessary action. It will be seen therefore that whilst everyone uses the term 'cost control engineer', his real function is one of *monitoring*, not *control*. Management should seek to control, using the information he provides.

## The role of the capital cost estimate

The economic viability of a project will be assessed at intervals during its development both before and after the project has been approved. At each reassessment a revised estimate will be made of the fixed capital estimate in plant and buildings: an estimate referred to as the *capital cost estimate*. Throughout the life of the project the capital cost estimate serves as the standard of reference, the basis for comparison, turning eventually into the completed cost of the project. It is *the* yardstick and the basic point of reference for project cost control.

However, this is not the only channel along which money will be invested in the project. Another possible fixed investment is land, and money will also be tied up in working capital. Working capital is the term used to cover the cost of the purchase of raw materials, materials in process, stocks of finished products and other cash requirements that may arise from time to time. It is very dependent, so far as its magnitude is concerned, on the manner in which the plant is operated and its products disposed of.

Fixed costs are, to a large extent, dependent upon the capital that has been invested in plant and buildings. Total operating costs and production costs are always subject to the most intense scrutiny. Every effort is made to minimise such costs, but there is little that can be done with respect to the fixed costs, a function of the plant and building investment, *after* that investment has been made. There is much that can be done, however, to prevent unnecessary fixed capital costs being incurred *during* project execution. The basic requirement for such preventive measures is *control*, and this control is the subject of this book. Practical and effective control of the capital cost is relevant throughout the life of the project, and still needs to be exercised after the plant has been physically completed and is being commissioned. Such control must be carried on to the bitter end: till the very last payment has been made.

The investment in plant and buildings is by far the greater part of the total investment made in any project and much of the other investment, in particular the working capital, is dependent to a degree on the design of the plant and buildings. Lower investment in fixed capital usually results in a lower investment in working capital, but not necessarily in lower operating or maintenance costs. This fixed capital element is not only the largest single element in the total investment but also the most important element, since once the commitment has been made, there is no going back. Within limits, land can be sold and working capital can be adjusted, but the plant and often the buildings have been designed for one end only. Indeed, even if it becomes apparent as the project develops, that the expenditure is going to be substantially greater than was first envisaged, it can be extremely difficult to avoid that extra expenditure. If the money is not spent, there is the very real danger that one is left with a partly completed installation, of no real value to anybody. This possibility emphasises the vital importance of adequate cost control, so that once the decision has been taken to create the asset, there can also be a confident anticipation that it will not cost more than was envisaged when that decision was made.

Having just stressed that serious cost overruns lead to almost unavoidable overexpenditure, we may have created the impression that it is always better to complete the project no matter what. This really should not be so. In retrospect, some of the project disasters described and analysed by us in the past (3) could have been less of a disaster had they been abandoned earlier. For instance, in the case of the supersonic plane Concorde it has been said in retrospect that it would have been cheaper to abandon it at almost any stage. The 'cost of failure', it was said, is 'more than the price of success'. But what is 'success' in such a context? In the case of serious prospective overrun, the project manager should do much more than just review the work to be done, seeking to cut cost. The project should be completely reassessed and its profitability reappraised. If it is no longer profitable, it should be abandoned, whatever the current investment. But this rarely happens. Davis, for instance, comments that all too often a plant that is an inevitable 'loss maker' is still completed. Such a situation called for hard decisions, but the number of bad projects that reach the operational stage is continuing evidence that many managers baulk at such decisions (5).

## Profile of a typical project

Process plant projects are steadily getting bigger, and certainly getting ever more complex. They are built bigger to achieve the economies of scale, and become more complex because of the urgent necessity to minimise operating, and particularly labour costs. This means that the stakes are growing all the time and there is ever more to gain or lose by completing a project on time, and within the budget. Let it 'drift' and tragedy can result. Cost control is therefore a vital ingredient for the 'health' of any and every project.

| ANALYSIS OF A TYPICAL PROJECT | | |
|---|---|---|
| | Total Cost % | Overhead & Profit included % |
| Initial costs: | 1.5 | |
| Design and engineering: | 7.0 | 1.0 |
| Project management & site supervision | 4.5 | 1.0 |
| Plant, equipment & subcontracts: | 35.0 | 10.0 |
| Construction & civil engineering: | 20.0 | 2.0 |
| Commissioning: | 3.0 | 1.0 |
| Shipping & insurance: | 6.0 | 1.0 |
| | 77.0 | 16.0* |
| Contingency: | 14.0* | |
| | 91.0 | |
| Finance, taxes & guarantees: | 9.0 | |
| | 100.0 | |

*These two items total 30%, and are the supplier's gross margin of 50% of the net cost of 61 (77 less 16) % of total project cost.

**Figure 1.4  Cost makeup of a typical project**
Cost analysis of a process plant project costing some £100 million.

Projects come in all sizes. Minor extensions could cost £10,000, a major international project from £5 to £10 billion! This question of size is discussed at some length in Chapter 13, but one thing to remember is that our concepts as to 'size' are continually changing. Ten years ago a £100 million project was rarely heard of: today such a project is becoming commonplace. But what are we talking about? In Figure 1.4 we give the typical makeup of a £100 million project. The greatest challenge to the successful completion of such a project lies in the need for the proper planning, coordination and motivation of the large numbers of people involved.

Let us try to get a 'feel' for what we are going to talk about by looking at a £100 million petrochemical complex built in the United Kingdom The volumes of materials and men involved are detailed in

A £100 MILLION PETROCHEMICAL COMPLEX

| | | | |
|---|---|---|---|
| Location: | United Kingdom | | |
| Engineering: | Manhours | — | 500,000 |
| | Flowsheets | — | 1500 |
| | Drawings | — | 2800 |
| | Suppliers | — | 1500 |
| Materials: | Structural steel | — | 2000 tons |
| | Piping | — | 240 Km. |
| | Buildings | — | 20 |
| | Tanks & spheres | — | 76 |
| | Pumps | — | 193 |
| | Weighbridges | — | 8 |
| | Electric substations | — | 5 |
| Construction: | Peak workforce | — | 2000 |
| | Concrete | — | 33000 m$^3$ |
| | Cabling | — | 4.5 Km. |
| | Roads | — | 13 Km. |
| | Railways | — | 5 Km. |
| | Perimeter fence | — | 8 Km. |
| | Workshops | — | 5 |

**Figure 1.5 Resources needed for a major complex**
This table illustrates the resources required in men and materials for a £100 million petrochemicals complex (1986 price levels).

Figure 1.5. The exact numbers and volumes of material will vary with the type of project, but these are indicative. Of course, all this effort is spread over time and the relation between manpower and time with such a typical project is given in Figure 1.3 (6). The manpower at peak is roughly twice the average manpower and this poses one of the major problems in efficient construction. Manpower on site has to be built up from zero to the peak, and then brought back to zero in relation to the workload. A major factor in cost control is to match the workforce with the workload. This demands careful and detailed scheduling of the materials coming to the site: usually the prime responsibility of a procurement department.

When the site is offshore the logistics become even more complicated. We have said often enough (although we did not invent the saying) that 'project cost control *is* project management'. The growing success in controlling the costs of offshore projects is undoubtedly due in part to the growing body of experience in the cost control of such projects. The *Estimating Check List for Offshore Projects* is now available, the first book of its type ever produced (7). It provides an 'aide memoire' for estimators and cost engineers, that they may check that all cost items and cost considerations have been included in an estimate for an offshore development.

A typical offshore development project is likely to contain all, or most, of the following elements:

> Platforms
> Drilling rigs
> Product loading systems
> Pipelines
> Sub-sea systems

The total investment for a major offshore platform with all the related facilities and including the initial exploration costs, is often in excess of £1 billion. Within the term 'platform', as above, will come what is called the 'topsides' and the related 'support structure'. We presented earlier (Figure 1.4) the cost profile for a typical process plant. The cost profile for typical topsides facilities will be rather different and the cost analysis is also different, as below:

|   |   | % |
|---|---|---|
| A | Equipment and materials: | 17.00 |
| B | Yard fabrication: | 23.00 |
| C | Load out and installation: | 14.00 |
| D | Hook up and commissioning: | 30.00 |
| E | Project management and engineering: | 16.00 |
|   | Total: | 100.00 |

These relationships are currently (1986) typical where a project is handled by a managing contractor. They completely exclude the costs of the main support structure and the owner's executive, project management and engineering costs. The normal approach is for the owner, usually a major oil company or a group of such companies, to form his own management team working with the project team established by the managing contractor. A platform installation can cost in excess of £300 million, so it is a major project. However, the relationships set out above can change, since there is an ongoing effort to reduce the amount of work done offshore: items C and D above. For instance, three very similar platforms have been built in connection with the development of the Statfjord field in the Norwegian area of the North Sea. It was said of the Statfjord 'B' platform, built by Norwegian contractors for Mobil Exploration Norway Inc., that at towout the topsides were 85 per cent complete. But when Statfjord 'C' was towed out it was said to be 95 per cent complete. The reason? To quote: 'Talk to anyone involved in Statfjord C about the reasons for its success and the same phrase keeps recurring: the learning curve' (8).

It is indeed true that offshore work has now reached a high degree of sophistication as was illustrated by the material provided for a one day seminar on 'Cost Engineering Offshore' offered by the Association of Cost Engineers in March 1985. One feature of many of these projects is that the client takes up the role of project manager, rather than handing over to a managing contractor, so we have a paper on 'Client Project Execution' (9). The presentation of the cost control aspects is delightful in its simplicity, despite the complexity of the projects for which it is designed. When discussing changes in scope – inevitable in any project, as we shall later discuss in detail – we meet the rule: no change without full evaluation and proper authorisation. We hope that it is *always* obeyed!

### An example from the North Sea

With this in mind, let us now look at the Brae Field, situated some 130 miles offshore from the coast of Scotland. Marathon Oil UK Ltd have the task of developing the Brae Field on behalf of seven other Co-Venturers, as they are called, with Marathon having the biggest single share in the development (38 per cent). Britoil PLC have the next largest interest: 20 per cent. Britoil have assumed responsibility for the oil and gas exploration and production interests of the state owned British National Oil Corporation and are now an independent private sector company.

Our attention was first drawn to this particular North Sea development by a headline: 'Brae Triumph' (10). Once we began to look, we found other articles with equally significant headlines, such as 'Brae: on time, on budget, on stream'. Here, very evidently, we have a successful project. The project now completed – it came on stream in July 1983 – is what is known as Brae 'A' Production Platform, in the South Brae field, and it is now being followed by the Brae 'B' Production Platform. The Brae 'A' Production Platform is a conventional eight-legged steel jacket with modular production facilities, standing in 111 metres of water, and supports topsides designed to handle 100,000 barrels per day (b/d) of crude oil, 12,000 b/d of NGL and 145 MMCFD of gas. Natural gas is used to fuel the 80,000 kW Power Generation Plant, that provides the electricity required to run the platform. The project has cost in total some US$2 billion, including the drilling of 36 wells.

This project is said to be the largest and most challenging undertaken by Marathon since the company was established nearly a hundred years ago. Despite the challenge presented by the hostile North Sea environment, the Brae project reached every milestone and met every successive deadline. Direct construction work in the North Sea started in 1982 and included:

- Installation of the massive 22,500-tonnes platform jacket.
- Driving all 36 of the jacket's piles, each 325 feet long, into the seafloor within 11 days, using the world's largest underwater hammers.
- Placement within 14 days of the topsides modules. The 34,000-tonnes topsides operating weight was among the heaviest deck loads supported by a steel structure anywhere in the world.

All in all, this work took 57 days, an impressively short time, taking advantage of the 1982 'weather window'. Meticulous planning contributed much to the success of this operation. 'Milestones' were set to monitor progress: a 'red flag' system gave early warning of schedule slippages: actual progress was scrutinised against planned progress: nothing novel. Just painstaking planning.

Then followed the platform hookup, a task calling for some five million manhours spread out over about 18 months. A workforce of some 4,000 was brought together for hookup and commissioning, at times with more than 1,900 of them out at the platform every day of the week, serving 12-hour shifts on a 14-days-on, 14-days-off basis. The work to be done included more than 30,000 tightly scheduled tasks and the completion of some 180,000 electrical and instrument connections. Thus we gain some appreciation of the scale of the work offshore. The platform, pictured during hookup, can be seen in Figure 1.6. Unfortunately, even an aerial photograph such as this hardly gives us an impression of the immensity of the project.

### Project management – the key to success

The secret of the success of the Brae Field project noted above has been ascribed by Marathon to their exercising direct control over

**Figure 1.6  Brae 'A' Platform**
This platform, located 155 miles north-east of Aberdeen on block 16/17a, is shown during hookup prior to it coming on stream. Also shown are two accommodation vessels, *Safe Felicia* (almost hidden) and *DB-100*. (Photograph by courtesy of Marathon Oil UK Ltd.)

every facet of design, engineering and construction. They decided at the outset to assemble the best possible team to run the project. Technical experts and people with long experience in offshore oil and gas projects were brought to their London offices from all over the company. The result was a collection of some of the most knowledgeable oilfield veterans to be found anywhere in the world. This group of managers, under the project director Mr. J. L. (Corky) Frank, in turn recruited and trained further engineers and specialists in the UK to fill out a project team that eventually totalled some 350 personnel. In addition, Marathon had a team of around 50 people permanently based in the offices of Matthew Hall Engineering, who were responsible for the design of the topsides facilities. Their design programme, which covered in all 14 modules, peaked at over 450 men, whilst the fabrication of the modules was spread across six yards, four in the UK and two in Spain. In all this, we see experience – previous experience in the same field – playing a key role. Matthew Hall Engineering, for instance, proudly advertise a series of eight 'North Sea epics now on release', of which Brae 'A' was the seventh.

What we wish to emphasise in relation to this project is that in spite of its magnitude and complexity everything was under control and those involved in the project *knew where they were going*! The task of the cost control engineer is to help his project manager to see where his project is going in terms of cost.

Yes, this is the lesson we will be emphasising continually and is the underlying theme of the whole of this book. There are two vital factors that must never be forgotten:

Simple controls applied Early

*not*

Sophisticated controls applied Late

One of the aspects of sophisticated controls is that they always *are* applied late: they are too complex to set up early. We feel so strongly about these two key aspects – simple and early – that two complete chapters, Chapters 8 and 9, are being devoted to the development of that particular theme. It will be shown that it is far, far better to act *early* on somewhat incomplete and inaccurate information than to act *late* on more precise information. The tools used to achieve this must be simple enough for the project team to have a 'firm grip' on the 'pulse' of the project: sometimes somewhat crudely referred to as a 'gut' feeling. The idea is to look out for the 'trends', as outlined in detail in Chapter 8 (Early warning signals) and thereby see where the project is heading in terms of cost and time. Action delayed until all the details are in is usually far too late to be effective.

## Cost cannot be controlled in isolation

Project cost control, or cost monitoring, whilst it elevates the word *cost*, has in fact three dimensions:

**Cost**
**Time**
**Quality**

These three factors are interrelated and interdependent. They can all be expressed in monetary terms. They constitute yet another of those 'eternal triangles', illustrated in Figure 1.7 (11). Shorter completion times and improvement in quality will inevitably lead to higher cost.

What, then, is to be our objective, seeing that we are being pulled three different ways? Our target can be defined as: Project completion in a reasonable time, at an economic cost, with adequate quality. This is, of necessity, a very generalised statement of a qualitative nature. However, for each and every project it has to be quantified. There is no escape from the series of decisions that have to be taken to achieve the appropriate compromise. Since the key resources, time and money, are both scarce and limited, one is inevitably driven to a compromise. You just cannot have the best of three worlds!

## It's a team effort

Cost is inevitably everybody's business, although some try to ignore it. All costs come back somewhere to 'people' and their activities. Costs are higher, or lower, according to the diligence and skill applied by those 'people': people with their strengths and their weaknesses and, above all, their attitudes. At the top of the tree, as it were, we have management. Management must have convictions: they must have faith in project cost control and trust it. Mere 'lip service' just will not do. There must be a complete commitment by management to the principles of cost control: a clear acknowledgement of its importance in the system of things. Then, and only then, can the project manager and his team be expected to apply and implement the cost control procedures, with the related techniques, such as those we are going to describe.

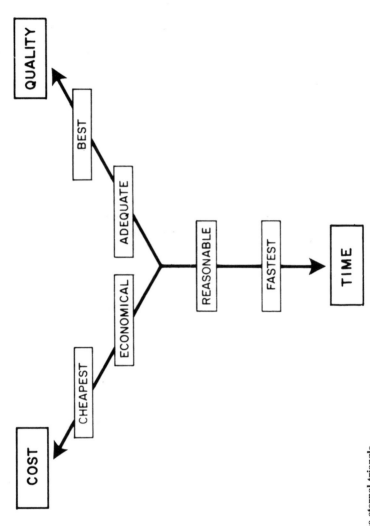

**Figure 1.7 The eternal triangle**
These three, cost, quality and time are essentially incompatible. The art is to maintain a proper balance between the three, so that quality is not sacrificed for either time or cost.

The role of the project manager in this is vital. He is the focal point for all decisions: all the data is directed to him. He remains one person, even in the most complex job with a workforce of thousands. Even then he *must* retain a 'feel' for the project as a whole. Even without the formal reports he will be able to say whether the project is going well or not. Reports will help him – help him considerably – particularly in giving him advance warning of the 'trend': whether his targets in terms of time and cost are going to be achieved or not. Such advance warning, early enough, will allow him to 'steer' the project along a course that will minimise, if not completely avoid, the potential damage.

The 'action', in relation to project execution and cost control, lies with the project team as a whole. Not only the construction team at site are involved, but also what are often called the 'home office' services, such as process design, the detailed engineering, procurement and expediting. The members of the team belong to various different disciplines and have very diverse functions. With their different backgrounds – procurement, accounting and engineering are all radically different in concept – communication is certainly not easy. Three different 'languages' – the jargon of their several trades – helps the confusion along.

But, nevertheless, if this problem is understood, and the appropriate effort made, then it can be overcome. One of us had the most satisfying experience of bringing accountants and engineers together, members of an internationally based engineering company, to spend time together developing a 'common language'. Our client counted the effort a success, and we ourselves even got paid for our efforts! The assignment: conversion of a 'cost centre' to a 'profit centre'.

All this but underlines the continuing difficulty that we have with communications. One of the major tasks of the project manager is to ensure quick and smooth communication among the members of his team, and between owner and contractor, where there are these two parties involved. The manner of its achievement is set out in Chapter 11 – Proper project management – so that all we need to say for now is that the key to success is to ensure that each member of the project team receives all the *necessary* information, but only that: information directly relevant and pertinent to his needs. Then only can the team operate effectively.

Perhaps we can draw a parallel: the first of many such comparisons we shall be making as we proceed. We can liken the project manager to the captain of a ship or an aircraft. Whilst at sea or in the air, he must make quick decisions, quite often without having complete information on the situation, and his crew have to implement those decisions without question and without delay, otherwise disaster would result. It is exactly the same with a construction project, except that the disaster is not necessarily 'total' and quite often a potentially hopeless situation can be retrieved if the 'early warning' signals are available and are heeded. But the information, on status and trends, must be immediate (directly after the event) and acted upon promptly. Only a competent and courageous project manager will fulfil this role. His major contribution is in the area of human relations, not his personal specialisation (say engineering). But more of this in Chapter 3, when we take a look at who *really* controls costs.

## References

1   Quade, E.S., 'A history of cost-effectiveness', Rand Corporation Report P–4557, 1971.
2   Novick, D., 'Are cost overruns a military-industry-complex speciality?', Rand Corporation Report P–4311, 1970.
3   Kharbanda, O.P. and E.A. Stallworthy, *How to learn from Project Disasters*, Gower, Aldershot, 1983, 273 pp.
4   Naisbitt, J., *Megatrends – Ten New Directions Transforming Our Lives*, Warner Books, US, 1982, 333 pp.
5   Davis, D., 'New projects – beware of false economies', *Harvard Business Review*, 64, March/April 1985, pp. 95–101.
6   Claxton, C., 'Planning major international projects', *Long Range Planning*, 11, April 1978, pp. 25–34.
7   *Estimating Check List for Offshore Projects*, published by The Association of Cost Engineers, 26 Chapel Street, Sandbach, Cheshire CW11 9DS, UK.
8   Gregory, Jenny *et al*, 'The Statfjord story', *Offshore Engineer*, July 1984, pp. 46–54.
9   Plumb, R., 'Client project execution', *The Cost Engineer*, Vol. 3, No. 4, July 1985, pp. 4–8.
10  Feature article: 'Brae triumph: now on to new $3 billion challenge', *Achievement*, May 1984, pp. 23–30.
11  Snowdon, M., *Management of Engineering Projects*, Newnes–Butterworths, 1977, 134 pp.

# 2　Why control cost?

This question may seem silly: too obvious to call for an answer. Of course one should seek to control cost. But it is a serious question, and directly relevant to our subject. Chapter 1 opened with one answer to this question:

> We all know that a business can only survive if it makes a profit. There is nothing one can do to *guarantee* that a profit is going to be made, but certain factors can go a long way towards making a profit a near certainty. Foremost among these factors is cost control.

But as we shall see, what is called the profit motive is only the beginning.

## Profit alone is not enough

In the 'good old days', when business conditions were simple and straightforward, making a profit was the sole criterion for survival. You made goods for which there was a market. You could sell *all* that you could make. You could decide on the profit margin and get it. It was, for most of the time, a seller's market and quite often a manufacturer had a monopoly with the particular product he was placing on the market. To put it briefly: 'Everything came your way'.

But this is no longer the case. The business world today is highly complex and fiercely competitive. This is true not only nationally, within countries, but also internationally, between countries. The game now being played is: 'The survival of the fittest'.

Because of these changed conditions, making a profit is indeed essential, but it is not all. It is, of course, a fundamental prerequisite to survival, but more is required. You *must* also have what the financiers call 'liquid assets'. We call it 'cash in the bank'. Without liquidity bankruptcy may well result. And yet you may still be making quite a good profit! There are a number of factors which have increased the importance and significance of liquidity over the years. One is what we call in estimating circles the 'economy of scale'. This fact of life has caused process plants to be built bigger and bigger. The larger a plant, the higher the stakes. Of course, the return on the investment is also higher, if we want it that way, and are willing to work for it. But we have to exert our efforts in the right direction. This can be assured if our investment decision takes into account the various factors we illustrated earlier in Figure 1.2, particularly those in the area we 'presume to have been completed' before cost control comes into play. As we said then we are not concerning ourselves here with the selection of projects, or the decisions that led to a particular investment decision. We are concerned with 'Project cost control *in action*', and the action begins *after* the project has been selected and the budget approved.

But we have to remember some of the guiding factors in that decision, since it is those factors that make the stakes so high these days, and so make the work of project cost control ever more critical in relation to successful completion of the project. Figure 2.1 shows us what it is all about. This portrays the potential cash flow for a typical process plant related to UK conditions, assuming the 'bare cost' of such a project to be of the order of £100 million. This excludes any interest charges, and is the basic capital investment to which the profitability calculations would have been related. When interest charges are added, because we have to build our plant and get it to work before we can make any money out of it, our investment has risen to £124 million. Once the plant is in operation, we should make a profit of £24 million per year, but the break-even point is still some eight years away, or some eleven years from the day we began to invest our money. If the project is delayed in completion by just one year, then the break-even point goes four more years into the future. Now you see how high the stakes, and how important timely completion can be. It affects not only the cost of the plant as such – the capital investment – but also profitability for many years to come. Delay in completion is prohibitively expensive, because of the immense sums tied up which are bringing no income. Can you doubt any longer how vitally necessary it is to 'control cost'. And, to control cost, you have to control *time*. Time is of the essence, as they say.

To further impress upon you the money value of time, let us take the case of a typical world scale fertiliser plant, such as are being built in India, and estimate the cost of just *one day's* delay in the completion of the project. The installation would be in all four major plant units: two 1,000 tonnes/day ammonia plants and two 1,350 tonnes/day prilled urea plants, using natural gas as a feedstock. The total project cost (1986 values) would be of the order of US$1 billion. Then the cost of one day's delay is:

| Direct cost to the project: | US$ million |
|---|---|
| (a) Interest | 0.5 |
| (b) Escalation | 0.6 |
| *Indirect cost (to the nation):* | |
| (c) Loss in taxes | 1.5 |
| (d) Loss in production: | 2.7 |
| Total loss: | 5.3 |

The loss in taxes relates primarily to excise duty and other levies that would be due to the government for one day's production. The loss in production is very serious for a country such as India, since it has to be made good by imports and is thus using up scarce foreign exchange resources.

Having seen the substantial cost of just one day's delay, what are we to think in relation to the many such plants not only in India, but in other developing countries, that have not been delayed by a day or two, but by months and sometimes years. It makes a mockery of project cost control and we see once again that it is preached far more than it is practised. So blatant is this particular example that we shall return to it again and again.

Delays can be avoided, and their effects minimised, by proper project cost control. We go into detail on this when we start to apply the principles we are now reviewing, and discuss 'Proper project management' (Chapter 11). For the moment let us just recognise that delay hurts everyone involved in the building of process plants – owner, consultant and contractor. How they share the responsibility we will examine in some detail in Chapter 3, when we turn from why to who – Who controls cost? We have pictured the cash flow impact on the owner, but the contractor is also affected. He has to maintain *his* liquidity. He needs working capital. Figure 2.2 illustrates the situation with respect to working capital over time. Payments will lag behind outgoings, unless the contractor makes specific arrangements with the owner to be funded in some way, and this the owner can well be reluctant to do. He from his side will do his best to keep payment lagging behind the work done for him by the contractor. So the contractor has to exercise care to see that his working capital, which may well run as high as 25 per cent of the

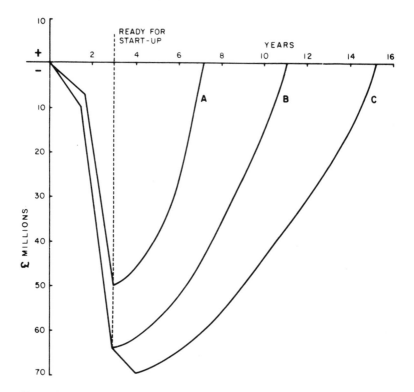

**Figure 2.1 Cash flow over time**
This graph shows the effect of one year's delay in completion on the time taken to recover the initial cash outlay.

total contract value, is rigorously monitored and controlled, otherwise he himself will have a liquidity problem. Liquidity is, in this day and age, essential to survival.

For the owner, too, the cash flow must be in accordance with the original planning upon which the project was approved, otherwise his long range prospects will be completely upset. But to maintain the cash flow within the budget detailed cost control is essential.

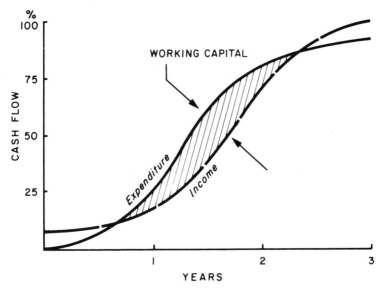

**Figure 2.2 Working capital**
Working capital seen in relation to income and expenditure.

## Parkinson's Law

Everyone knows Parkinson's Law, but it is no joke. It is a deadly serious subject, even if Mr. Parkinson dealt with it in a lighthearted manner. What was Parkinson's Law? 'Work expands to fill the time available'. The same law applies when building a process plant. By analogy: 'Cost expands to fill the budget available'.

Time or money used unnecessarily is of course time and money wasted. Man's ingenuity and imagination seem to know no bounds, yet he cannot eliminate waste. It is a simple fact of life that we waste more when we have plenty. We waste at a feast, but can be frugal in time of famine. Perhaps because we have to be! But the fact demonstrates that it can be done. The same applies to the building of a process plant. Parkinson's Law could be undermined, and that is the objective of project cost control. Cost control is an effective tool to avoid, reduce and minimise waste. It is a set of procedures whereby the actual results being achieved in terms of time and money are compared with the targets set, and the appropriate action indicated. And every effort must be made to set realistic targets in terms of time and money. This, in effect, brings the target into a region where, if it is met, there will be no waste: no expansion of work to consume the surplus. This, indeed, is the 'trick' of the trade. The standard set *must* be realistic. Not one that is too easy to achieve, nor one that is impossible to achieve. The prime standard in relation to cost is, of course, the cost estimate.

In Figure 2.1 we have illustrated the effect of one year's delay in the completion of a typical plant. As we said, that delay shifts the break-even point by some four years. This illustration is in no sense extreme. It happens all the time. It is indeed unfortunate, but such overruns occur far more often than we realise. We discuss this in some detail in Chapter 5 (Forewarned is forearmed), but it seems strange that even when the consequences are disastrous, we do not seem to become any wiser. We continually repeat the same mistakes, make the same errors, time and time again. It is almost like hitting your thumb with a hammer, knowing it is going to hurt. You would think anyone foolish indeed who did a thing like that deliberately. But what about the person who does it time and again? Yet that is what is actually happening. In Chapter 5 we have purposely chosen a long string of similar cases (Figure 5.2) in illustration of this very fact: that we just do not seem to learn. We keep on 'hitting our thumb'! Finally, in Chapter 14, we seek to examine why this is so, in the hope that that will help us to do something about it.

Learning is certainly not easy for the individual and it seems to be even more difficult for an organisation. The organisation will make the same costly and sometimes destructive mistake time and again. The organisation seems also to repeat the same mistake in different forms (1). This seems the inevitable conclusion if one considers two great disasters that have occurred in recent years – that at Bhopal in December 1984 and the loss of the space shuttle *Challenger* in January 1986. It turns out, in retrospect, that both could have occurred at any time, so that those involved were in effect sitting on a 'time bomb'. In both cases there were a number of patent warnings that went unheeded. In the case of Bhopal not only had there been numerous leakages of the deadly gas at that plant, but also at similar plant at institutes in the US, run by the same multinational, Union Carbide, and manufacturing the same product. Similarly in the case of the shuttle: there had been a number of snags leading to the postponement of the launch on several occasions in the past.

The reaction of management in both cases is also significant. We have always said that a policy of frankness, particularly in relation to the media, is always the best, but the initial reaction of the management in both cases – Union Carbide and NASA – was utterly confused and a number of contradictory statements were issued initially that made confusion worse confounded. Real information was very slow in coming, although it was there, and there was a general reluctance to talk about the tragedies. In the case of Union Carbide, despite their having spent considerable sums on additional safety equipment at their similar plant in the US, a 'mini-Bhopal' occurred there some eight months later. This lowered the credibility of the company substantially, causing those who till then had given the company the 'benefit of the doubt' to wonder. Headlines in the national and international press proclaimed of both Union Carbide and NASA that they were 'ill-prepared to cope with such a disaster'.

## No sudden shocks, please!

With any and every investment in a new process plant all the effort involved in design and engineering, procurement, expediting and the supervision of construction in the field is ultimately reflected in a mounting complexity of worked materials on the site, paralleled by a mounting cost. The final cost, as we have just seen, may or may not be within the first estimates that were made and approved. But to quote: (2)

> Great is the grief of one who is deeply entrenched in a capital spending programme and *suddenly learns* [our emphasis] that the cost will exceed expectations.

This statement demonstrates that in connection with the control of investment the most meaningful of all the information that can become available in relation to cost is the 'trend' – where are we going? Management never likes to suddenly learn that the budget is going to be exceeded. Much, much better to know ahead of time if that is really going to happen. Data that contributes to the early assessment of the cost trend is therefore very valuable indeed, since it can provide an early warning system to management in relation to the estimates of time and cost.

All estimating and cost control techniques depend to a greater or lesser extent upon the analysis of historical data for their validity. The factors, cost ratios and quantity ratios that are developed thereby are, whilst a plant is being built, not static but dynamic. Not only the relationships themselves, but also their changing value during the life of a project can be used to facilitate project cost control. So we shall show you later how to use them in order to make sure that you and your management do not get any sudden unpleasant shocks.

## Cost reporting is not cost control

It is all too easy to establish a system of project organisation and administration, with a regular flow of reports, and then believe that costs are under control. The greater the detail in which the reporting is done, the more convincing the paperwork, and the stronger the impression that everything is under control. But, beyond a certain optimum point, the reverse is almost invariably true. Later, when discussing the basic principles of site administration, we put forward the proposition, 'More men, less work!' (Chapter 5). We cannot now say: 'More paper, less work' because we have to handle the paperwork, but we can well say: 'More paper, less control!'

The fundamental difference between cost reporting and cost control, is illustrated in Figure 2.3. With Case A, the project is reviewed at intervals and revised estimates of the final cost are then prepared. To prepare these estimates, an appraisal must be made of the time that is still required to complete the project, so that both cost and time are under surveillance when the revised estimate is being prepared. If successive estimates indicate that costs are rising,

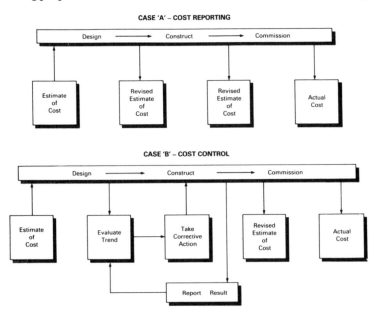

**Figure 2.3 Cost reporting versus cost control**
Reporting is the comment on the activity which is proceeding or has been completed. Control must influence as well as comment.

and we give you a splendid example of this in Figure 5.1, or that the project is taking longer to complete than we first anticipated, then steps will be taken in an attempt to remedy that situation. But such corrective action can only be minimal in its effect, since it comes very much 'after the event'. The decisions or circumstances which have given rise to the new situation, now reflected in the revised estimate, will already be largely a matter of history. The estimate reflects the situation at the time it is made, reflecting therefore a situation that already exists, and can hardly be altered.

But there *is* another approach. Case B in Figure 2.3 illustrates a process of evaluation, followed by corrective action as indicated. In order to evaluate a trend, a forecast has to be made not only of the anticipated end result, but also of the route by which that end result is going to be reached. Comparison of the route that is now going to be followed with that forecast earlier allows the trend, either along the route we want to follow, or away from it, to be seen. Any potential divergence can be studied before it becomes too significant and the appropriate action taken. The result of the action taken has also to be ascertained as it occurs if the system of control is to be fully effective. If we do this we then have a cycle:

1   Evaluate
2   Correct
3   Report

This cycle of events, constantly repeated, is fundamental to effective project cost control.


**The management approach**

Before coming to consider project cost control in any detail it should be set into context. There will always be a *promoter* of the project, who could be the owner, 'employer', sponsor or user, but will always be referred to by us as the 'owner'. Once the owner has decided to proceed with a project he always has to first establish feasibility and then ensure that the necessary funds are available. When a decision has been taken to proceed a project manager should be appointed. It is indeed implicit in the concept of project management that a project manager be appointed by the owner at a very early stage to 'manage' the project. Referring back to Figure 1.1, the project manager should be appointed once the project is 'go': very soon afterwards a project cost control engineer should also be appointed. Once a project has been defined and is in preparation the project manager should become involved and it is

he who will ensure that the project organisation appropriate to the
project is set up. Part of his responsibility must be to consider the
facilities available to him and assess what help he needs.

As he begins his work he has a variety of choices open to him, his
choice being determined to some extent by his own capability – or,
more often, his own judgement as to his capability, which may well
be at fault. He can:

1   Do it all within his own company
2   Seek the services of a consultant
3   Seek the services of a contractor
4   Seek the services of both consultant and contractor

Since alternative 4 is the most complex, it is that which will be used
by us as a basis for illustration in relation to project cost control.
This means that at least three separate parties can be involved in a
project. These are: (a) owner (b) consultant and (c) contractor.
Their specific functions can well vary from case to case. No two
projects are ever the same, even when they may appear to be. Each
and every project is unique and so, therefore, are the roles of these
three parties. These three key participants have three distinct and
separate roles to play, thus:

The owner        –    oversees and pays
The consultant   –    advises
The contractor   –    does the job

The potential relationship between these three parties is illustrated
in Figure 2.4. The boundary between consultant and contractor
has become somewhat blurred these days. At times a contractor will
take on what amounts to a consultancy assignment, whilst on the
other hand a number of major consultants have entered the
contracting field. However, we are going to look at project cost
control within the orbit and under the direction of the 'contractor'
(often a 'managing contractor'). Nevertheless the owner will still
have to set up an organisation of his own, that must be interrelated
with the organisation set up by the contractor. Both should have a
project manager. Were the owner to decide to 'go it alone' then his
project manager would have to establish his own project organisation in its entirety.

When a contractor is used the project manager appointed by that
contractor should be made responsible, within the contractor's
organisation, for every aspect of the project. Listen to what one
such contractor says of him:

He is responsible for every aspect of the job from inception to completion. He is

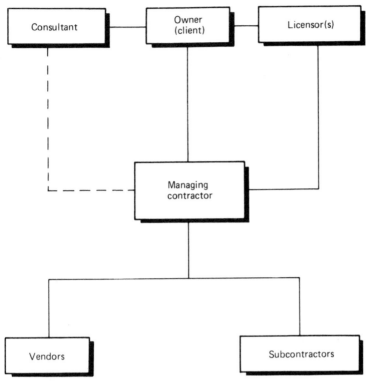

**Figure 2.4 The basic relationship**
Here the relationship between the various parties that can be involved in a project is presented diagrammatically.

> responsible for every service required to carry out the work: planning, scheduling, costing, designing, engineering, purchasing, inspection, shipping, construction and commissioning. And he is responsible to you, our client. He is your direct contact. And you will know him personally. His position calls for wide experience, broad knowledge of every group within the organisation, the ability to control progress and make decisions.

However, the owner still has certain responsibilities which he cannot delegate to the contractor. These are effected through his own project manager. The organisational setup to achieve this is illustrated in Figure 2.5. From this diagram it can be seen that the owner and the contractor should be mutually supportive. This is indeed the way in which the relationship is seen by the contractor himself, since the layout shown in Figure 2.5 has been copied faithfully from a brochure illustrating the project team as proposed by one such contractor. The interrelationship shown in light rule is

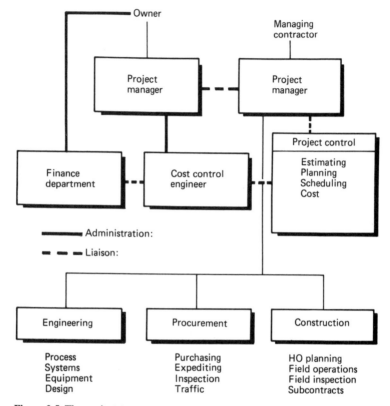

**Figure 2.5 The project teams**
The chart shows (in light rule) a typical project team (with acknowledgements to the M. W. Kellogg Company, Houston, US). Added in heavy rule are the key functions that should be provided by the owner to support his project manager and provide his project cost control.

from the brochure. The heavy rule has been added to the chart as originally prepared and its purpose is explained below.

There is no doubt that this method of working both alongside and in parallel, just like a team of horses 'in harness' is highly successful and should therefore be completely acceptable to all the parties involved. How does it work? To quote once again from a brochure issued by a contractor:

The Project Control Team [refer to Figure 2.5] under the direction of the Project Manager sets the control guidelines for the project. On major projects a Project Control Manager heads the Project Control Team. Each supervisor within the Engineering, Procurement and Construction areas is involved in the development of the project controls which affect his area of work. Thereafter, he is responsible for the execution of the project within the control plans and budget established for his area of work. The Project Manager, the Project Control Manager and his Project Control Team constantly monitor performance, making adjustments as may be required to plans as they may affect the interfaces between the specialty groups.

It is very clear that this contractor knows the road he has to follow. But the owner has a positive role to play and this is also demonstrated in Figure 2.5. It is the 'heavy rule' addition to the original organogram produced by the contractor. Two key functions should be exercised by the owner, both functions that he should have or should establish within his own organisation. These are the finance department and the cost control engineer. They will have to work alongside the managing contractor's personnel, day in, day out for the next three years – or however long it takes not only to bring the project to completion and commission it, but to pay the very last invoice. They will still be busy when the contractor's team has packed up, left the site and gone off to the next project. To facilitate the task of selecting a project cost control engineer, we present a typical *Job Description* as Appendix A.

**The earlier the better**

The real trick in effective cost control is to start at the beginning, if not before, and to act early. Early action, even on information that is incomplete or only partly processed, is far, far better than delayed action. Delayed action is subject to the law of diminishing returns, as we illustrate later in Chapter 5 (see in particular Figure 5.6). The point we have to appreciate is the powerful impact of early action. This can be seen by considering the influence of pre-design studies. Such studies, although constituting only some three per cent of the total cost of a project, can easily contribute as much as 50 per cent to the total profitability of a project. We have set this out graphically in Figure 2.6 in the hope that such a diagrammatic representation may bring the relationship home more vividly. This emphasises that the pre-design engineering stage is the time for *action*. That is the time when the maximum influence is possible on cost, and the chance of cost reduction is real and substantial. This is an area where cost control can really be *in action*. Consider, in this context, all the implications of Figure 3.3, in the next chapter – yet another example of this law of diminishing returns.

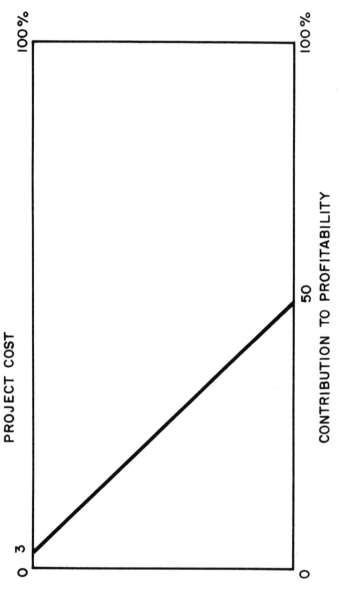

**Figure 2.6 Catch the 'early bird'**
Early studies, though costing less than 3% of the total project cost, can contribute 50% or more to the ultimate profitability of the plant. (Diagram based on an idea presented in *Management of Engineering Projects* – Snowdon, Newnes-Butterworths, 1977.)

40

So there is no doubt that when it comes to project cost control, the earlier the better. Whilst the old adage 'better late than never' is certainly true, and some effort at cost control, even when applied late in the day, in the field, when construction is underway, as is so often the case, is better than none, why not listen to the exhortation? Start thinking about cost control at the same time as you start thinking about the project!

## Do we 'crash' or 'control'?

In order to secure the maximum benefit when it comes to the execution of a project, there must be control, preferably in the context of 'total project management' as discussed a little earlier in this chapter. There are, however, times when the most important thing of all is to get the plant on stream. The benefit in terms of early availability of the product can outweigh the possibility – nay, the certainty – of increased cost and wasted effort that will accompany an all out effort to complete the project as early as possible. This applies, in particular, to cases such as the 'debottlenecking' of an existing, operating plant. The plant has to be shut down in order to make the necessary changes, and execution on what we call a 'crash' basis must be resorted to in order to minimise the loss of production. Cost becomes a secondary consideration. But does that mean that cost control must 'go out of the window'? Of course not. All we say is that cost considerations must not hinder quick completion. The fundamental difference between what we can call the 'controlled' approach and the 'crash' approach are set out in Figure 2.7 (3).

Once again, if only we will think before we act, *then* plan and approach the problem methodically and then proceed to monitor what we are doing, then we are on the road to achieving the best possible solution in all the circumstances. We have brought out this aspect of project development because it is something that happens fairly frequently, and all too often the 'crash' approach is allowed to lead to a complete and utter disregard of the cost implications of what is being done. As we indicate in Figure 2.7, there should still be opportunity for a *little* cost control.

## Cost – benefit

The question of the benefits that accrue is, of course, the acid test in relation to project cost control. Does it pay for itself? Do the

| ACTIVITY | "CRASH" APPROACH | "CONTROLLED" APPROACH |
|---|---|---|
| Define objectives | Recognised | Defined |
| Establish priorities | Controlled | Set |
| Planning emphasis | On coordination | On task assignment |
| Administration | Centralised | Devolved |
| Project duration | Unknown | Known |
| Planning | Little | Detailed |
| Control | Little | Each task controlled |
| Completion | Immediate | On schedule |
| Ideal for: | Operational problems | Complex projects |

**Figure 2.7 The 'crash' versus the 'controlled' approach**
This table shows the difference between these two approaches in relation to the various activities in which we are involved when developing a project.

benefits exceed the cost? If they do, and especially if the return is substantial – say four or five times our initial investment – then the quesion Why control cost? receives a resounding answer. The problem here is that assessment of the benefits is usually qualitative rather than quantitative. Good cost control is so much a team effort that the source of the benefits will seem widely dispersed. But those who have made a study of this aspect say that cost control more than pays for itself.

When we talk of 'benefits', we mean, in the first place, the monetary benefit: benefits that can be quantified. But in addition the application of cost control techniques brings fringe benefits, not quantifiable, such as: (a) better communications and (b) better human relations. This will lead in its turn to smoother project execution and both morale and productivity increase quite considerably. The direct cost of implementing the cost control activity, as compared with the related benefits, is illustrated diagrammatically in Figure 2.8. Both change quite rapidly over time, so once again we see the desirability of applying the principle enunciated earlier: 'the earlier the better'.

The indication given in Figure 2.8 is necessarily very subjective. It is most difficult to establish objective quantitative data on this subject, because whilst we know what happens on a project where the cost control engineer is deployed and also what happens when he is not, we cannot compare what would happen on a project with and without his services. No two projects are alike. Each project is *unique*, with the result that the experiences of one project cannot be

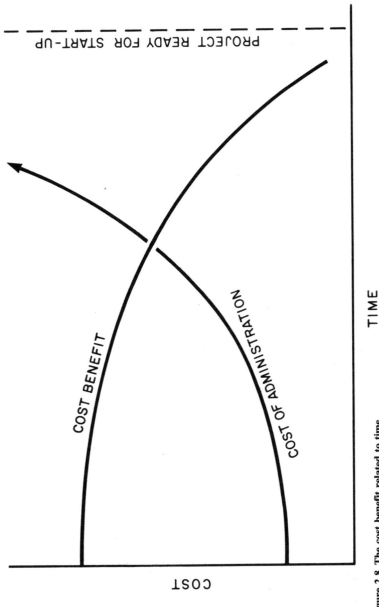

**Figure 2.8 The cost benefit related to time**
Figure 3.3 demonstrates that the ability to control cost diminishes rapidly over time. At the same time, the cost of such control will escalate, as we see here, unless the futility of the further effort is realised.

| SAVINGS THROUGH COST CONTROL | | |
|---|---|---|
| Technique | Traditional method | Total cost management |
| | Months | Months |
| Design, then start construction: | 32 | 13 |
| The design/construction overlap: | 0 | −10 |
| Construction time: | 31 | 33 |
| | 63 | 46 |

Net saving:    =  17 months, or 27%
Money saved:  =  15% on inflation alone
                        23% in total.

**Figure 2.9 Savings through cost control**
This table sets out the potential saving in project cost with proper cost control, operating as an integral part of the project management structure.

directly transferred to another. They can only ever be 'tailored' in order that comparisons may be made.

However, attempts have been made to do just this. Miller (2) has tried to quantify the benefits that come from cost control with a typical process plant project and we present the data he puts forward in Figure 2.9. It will be seen from the table that the saving in time and money are as much as 25 per cent. The extra cost of instituting cost control on the scale necessary to achieve this sort of result has not been indicated, but it is our feeling that a most rigorous and detailed cost control administration will not exceed say a half per cent of total project cost. Thus the benefit–cost ratio is of the order of 50:1. Another source (4) claims a five per cent saving in field costs at a cost, for control, of 0.4 per cent of the total field expenses. In that case the benefit–cost ratio would be 12.5:1. These figures are all on the basis of the *direct* saving in cost: a real, not a notional saving. If, in the absence of a cost control system there was an *extra* overrun of some 15 per cent, apart from any overrun that might occur if cost control was deployed – and such overruns are not at all unusual – then the benefits of project cost control are actually much higher, because of the 'rolling on' effect. The delay and cost increase has serious effects on profitability, delaying start-up, increasing product cost, and endangering markets.

The consensus of opinion seems to be that direct savings can well be of the order of say 20:1. If the related influence on matters such as product cost and the market are taken into consideration, it is easily possible for this primary saving to be more than doubled, and we are in the area of say a benefit–cost ratio of 50:1. What was that question again? 'Why control cost?' The answer is indeed plain for all to see. The savings are more than significant: they are substantial.

## References

1 Shrivasava, P., 'The lessons of Bhopal', *Bus. & Soc. Review*, No. 55, Fall 1985, pp. 61–2.
2 Miller, W. B., 'Fundamentals of project management', *Jnl. of Systems Management*, 29, November 1978, pp. 22–29.
3 Snowdon, M., *Management of Engineering Projects*, Newnes-Butterworths, 1977, 134 pp.
4 Bromberg, I., 'CIR: Construction control system', *Eng. Proc. Econ.*, 1, June 1976, pp. 113–122.

# 3  Who controls cost?

We have already noted in Chapter 2, in the section titled 'Parkinson's Law', that cost control is, in essence, prevention of the waste of basic resources. These may be broadly identified as time, materials, and energy: and all can be expressed in monetary terms. Waste is caused by people, hence it can be controlled, if not prevented, by the people who are wasting these resources. This means, in effect, that everyone concerned with the project, whoever they are, and whatever they do, is in a position to influence, and hence contribute to the control of cost. This is the *primary* role of the project team, but it does not end there. It extends to the copy typist and the janitor. It involves the sub-subcontractor as well as the managing contractor.

Yet, despite this basic fact, there is the tendency to look to one man to control cost, usually the accountant. This is a great mistake. The accountant, sitting in the comfort of his chair in an office remote from the major activity, is hardly in a position to control cost. He has no feel, probably no authority, and hardly the competence to change the course of a project if it is headed in the wrong direction. The accountant, however, can produce valuable information which is of great help in controlling cost. He can keep the 'score', producing the results, and an analysis of these results, promptly. This 'scoring' must be of the right kind and be available at the right time – preferably 'yesterday'! This is *vital*.

## The project 'trio'

Executing a project is both a mission and an adventure. A project, in its broadest sense, is any task which has to be accomplished within a scheduled time and within the available budget. Climbing

Mount Everest was a momentous project, surely as difficult, if not more so, than the successful completion of a billion dollar petrochemical complex. The comparison is just: those involved in the latter should have the same approach as those involved in the former exercise. Let us see it as the 'project game', with three players, each having their specific functions to perform if we are going to achieve the desired goal. The trio are: (a) owner (or client) (b) consultant and (c) contractor. Their specific functions can well vary from case to case. In the process plant field, no two projects are ever the same, or ever will be. Each project is *unique*, and so are the respective functions of the several players. However, certain basic patterns can be readily recognised. The pattern that takes shape in any particular case determines who leads: determines 'who controls cost'. The owner will decide to proceed with the project on the basis of the feasibility studies that he has made (see Figure 1.2) and he can then choose one of three broad alternative approaches to project execution:

1   Design and build the plant himself
2   Design the plant and get it built by a contractor
3   Get a consultant to design and a contractor to build

We have already noted in Chapter 2, in discussing 'The management approach', that the demarcation line between consultant and contractor is not very clear cut. They tend to intrude upon the activities of each other these days. It is therefore possible, with our third alternative, to find that one company, the managing contractor, will combine the roles of both. However, assuming we are maintaining the division of responsibility outlined above, the basic responsibility for cost control in the three cases outlined is as follows:

| Designer | Builder | Cost controller |
|---|---|---|
| Owner | Owner | Owner |
| Owner | Contractor | Contractor/owner |
| Consultant | Contractor | Contractor/owner |

The owner is spending his own money, so he is the one primarily interested in controlling the costs, but he does his best to make the contractor share his interest by the type of contract he uses: but more of that shortly. However, the power and authority of the owner to control cost is practically nil when he is not building the plant himself, and even more so when he is not designing it. As we noted earlier, it is at the design stage that the key decisions are taken and the project effectively 'cast in concrete'. There are, however, means whereby he can take some steps to safeguard his interest, as we shall see.

Perhaps we should say as an aside at this point that we have, throughout this book, when illustrating the various procedures and approaches to project cost control, assumed that the roles of consultant and contractor have been combined into that of the managing contractor, managing on behalf of the owner. However, we believe that the owner should have his own cost control function, despite that, and the procedures outlined are designed to that end. For instance, the administrative procedures outlined later in Chapter 6 should be implemented by the owner, whether or not his managing contractor, or contractors, fall into line. This is, indeed, an aspect he can ensure by bringing in the appropriate requirements in the project specification or the conditions of contract.

### Types of contract

There are broadly two major types of contract that can be set up for project execution, assuming the owner is going to employ firms outside his own organisation. These are firstly the turnkey and secondly the departmental. In the case of a turnkey contract, the entire responsibility, starting from the 'green field' site to the operating plant rests with the contractor. This is the origin of the term 'turn key': all the owner has to do, it is said, is to 'turn the key'. In the case of what we have termed the departmental approach, the owner himself assumes responsibility through his engineering department. The project is 'departmentalised', a series of orders, or contracts, being placed with various companies on behalf of the owner, and coordination of all the contracts rests wholly with the owner. In this area we meet two specific types of contract, the difference lying fundamentally in the method of assessing and paying for the work done. These are (a) lump sum contract and (b) cost plus (or schedule of rates) contract. There is a very wide variation in the nature and type of contract that can be established, even within these two broad classifications, so that no two contracts are ever identical.

With a turnkey contract, the owner–contractor relationship may well be likened to that of patient and doctor. A patient's faith in his doctor is half the cure: the other half medicine, or more probably, nature! It is just the same with owner and contractor. Faith is fundamental to the relationship, but the other half is competence and capability on the part of the contractor – though here, too, nature can play a vital role. The weather can have a profound influence on project cost. With a true turnkey contract there can be no 'buck-passing', as the Americans say. Whilst it is true that the contractor's problems become the owner's problems, this is not in the contractual sense. But delay in completion hurts the owner far more than it can ever hurt the contractor. Therefore, despite the fact that the contractual responsibility sits wholly with the contractor, the owner should still work with him to reach their common goal: project completion within the scheduled time and budgeted cost.

When we turn to consider the departmental approach, the engineering department of the owner assumes the role otherwise played by the managing contractor. The owner may, and often does, subcontract key elements of the work. He can let a part, or all, of: (a) process engineering (b) detailed engineering (c) procurement and (d) construction. The departmental approach is adopted sometimes for reasons of secrecy, when a new process is involved, or for economy. In practice, however, the latter reason is almost always fallacious. The apparent savings are not real, because the full internal costs are rarely identified and set against the cost of the project. Some of the major international companies turned to the departmental approach a few years ago, and learnt their lesson the hard way. That approach not only cost them more in real terms, but in addition they were burdened with a number of headaches that the seasoned contractor is far better able to tackle. That is his forte. A secondary problem is that the owner does not always have enough capital projects on hand to keep his engineering department busy, yet he ought to maintain his staff levels to cope with the major project when it arrives. If he does just that, then his staff becomes demoralised when work is slack.

However, the two modes of approach just detailed can in fact be combined, and that with advantage. The key factor for success if this 'mingled' approach is adopted is a close owner–contractor relationship, associated with a complete understanding by both of the project scope. It is this combined approach which we use as a basis for the development of the relevant procedures and techniques for project cost control.

A number of devices of a financial nature can be employed to give the contractor some incentive to keep costs under control, but the best guarantee remains the name and reputation of the contractor himself. The contractors' own stake in this game of project execution is in fact quite high. A project executed within time and on budget is the best thing for him by far: it leads to repeat orders. He does not have to advertise the fact: to 'blow his own trumpet'. The completed project does that for him far more effectively. On the other hand, a project overrunning on time or cost is enough to 'kill' repeat orders, particularly from the same owner. The repercussions extend far and wide. One bad job by a particular contractor can well have the effect that he is 'black-listed', even though it is all unofficial: merely the reaction to bad news.

Of the various devices that may be employed to induce the contractor to share an interest in final cost with the owner, the most usual is the bonus/penalty clause. Whilst this is good in intent, it is hardly ever effective. A repeat order is the best bonus for any contractor, and a lost order the worst possible penalty. A monetary bonus or penalty, related to certain factors in the progress of a project, acts neither as an incentive nor a deterrent. It does, however, have a token value. On the other hand, incentive at the design stage can pay rich dividends, because the benefit–cost ratio here is so much higher. There is real scope for the contractor to make an impact on the situation. Whilst design itself is only perhaps ten per cent of total cost, meticulous attention to the effect of design on cost at that stage could well bring savings of 20–30 per cent in the final cost of the project. And the extra cost? – usually well less than one per cent!

### Project organisation

The way in which a project organisation develops will vary from project to project and from company to company. It is also very dependent upon the type of contract that has been set up. Ideally, the project organisation should be 'tailored' to each specific project. Figure 3.1 shows the typical project organisation when a managing contractor is being employed. For the sake of simplicity and in view of our special interest, details other than those related to cost control have been omitted. Figure 3.2 takes us a step further, illustrating the relationship between owner and managing contractor. Both Figures 3.1 and 3.2 demonstrate the vital role inevitably played by the project manager. He is the fulcrum around whom all the key activities must revolve. He is the 'kingpin': without him the project must collapse. A major part of his work will relate, of course, to that most vital of functions: cost control.

### The project manager and control

Effective control of a project team requires a good leader who has the complete confidence of his management and who has been

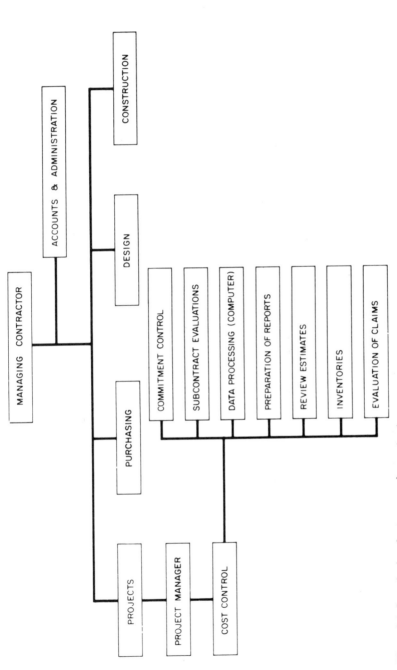

**Figure 3.1 Organisation chart – managing contractor**
Typical outline organisation, highlighting the functions of cost control. A more detailed development is to be found as Figure 11.1 (Chapter 11).

51

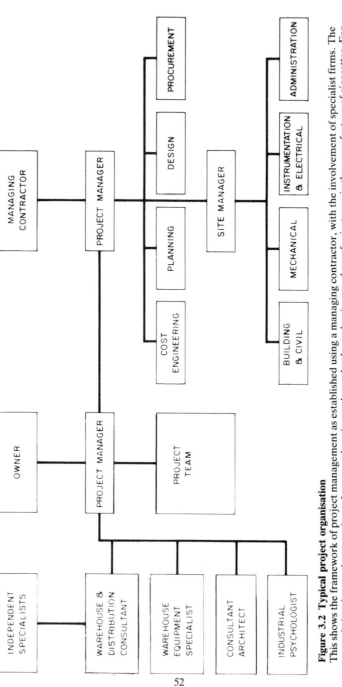

**Figure 3.2 Typical project organisation**
This shows the framework of project management as established using a managing contractor, with the involvement of specialist firms. The example is orientated to a project where warehousing and people play a dominant role, as for instance in the manufacture of cigarettes. For yet more detail, refer to Figure 11.8 (Chapter 11).

vested with full authority. This leader we call the project manager. It is possible that some of the members of the project team are not administratively responsible to the project manager. The project manager has their services as part of his team, but their functional control, or technical guidance, comes from the manager of their particular discipline. Nevertheless, an effective project manager, with tact and diplomacy, will get his leadership accepted despite his lack of direct authority over such people.

For the project manager to be effective in relation to cost control, a clear understanding of the end in view is required. It must be recognised that for cost control to be successful it must continue throughout until that end is achieved. Further, each and every one engaged in the project must be *cost conscious*, realising above all that the savings of cost in one area can easily lead to extra costs in another. The project records must be impartial, clearly reflecting the project scope, the real costs, the related relevant conditions, such as the time to completion, in a concise and comprehensive manner. This demands method: systematic tabulation and forms that set out the relevant data clearly. It also demands courage and honesty. Once that data is 'fudged', to hide something from management, cost control is going out of the window. These practical aspects of cost control are, of course, going to be developed in detail later, in Part 2 of this book. For the moment, let us remember the golden rule, 'prevention is better than cure'.

There is no doubt at all that unnecessary restraints can impose a serious burden on the project manager and his team, and impair their efficiency. A proper balance must be maintained between a freedom to 'get on with the job' and the necessity of reporting what is happening. Cost factors are paramount, but safety, operability, quality, capacity and time are also important and cannot be ignored. You will remember that we made this point early in Chapter 1, and we dare to reiterate it in this context, asking you to study Figure 1.7 once again and appreciate its potential tensions.

We also made the point earlier, in Chapter 2 (see Figure 2.3) that cost reporting is *not* cost control. For effective project cost control certain basic principles are axiomatic, namely:

1  Real cost control will only be achieved by sound management of the project.
2  The accountant, and others directly concerned with costs, cannot control them. However, their reports will assist the project team to do so.
3  Constant and continuous effort to control cost is required, throughout the life of the project.

4  All members of the project team must be *cost conscious*.
5  Initial cost targets set should be seen as a challenge to be beaten.
6  Control is far too late, if it is initiated once the costs start coming in.

A study of these 'axioms' should be accompanied by the realisation that the ability to have any influence at all on cost, let alone *control* costs, diminishes rapidly as the project progresses. We have illustrated this point graphically with a well-known and widely publicised diagram – Figure 3.3. You will see from the note to this particular illustration that this diagram first saw the light of day seventeen years ago now, but it is still as true as ever. As a project progresses, the number and detail of the cost control reports increases in inverse ratio to the effect that such reports will have on the cost of the project. When the project is complete the most detailed cost analysis can be made, and a book can be written about the reasons why the project has cost what it has cost, but the money has already been spent and the time when one could influence cost has long gone. Any analysis at that point in time is, at best, a 'post mortem' for *that* project: but perhaps a good lesson for the next, if only we will listen!

This chapter began with the statement that cost is everybody's business and it is indeed true that each and every one can play his role in this area. But it is the project manager who is the focal point. It is he who sets the pace and gives the example. He, above all, is the one person who can 'make or mar' a project. Right at the beginning (Chapter 1 – It's a team effort) we ventured to liken the project manager to the captain of a ship or the commander of an aircraft, and this describes his real function quite accurately. Of course, he has available to him a wide team of specialists to help him achieve his objective – the completion of the project on time and within the budget. To continue the analogy, he has his cost engineer acting as the 'navigator'. He keeps the 'log' (the cost records) and pores over the 'maps' (the budget) and then submits his conclusions – the trends and projections as to where they are going – to the project manager. This information helps the project manager to see where the project is heading and whether, left on course, it will reach 'port'. That rarely happens if things are left to take their own course. The project manager finds that he has to set new 'bearings' to reach his target and then has to get his team to realise that they are on a new course. This is achieved by persuasion and motivation: seldom by directive.

Building a process plant is indeed a 'battle royal'. The resources of men and money are lined up, and it is the 'players' – the project team – led by their captain – the project manager – who have to win the battle. They have to complete the project in time, and within the set budget. Thus the entire team is working together to control cost, though the project manager is the initiator and the motivator. The crux of the matter: can he get his people to work as a team to strive towards their key objective?

## Accountants can do much more

We have pointed out earlier in this chapter that the normal function of the accountant is that of monitoring and recording. He cannot control costs any more than can the project cost control engineer. This is a view with which accountants in general seem to concur (1). However this need not be so. Accountants can, and some do, play a more forceful role in relation to cost control, and the cost control engineer should both facilitate this and cooperate as far as he can. The sphere of influence for the project accountant is well set out in a book by an accountant (2). It has a pointed and most appropriate subtitle: *A Preemptive Audit Approach*. Whilst the technique is still being developed, it is clear that the accountant, acting as auditor, can transform his role from that of mere 'figure crunching' to that of an active and concerned 'hearer', listening to managers at all levels and participating actively in the control of project cost.

The process described by Pomeranz as the 'preemptive audit' has many similarities with the system of 'early warning signals' used by engineers and described here by us. Accountants and cost engineers have much to learn from one another and they can, working together, be a very powerful team, but to achieve this the technical jargon has to be abandoned, so that they speak a 'common language'. It is considerations such as these that have led to a new and ever-increasing breed: the Accountant-Engineer or the Engineer-Accountant. Such individuals, once they have the appropriate experience, have a most useful part to play wherever engineering and finance meet – and this includes our present subject, project cost control.

Preemptive auditing is 'constructive in both intent and execution'. This is in sharp contrast to the normal auditing function, which is almost always a 'post mortem'. Preemptive auditing increases and facilitates the ability of management to make proper, sound financial decisions. It is normally performed in two phases:

Design engineering phase
Execution phase (construction)

To be effective the preemptive audit team must be involved with a project right from its inception. The emphasis is on audit *before* spending instead of the conventional approach: audit *after* spending. This is indeed a refreshing approach and can add a new tool to the project manager's armoury, since it provides another, independent check on the growing project cost. The concept has been taken right back to the initial 'project approval' stage, with a considerable improvement in capital resource allocation. For instance, one specific proposal for a project costing some US$50 million was said to give a DCF of 22.6 per cent. However, when examined afresh by an audit team that took its members not only from the finance department, but also from research, marketing and planning, with due correction being made for capacity utilisation and other factors outside the project itself, the DCF came down to a mere 14.2 per cent. Since the introduction of the preemptive audit approach in 1978 some twenty proposals have been subjected to this process with the following result:

5 rejected
5 approved with modifications
2 partially approved
8 approved as submitted

There is no doubt that this new approach provides an independent evaluation of the capital budget proposal, leads to orderly and more effective decisions and is a welcome complement to the work of the cost control engineer.

### Size is not significant

The philosophy and the mechanics of project cost control are basically the same, no matter how small, or large, our project. Project Mount Everest involved months, possibly even years of detailed preparation and planning. A lesser peak would only need weeks of planning. But the basic requirements are no different in the two cases. It is just the same with building a process plant. Small or large, meticulous preparation and planning is the key to success – and successful project cost control!

Size as such really does not influence the situation, except that the larger the project, the greater the resources that are required in terms of men, money and materials. The stakes are therefore much higher, and there are more things to go wrong. This fact, coupled with another well publicised law – we have already mentioned Mr. Parkinson in Chapter 2 – we now turn to Mr. Murphy. His maxim

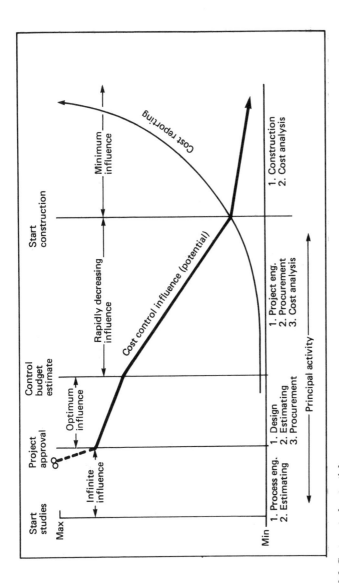

**Figure 3.3 Cost control potential**
We make no apology for reproducing this classic curve once again, since it represents an axiom that must never be forgotten. (Originally attributed to Mr. G. Azud, this diagram first appeared in his paper 'Owner can control costs', included in the 1969 Transactions of the American Association of Cost Engineers.)

57

is: 'If anything can go wrong, the chances are it will!' This means that the chances of failure are that much greater, for that probability is a product of the various individual probabilities. Having said that, it does not sound right: yet Mr. Murphy *is* right. The mathematical approach tells us that the multiplication of a series of high probabilities becomes a low probability, a fact we take advantage of in estimating. Perhaps we could better say that when there are more things to go wrong, then the chances are quite high that something or other will always be going wrong. The fact remains: things do go wrong! We noted just now that the bigger the project, the more men will be required. But watch out! The law of diminishing returns is universal: a subject we will revert to in some detail later. (Chapter 5 – More men, less work!).

A small project, say up to the order of £1 million or so, may well need very little in the way of documentation. The project team can be kept small and compact and it is quite often possible for one man to keep all the significant information in his head. Of course, it is still very desirable to have the key information on record, so that the second-in-command can take over at need, but the fact remains that a small project can be run extremely efficiently without recourse to detailed documentation and sophisticated control techniques. But the basic features of project cost control must still be constantly in mind:

1 Start control early, before design begins
2 Plan meticulously, before construction starts
3 Watch out for the early warning signals.


**Simplicity is the key**

Although project cost control is as old as history – that was where we began – it is a topic that has really come to the fore in the last twenty to thirty years. Interest was triggered by a number of dismal failures in terms of time and cost. Cost engineering and cost control have now developed into fully fledged disciplines. There are already some twelve separate national cost engineering associations and also an International Cost Engineering Conference. National conventions are held in a number of countries every year, and there is an international conference in alternate years. All these meetings produce an enormous amount of paper in the form of articles, technical papers and reports of seminars. For example, the last few international congresses, held in cities as widely separated as Utrecht, Mexico City, London and Montreal, have each attracted hundreds of delegates from up to twenty-five countries. The proceedings are published as books running to 500 or more pages.

It is our view, however, that in all this those most concerned with cost control are in danger of getting ever further away from reality. There is a very real danger that those directly responsible for cost control could be losing the 'feel' for the subject. Some of the techniques and 'tools' being devised and offered are too elaborate, too sophisticated. They seem to attempt 'too much, too late', instead of 'a little, very early'. We have just seen (Figure 3.3) that the ability to control costs diminishes very rapidly as the project proceeds. Of course, these terms 'early' and 'late' are comparative only. The actual time involved in being early, as opposed to being late, will vary quite considerably from case to case.

Accepting the fact that cost control is most effective in the early stages of project development, it has to be recognised that costs are controlled, in the first place, by controlling the *scope* of a project. Scope is determined initially by the process design and its further development as engineering design. The parameters in this context are most certainly fixed in the early stages, if not the very early stages, and once established all subsequent effort will have only a marginal influence on cost. This is the basic message of Figure 3.3, a message that must never be forgotten. However, as a project proceeds, scope changes are almost inevitable. Often, they are the inevitable consequence of the initial decisions: requirements that were overlooked at the earlier stage. This but serves to reemphasise the critical importance of those early decisions.

For major projects, say those involving a capital investment of £100 million or more, the number of items to be purchased can well be in the tens of thousands, and the number of separate planned activities will be in the thousands. The information relating to all this will inevitably generate an enormous amount of paperwork, which *must* be processed expeditiously and systematically if it is going to be of any use. A computer is often employed to facilitate this data processing, and can be of very great help, provided we do not get 'drowned' in a flood of printouts. Having noted that 'a little, very early' is far more effective than 'too much, too late', let us realise that this flood of information could well defeat its purpose: cost control. So whilst the detail may be necessary and inevitable in areas such as procurement and construction, we should seek a simple approach to project cost control. An answer today may not be so precise, nor as detailed, as an answer in three weeks' time, but it is close enough to the truth to be quite effective for cost control purposes. This aspect is developed in detail in Chapter 6, when we get down to the 'nitty-gritty' of project cost control administration.

## Communications

Good communications are basic to successful project management and play a very important role in completing a project on time, and within the budget. Every member of the project team must know his specific role, and the purpose it serves in the overall context of project administration. What *exactly* is expected of him? How vital is his (*each* individual) role in the total picture? What will happen if one link in the long chain fails? Yet more important, what rewards, monetary and otherwise, are to be accepted if each person performs his assigned task to the best of his ability within the overall schedule?

It is well recognised by management experts that our communications are very poor. Perhaps poorer today than fifty years ago. This is but a 'hunch' on our part: we have no proof. But we are sure that communications are the weakest link in the chain of requirements for effective project management and its concomitant benefit, effective cost control. It is *the* factor that invariably appears when the causes of failure are studied. The major reasons for projects not being completed on time, and within budget, are:

(a) Poor morale
(b) Poor human relations
(c) Poor labour productivity
(d) No commitment by those involved.

All of these owe much to, and are even generated by, poor communications. So much has been written about the theory and practice of communications, yet the years pass without any significant improvement. Peter Drucker in his Foreword to the recent book on the subject states quite bluntly that poor communications are a direct result of our ignorance. We do not know: what to say; when to say it; how to say it; or to whom to say it. There is certainly no mincing of words here!

Information regarding any project can be generated in only two ways: (1) by written communications; or (2) by word of mouth. But people rarely read carefully what is written and, what is worse, hardly ever listen. Worse still, they only read and listen to what they want to read and listen to! We tend to read and to listen to what suits us, and fits in with our own ideas. Just in case you doubt this, just try a little experiment. Next time a friend greets you with the words:

'How do you do?' say in reply: 'I died last week.' The chances are better than 50 per cent that your friend will hear you say: 'Fine, how are you?' This is because that is what he *expects* you to say. Because that is what he expects, that is what he hears. Do you still doubt that it is so?

It has been estimated that half our waking hours are occupied in listening, or what is called 'listening', to others. The other half of our time is spent reading, writing or speaking. We know, it seems, the reason for poor communications, but not the solution: how to make people *really* listen. There is an enormous volume of literature on this subject – over 200 books on listening alone – but we still go on in the same old way. Suffice it to say for the moment that there remains a lot to be desired in this matter of communications. If, therefore, we will only recognise that fact, and allow for it – by saying the same thing ten times over, in ten different ways, for instance – we are on the way to solving the problem. Let us let you into a secret: we have done just that in this book.

Why have we dealt with this subject of communications at some length? The instructions and the information from the project manager to the members of his team can only come to them in writing, or verbally. If they neither read nor listen carefully, then he is getting nowhere. What chance has he of getting the right things done at the right time? So it will pay real dividends to give a great deal of attention to communication within the project team, and between owner and contractor.

## Cost control is everybody's business

Who controls cost? Those who incur those costs. This includes everyone connected with the project, whether at site or at the head office, together with all the suppliers and subcontractors. Earlier we emphasised that cost control is in effect the prevention of waste and since waste is caused by people, it can only be controlled by them. Most of the waste is potential to begin with: a design that has not been optimised. So that is where cost control must start. Leaving it to the construction stage is far too late.

Each member of the project team, to begin with, is in a position to affect, and thus control cost. But they cannot act in isolation, because we would then have 'too many cooks', and we know what that leads to. The key person, in cost control, as in every other aspect of the project, is the project manager, for he should have the 'helicopter view', and realise the impact of what is being done on all aspects of a project. We have already likened his role to that of the captain of a ship or aircraft. When we come to consider the specific area of cost control, where everyone should be 'cost conscious' and play their part, perhaps a more appropriate analogy would be to consider, or compare the project manager to the conductor of an orchestra. The best result will only be produced when all are playing in 'harmony', following the lead (baton) of the project manager. Each member has his individual and valuable contribution to make: if any one was missing there would be something lacking. But they *must* play in unison. The conductor succeeds because he has direct and instant communication with each and every member of his orchestra. The project manager needs just that, and we see yet once again the importance of communications in effective project cost control.

The project manager leads in controlling cost. But without the full cooperation of every member of his team he can control nothing. So who controls cost? Everyone connected with the project, we then say. But let us think a little further. Let us think a little more about this word 'control'.

### The real constraints

Our basic concern throughout this particular chapter has been to try and bring home the all pervading importance of cost control, but it is very easy indeed to be unable to see the wood for the trees. This is a potentially dangerous situation and can be of major significance in multi-project developments, because the bigger the investment, the more sophisticated the systems that are employed. Hereby a delusion develops. The flow of data can create the illusion that events are 'under control'. In fact, of course, they have their own momentum. The real trick in effective project *management* (rather than 'control') is to find out where that 'momentum' is taking one.

Any company proceeding to implement a series of capital projects operates under two basic groups of constraints: one internal, the other external. The internal constraints are largely the result of company policy (or the result of a lack of policy). The external constraints motivate some of the internal constraints and also constrain the contractors, subcontractors, manufacturers and others who contribute either directly or indirectly to the progress of the project.

Whilst a project is under study, and during the early stages of design and order placement, the internal constraints are all important. Once, however, the project is largely committed, the external constraints assume the dominating role. What are these constraints? They have been summarised as: (a) sociological (b) inflationary (c) ecological (d) political (3). The relative impact and importance of these several factors will vary from country to country. Typical of the sociological constraints are the availability of natural resources, the availability of labour, the quality of labour, the population trend, and the quality of life in the country concerned. We bring things closer to home by reflecting that all these things influence the frequency of strikes, the availability of transport to the site, the need to build canteens and toilets on site: and it is all these things that determine the cost and rate at which a project is brought to completion.

The ecological? As we shall see, despite facile communications and the many similarities, there is still a great difference between building a process plant in the United Kingdom as compared with either Western Europe or the USA. We highlight this in Chapter 5. Why should this be? The fundamental reason is ecological: that water that separates and still insulates the islands of Great Britain, even though in one place it is only twenty miles wide. This is a critical constraint.

All the efforts to overcome these constraints, or work within them, are ultimately reflected in what is accomplished: what is built. In this book, as the work progresses, we call that accomplishment 'value of work done'. Plotted over time, it takes the form of an S-curve, and the end result of the constraints we have been discussing is to lead us inevitably to the 'Law of the S-curve', a key section in Chapter 7, when we come to discuss our targets, and how we get there. A *law*, indeed! So *who* controls costs? We will be a long way along the right path if we can but recognise our limitations, and work within them. It never helped to attempt the impossible.

## References

1 Bentley, T. J., *Making Cost Control Work*, MacMillan, 1978, 152 pp.
2 Pomeranz, F., *Managing Capital Budget Projects – A Preemptive Audit Approach*, Wiley, New York, 1984, 258 pp.
3 Guthrie, K. M., *Managing Capital Expenditure for Construction Projects*, Craftsman Book Co., USA, 1977, 624 pp.

# 4 Designing to cost

Necessity *is* the mother of invention. During World War II the supply of certain critical materials was either cut off or reserved for defence purposes, and manufacturers were compelled to look for substitute materials. Man's ingenuity rose to the occasion and substitute materials were found or created. With the war over and the supply of the previously critical and scarce materials resuming their normal availability, the users reverted to the original materials. The substitutes were discarded without a second thought: discarded, that is, by the great majority. The firm General Electric in the USA was a notable exception.

### How did it all start?

General Electric noticed that in many cases the substitute was less expensive and/or more reliable than the original, traditional material. So they asked the basic question: Why discard the substitute? Why not use this alternative material voluntarily and so get better value for money? As a result of this thinking, a General Electric purchasing agent, Mr. L. D. Miles, together with a team of three, was assigned to this task in 1947. Their analysis of products and materials to determine which was the better value for money – that is, achieve the required function at the lowest cost – led to the founding of a new discipline. This new discipline was called value analysis (VA) and through its application to their business General Electric saved more than US$200 million in seventeen years. The US Navy adopted the technique, calling it value engineering (VE) and in the first year of its application they achieved a saving of some US$18 million. Then came the US Air Force, in 1955. Then value engineering got a further boost in 1959, when Mr. Robert

McNamara, then US Secretary of Defense, gave it the further strength of official policy, resulting in a saving of US$14 billion in the first five years of application throughout the department.

Mr. Miles and his associates in General Electric, who began it all, value analysed each product or item of equipment *vis-à-vis* its function systematically, starting from scratch and without taking anything at all for granted. It is in this respect that value analysis, or value engineering, differs significantly from the conventional cost reduction techniques that were current at that time – and still are in many quarters. The emphasis is on function rather than on product and the search is on to see what else could perform that function. The main criterion is *value*, and *not* cost. Cost is determined by what an item is, whereas value is determined by what an item *does*. Value is always relative and its assessment somewhat subjective. It is related to utility and cost, and can only be assessed by the user.

How then does value engineering differ from other cost reduction techniques, such as works study? First and foremost, the latter 'clips costs', whilst value engineering 'blasts costs'. Secondly, value engineering is a disciplined and organised approach which takes nothing for granted. Thirdly, its utility lies, above all, in teamwork. Lastly, the emphasis in value engineering is laid on function, and the function, once clearly established, has to be fulfilled without sacrificing quality. The technique peels the 'cost onion' layer by layer, identifying each unnecessary cost. Under such detailed and powerful scrutiny, the cost pyramid tumbles down.

## Value engineering in a nutshell

Putting the subject in a nutshell, value engineering asks a series of simple, direct questions:

> What  –  is it?
>        –  does it do?
>        –  is it worth?
>        –  does it cost?
>        –  else will work?
>        –  does *that* cost?

This series of questions has to be asked and answered in a logical sequence, as illustrated in Figure 4.1. You will see that answers are expected. This illustrates the basic philosophy of value engineering. There *is* a better way to do it. Find it! In fact, in value engineering one never rests on one's laurels. There must be a continuous

| A. | COLLECT INFORMATION | |
|---|---|---|
| | What *is* it? | — Gather the facts |
| | does it *do*? | — Determine function |
| | is it *worth*? | — Evaluate function |
| | does it *cost*? | — Evaluate cost or worth |
| B. | SPECULATION | |
| | What *else* will work? | — Brainstorming |
| | | — Eliminate |
| | | — Simplify |
| C. | ANALYSIS | |
| | What does *that* cost? | — List pros & cons |
| | | — Assign value to each |
| | | — Select best ideas |
| D. | PLANNING | |
| | Alternate solutions | — Analyse specifics |
| | | — Assess feasibility & savings |
| E. | REPORT AND IMPLEMENT | |
| | Define | — Prepare report and proposal |
| | | — Discuss with management |
| | | — Translate ideas into action |
| | | — Schedule & funding |
| | | — Monitor to completion |

**Figure 4.1 The sequence for answers**
The questions posed by value engineering should be presented and answered in a logical sequence.

attempt to improve on the 'best' solution, for how can one ever know that the 'best' has in fact been achieved. The answer is always somewhat subjective. The technique can therefore be summarised as:

Blast – Create – Define

Value engineering is *the* way to reduce costs! It can be applied not only in the engineering field, where it originated, but also to services, management control, information resources and capital projects. Properly applied, value engineering does more than maintain quality at reduced cost: it can actually enhance quality.

Quality engineering and value engineering, indeed, are but two sides of the same coin.

The basic objective of value engineering is to provide a specific function at the lowest cost *without affecting quality*. Quality engineering, on the other hand, seeks to improve quality, naturally without increasing cost if at all possible. To be effective, value engineering must be applied to the heels of quality engineering: only thus can the maximum benefit be obtained. This fact is illustrated diagrammatically in Figure 4.2. The later the change is made, the more it costs to make that change and the less the saving that can result (1).

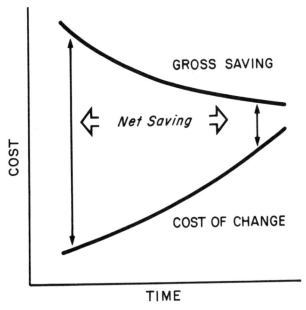

**Figure 4.2 Saving through value engineering**
The saving made is subject to the law of diminishing returns. The cost of making changes rises ever more rapidly, whilst the scope for economies steadily decreases.

## The value engineer

Value engineering is an attitude of mind and a way of thinking. Dare we say that value engineering is only used by champions – they become the champions in the process! The difference between a winner and a runner-up in a race is sometimes very small indeed, but what a difference in the reward. But winners need a coach: experience always has a role to play. This is where the value engineer, or value analyst comes in. He must combine youthful imagination with mature judgment and sound technology. He must be a psychologist, engineer and salesman all rolled into one, yet at the same time he must have the ability to see the problem through the eyes of his management. He must be able to lead and direct a multi-disciplinary team, with perhaps members from the design, production, estimating, purchasing and sales departments. He must be an innovator, *not* an inventor. The invention must already be available to him.

Does such a super-being exist? Most certainly. There is one in every organisation, but real managerial ability may well be required to pick the needle out of the haystack. And then, to crown it all, our value engineer must be humble, that most difficult of qualities. It is worthy of note that Mr. Miles, credited by most writers on this subject with being the father of this new and most valuable discipline, hardly mentions his own personal role in his classic work on the subject (2).

Value engineering will only be successfully applied if it receives something more than top management support. It must have top management *involvement*. Mere paying of lip service to the principles we have outlined – and who would not assent to them in principle – mere lip service is just not enough. But of course and as usual, management must be properly informed. They should not be called upon to make decisions 'blind'. Thus, when reporting, or making proposals, the value engineer should see that management is told quite clearly:

> What    –   is the cost
>          –   is the benefit
>          –   is the risk

The order above is quite significant. Putting it candidly, our value engineer has first to say: 'Look, what a beautiful rainbow', and then demonstrate where the rainbow ends! That is why he has to be a salesman too!

Value engineering is inter-disciplinary and all embracing. A typical VE team would comprise: a designer, an estimator, a producer, a purchaser, a salesman and a value engineer. The value engineer acts as the coordinator in the team. One member from each function is quite sufficient, although it is advisable to rotate membership in order to generate fresh ideas. The value engineer will normally act as chairman of this little committee, as well as coordinating their work. He may be a specialist in any branch, although when we come to process plants engineering knowledge will be desirable. In addition, he should have had reasonable exposure to the other disciplines with which he now has to work, and extensive training in value engineering as such. The other members of the team should also be initiated into the mysteries of value engineering before they start working together: a sort of orientation course. The team have to work as a team: so they all have to get on to the same 'wavelength'. Probably the best person to conduct such an introductory course is the value engineer himself, or perhaps an outside consultant can be used. All this demands that the value engineer must be fairly senior in his organisation, reporting directly to top management. As we have said earlier, the involvement of top management is fundamental to effective value engineering.

**Value engineering in action**

Our subject is cost control *in action* and value engineering has also been seen in action, with great benefits. It has been most publicised in relation to government contracts in the US, and has given real incentive to both contractor and client. The Department of Defense contracts there include a VE clause inviting contractors to challenge unrealistic specifications and requirements and suggest changes to reduce cost (3). Any savings are then shared between the two parties. As a consequence some 5,000 *Value Engineering Change Proposals* were submitted by contractors over a four-year period, of which some 55 per cent were approved. These resulted in overall savings of some US$50 million, of which the contractor's share was nearly half.

It is very clear from these figures that value engineering works and if properly applied provides a real incentive to devise and propose cost reduction changes. The contractor's cost in developing the proposal may well be lost if it is not approved, but that is a risk well worth taking, since the gain from an approved change is substantial. It was also found by experience that the greatest opportunity for successful VE came in the *preconstruction phase* of the project. In other words, the earlier the better, a point we have been striving to emphasise. Project cost control should always start at the *beginning* of a project, the benefit being demonstrated graphically in Figure 4.2 and in real financial terms by the illustration of VE in action that we have just given.

The approach has now been developed to the extent that a

specific terminology is in common use, much as has been the case with network analysis in planning. Just as there we meet terms understood only by the initiated, such as 'free float', with value engineering one meets terms such as 'blast' (which we have already mentioned), 'use value', 'cost value' and 'esteem value', all of which have precise definitions. For a simple outline of the technique, we would refer you to a paper giving an outline of the subject by P. Saint, first published in 1973 but of such interest that it was reprinted in 1986 (4).

### Designing to cost

The crux of VE is to design to cost. This was the philosophy of Henry Ford, who perhaps anticipated VE by a quarter of a century. The industrial world may have lost a great deal by not paying more attention to Mr. Ford's concept. The conventional approach is to design an item, then cost it and on that basis fix the selling price. Is it any wonder that many ventures based on this traditional method of approach have failed? The selling price that comes out of that particular mill may be such that the customer does not consider the item 'good value for money'. The outlook adopted by Henry Ford and the value engineer is the very reverse of this. Start rather with the price that the market can bear: work backwards to cost and so finally, to the design. This is the 'design to cost' concept. It is pragmatic, down to earth: the realistic approach. With this concept, the cost of production, based on the selling price, is the established price. The designer is therefore required to develop a design that can be produced at, or under, the predetermined cost target.

To illustrate, let us consider the example of Mr. Ford. He started with the premise that cost is *not* fixed. In fact, the real cost is seldom known. The selling price, once fixed in relation to the market, forces the cost down, and the design is geared to meet that cost. This is not only common sense, but also good business sense, judging by the phenomenal success of the Ford 'Model T'. Surely it is strange that Henry Ford's philosophy, first exercised in 1923, restated and termed value engineering some twenty-five years later, has still not achieved the wide acceptance it deserves. How many organisations outside perhaps Japan and the USA, really practise VE, as apart from just paying it 'lip service'?

There is no doubt at all that the use of VE techniques early on in the design process can result in drastic reductions in the cost of the final product. A good VE team will challenge the user's criteria and eliminate those standards and specifications which do nothing to improve performance, but merely add to the final cost. A second, and even a third look by a VE team during the design process will almost invariably provide less expensive alternative approaches to the original design concepts. In addition, and going alongside this work, efforts are also being aimed at reduction in operation and maintenance costs, and this always produces good results. However, because of the lamentable lack of experience in the application of these techniques, the more usual course of events is as we describe below.

Right at the beginning the user sets standards that are so high that the cost is phenomenal. The construction of the nuclear reactor and its ancillaries are – or rather were – a glaring example of this approach. The specifications in the beginning were 'Super Rolls-Royce'. The designer, coming to detail, takes a pragmatic view of the whole issue – he has to get the design finished – and arrives at a design with a moderate cost, but one still far higher than that which would lead to a selling price which the market can happily bear. What is the alternative? We are already too late. The construction team can reduce costs by applying VE concepts in their area: a further VE exercise applied once the plant is in production can no doubt reduce maintenance costs, and so produce further savings. This process is logical, but the big opportunity has long been lost. It is no substitute for the full use of VE right at the beginning, during design development.

The conclusion? A little extra time and effort spent at this stage can pay rich dividends. This is one of our *basic* messages to you, and it will be emphasised time and again throughout this book. A fundamental principle in project cost control is to *act early*.

## Parametric cost estimating (PCE)

A key factor in the application of VE techniques to process plants is the ability to make reliable, consistent, *comparable* estimates at an early stage. It is here that parametric cost estimating comes to our aid. This technique relates cost to certain parameters or characteristics of a product or process system, and the approach is based on historical data. The parameters used obviously depend on the industry and on the product. For example, in the steel industry the parameter chosen could be cost per ton, which is in effect a measure of productivity. The same yardstick could also be used for the fabrication of process equipment, provided reliable, accurate historical data was available. To illustrate further, so far as the process plant and equipment industry is concerned, parameters can be selected reflecting physical characteristics, or performance characteristics. Thus:

Physical      –   area : volume : weight : capacity
Performance   –   heat : duty : HP : KVA

Parametric cost estimating has a particularly important part to play in the very early stages of design, and hence in VE, when the preliminary design characteristics are being established and one needs to know the probable cost quickly. The cost developed from the historical data will refer to some specific base year, and be updated using escalation factors. As the design work proceeds, and more time is available, these preliminary estimates can always be firmed up by enquiry of manufacturers. The cost data available also needs to be corrected for what is called the 'learning effect' and general technological advance. However, this is a most difficult area, since such correction factors are seldom available, except after the event, when they become incorporated once again into our historical data.

The extent to which such data is available will vary from company to company, but such data as *is* available should be very carefully documented and updated whenever possible.

The process plant and equipment industry has been using PCE for many many years. This particular industry uses capacity/cost and performance/cost curves extensively in cost estimating, and even to establish a price. Most contractors in the industry have a wealth of such information, locked up in their secret data banks – the so-called 'black books'. The data will have been accumulated from the various projects that they have built over the years, in various parts of the world, over several decades. It is continuously being collated, analysed and updated by specialists (they call them estimators) for use on new projects as they come along. Fortunately, contractors and sometimes even fabricators, are kind enough to publish data of this kind from time to time, but unfortunately the great volume of such data relates to the USA.

### The vital few and the trivial many

A complete process plant consists of many thousands of separate items. It is the same, of course, with a car or a plane. The application of VE, as discussed earlier, to each and every item would be a tedious, laborious and unending job. Fortunately, there is a well-known principle, first enunciated by an Italian born Swiss economist, one Vilfredo Pareto, in 1898, that comes to our rescue here. Whilst he was studying the distribution of income, Pareto found that just a few people had most of the money. This is, of course, nothing new in itself: many people over the centuries have observed precisely the same phenomenon in their own locality. It is true even today!

Unfortunately, however, this important principle lay buried for many years, until it was rediscovered and applied to the current industrial situation quite recently. The principle was then enunciated in numerical terms, and became a law. It was known as the famous 80:20 rule, which states, in effect, that relatively few causes are responsible for practically all of the effect observed. More recently still, this same principle has been reduced to one terse statement: 'Vital few vs. Trivial many'. The scope of the rule, in numerical terms, is illustrated diagrammatically in Figure 4.3. In any situation, therefore, if we listen to the rule, it is sufficient to concentrate on the 'vital few' items. Nothing will be lost if this approach is adopted. The use of the same principle led to the very popular A–B–C analysis used in materials management. Figure 4.4 lists the application of the principle to a series of items to illustrate its wide and general use. Of course, the list started in Figure 4.4 is actually unending. It is a pity that such a simple, powerful and timesaving tool remained hidden and failed to be utilised by industry for several decades after it was first stated. But this prolonged delay in application of new principles has a number of parallels in history, science and engineering. It could be quite an interesting piece of research to ascertain how long a time elapsed between certain inventions or discoveries first seeing the light of day and their eventual application on a wide scale. The time may be growing ever longer these days, with the so-called 'knowledge explosion', which makes it ever more difficult to find out anything about anything. This is the intractable problem of 'information retrieval'.

But to return to our prime subject – the process plant. A process plant, once again, consists of a great many individual and different items – items of plant and equipment – and we have to consider not only the individual items but also their interrelationship. Change one and you have to change another. It would be virtually impossible to 'value analyse' them all. However, applying the rule, it is quite sufficient to concentrate one's attention on the 'vital few', perhaps even less than 20 per cent in number. The 'trivial many' can then take care of themselves! Look at Figure 4.5 for a moment: a typical

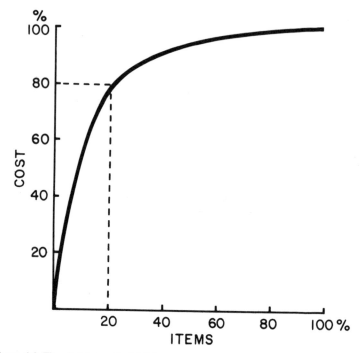

**Figure 4.3 The vital few – the trivial many**
Within the area bounded by the dotted line (80:20) lie the vital few. The rest, the trivial many, can be safely ignored.

| THE FEW (normally 20%) | | MOST (normally 80%) |
|---|---|---|
| Employees | contribute to | Absenteeism |
| Products | contribute to | Sales & Profits |
| Items | contribute to | Cost |
| Suppliers | contribute to | Problems |
| Employers | contribute to | Sales |
| Tasks | take up | Time |

**Figure 4.4 The vital few highlighted**
Here we see the way in which the 'vital few' can contribute to cost savings.

---

### COMPONENTS OF PRODUCT COST

| | |
|---|---|
| Materials, including bought out: | 40% |
| Direct labour: | 10% |
| Overheads and administration costs: | 45% |
| Profit, gross: | 5% |
| Selling price to wholesaler | 100% |

---

**Figure 4.5  Components of product cost**
This analysis lets one see where to look for the significant savings.

analysis of product cost. All materials still only total 40 per cent of total cost, but of course, savings there bring consequential savings in the other items that contribute to total cost.


## Value engineering and process plants

The VE technique has been used more recently in the building industry and in the construction of various types of process plants. The construction industry, although one of the biggest in terms of volume, is one of the most conservative of industries. Although design engineering, as such, constitutes perhaps little more than five per cent of the total cost of a project in the construction industry, the decisions made at the design stage have a profound influence upon the final project cost. It is therefore well worth while offering considerable incentives, and making a material investment, in efforts that will lead to a more economic design. It is also possible to appy VE to the construction phase in the field, and a formalised documentation that would give a basis for its application could pay rich dividends. The VE approach is without a doubt invaluable in decision making on major capital projects, including process plants. Its merits are slowly being recognised, but its application is still very limited.

To illustrate the way in which the VE concept can be applied in the process plant area, we can take the study made of the standard 1,000 tonne per day ammonia plant. A series of competitive bids was received, and selection was not easy. So a consultant was engaged to facilitate the decision. The cost analysis made by the consultant, as illustrated in Figure 4.6, demonstrated that there were savings in capital cost as the hydrogen content of the feedstock increased. However, the price of the feedstock rose inversely against the hydrogen content, with the result that the ultimate

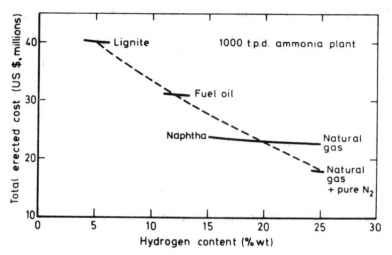

**Figure 4.6 Capital cost versus hydrogen in the feedstock**
Relationship between feedstock specification and capital cost. The general trend between investment cost and hydrogen content can be seen from the broken line. The heavy lines show the local relationship within the rather narrow limits of a specific feedstock. (With thanks to Dolphin Development Company, Beaconsfield, UK, for permission to publish.)

production cost was about the same, whichever feedstock was chosen. But the consultant, using VE techniques, went one step further, and analysed the possibility of using pure nitrogen instead of air in the synthesis step. This suggestion arose from the fact that the primary product of air separation plants is oxygen and the nitrogen a by-product in surplus. It should therefore be available in volume at low cost. Adopting this suggestion led to substantial savings in the investment cost of the natural gas feed plant. The production cost still remained essentially the same.

Another recent application of VE in the process industries which came to our notice relates to the new mechanical vapour recompression system (MVR), as compared with the traditional multi-effect evaporator (MEE). Evaporation requires very considerable energy, so that any means of conserving energy in the process is more than welcome. For instance, an MEE with four effects requires some 250 Btu per lb. of evaporation. Additional energy is required for pumping the very substantial quantities of cooling water required, which amounts to from 3–6 gallons per lb. of evaporation.

With MVR however, the modern concept, the first stage vapour is mechanically compressed and then used as the heating medium in the same stage. As a result the vapour is condensed in the evaporator itself and no external condenser is required. The energy requirement therefore falls – falls quite dramatically – to some 30 Btu per lb. of evaporation. However, due to the low overall temperature difference, the surface area in the evaporator is larger and the capital cost of the equipment in consequence higher than that for the traditional process. However, the operational economy is such that the extra investment can be recovered in the first year of operation, and the new process remains exceedingly attractive.

The multi-effect evaporator still remains the more economical process overall for thick, viscous solutions, because of the higher temperature differences and better heat transfer that can therefore be secured. But VE does not rest content. That situation is examined, and the application of VE pointed to a combination of the two systems in such a case, the new system being employed in the initial stage and the traditional system in the final stage. Such a combination may well sound complex, but that approach gave the optimum result.

We do hope that we have not been too technical, but these two cases have been quoted in some detail to give a little idea of the interplay that goes on between process, capital cost and operational cost. All this has to be analysed by the value engineer in order to secure the maximum benefit from the technique. It is of no use to reduce capital cost, for instance, if operational cost soars as a consequence.

Whilst we have laid substantial emphasis on the application of VE early, we would not wish to create the impression that that is the only time when it can be effective. The same approach should be made to all the activities, throughout the time that the plant is being built. Figure 4.7, for instance, illustrates the result of VE analysis in the construction phase. As will be seen, the cost/time curve has minima related to normal time of completion, and minimum cost. If, however, there is reason to put pressure on, and complete the plant in 'crash' time, then the capital cost of building the plant goes up considerably. The VE approach analyses the merits of the situation, looking not only at the capital cost, but the benefits that will accrue from early completion, to recommend the most advantageous approach in a given context.

The very real significance of time in relation to the VE effort is illustrated in Figure 4.8. We have said that with VE, as with everything else, the earlier the better, but of course situations arise, such as we have just mentioned, where VE can be applied with profit in the later stages of development of a project. Figure 4.8 relates the cost reduction due to VE to the corresponding cost of the recommended change, both as a function of time. The graph,

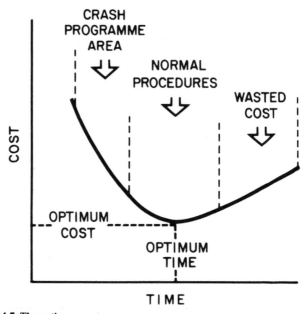

**Figure 4.7 The optimum cost curve**
Expenditure to achieve a 'crash' programme can be justified if the saving in time is valuable enough, but money spent after the optimum time has passed is just money wasted.

though typical only, clearly demonstrates the principle that we have been at pains to emphasise and demonstrate throughout this chapter: the earlier the better. Application of VE brings the greatest economy in the early stages of design. Delay reduces the options that are open to one, and hence the potential benefits, quite drastically.

## Benefits and incentives

General Electric, who were the first to introduce the VE concept, claimed to have saved some US$200 million in seventeen years through its application. As we said earlier, the concept was also used widely by the Department of Defense in the USA, with savings of more than US$14 billion in the first five years of the programme. With such colossal savings in prospect, VE spread like a tidal wave across the USA, and its ripples reached Europe in 1960. Dunlop in the United Kingdom were the first to take up VE there. Two associates of Miles left GE in 1958 to form their own company,

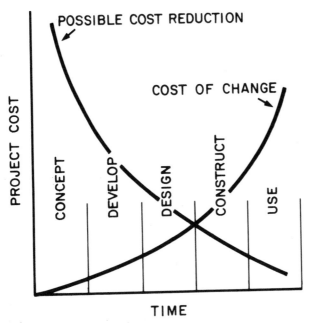

**Figure 4.8 Typical project execution**
As a project moves from the initial concept through all the phases of design and
construction to ultimate use, the ability to reduce cost falls, while the cost of change
rises sharply. This aspect is further discussed in Chapter 9, under the heading 'The
work cycle'.

Value Analysis Inc., and in 1962 the firm Value Engineering
Limited was set up in the UK. A survey of several firms using VE in
the UK indicated savings of the order indicated in Figure 4.9. With
the possibilities being in the ranges indicated, one can expect, for
process plant construction, savings of the order of 30 per cent or
more. This is quite substantial and perhaps even incredible, but it is
possible. In fact, the saving on the application of VE is seldom less
than 5 per cent, frequently from 10 to 20 per cent, and sometimes
even exceeds 30 per cent. And let us not forget that the savings
indicated in Figure 4.9 are the direct, measurable savings. In
addition there are other indirect and intangible benefits and savings
which, if they could but be quantified, might well exceed the direct
benefits. VE can improve the entire climate and attitudes in an
organisation. Being essentially a team effort, it leads to better
communication, better understanding of one another, and thus
better human relations and fuller cooperation. These factors are
vital to the successful operation of a company, although most

```
SAVINGS THROUGH VALUE ENGINEERING

Type of Product                                    Saving
                                                   %

Consumer:                                          26–28
Light engineering:                                 29–32
Heavy engineering:                                 30–34

Heavy engineering is the class in which most process plant &
equipment falls.
```

**Figure 4.9 Savings through value engineering**
A table designed to demonstrate the potential for saving by value engineering
techniques in various major areas of the economy.

difficult to measure. They undoubtedly contribute to an improved
balance sheet – and all this is only a by-product!

How can companies be encouraged to use VE? Here the
purchasing department has an important role to play: that is where
it all began in GE, after all. Suppliers can be asked formally or
informally to apply VE, and given certain incentives to do so, such
as increased business, or orders without competitive tendering.

**Quality assurance and quality control**

Having discussed value engineering and the importance of designing to cost at length, our survey of the subject would not be
complete without some mention of *Quality Assurance* (QA) and
*Quality Control* (QC). Referring back to Figure 1.7, you will see
that there is a continual 'tug of war' between quality, cost and time.
Yet quality must be maintained. This is the function of Quality
Assurance, which relates to the entire range of activities and
functions involved in project implementation, including project
control, design, engineering specifications and the supporting
systems, all necessary to assure quality. Quality Control, which
should not be confused with QA, is a part of that function, relating
to the control and verification of the required quality.

It is now common practice for QA/QC policies to be formally
drawn up within a company as part of its overall directives in
relation to company policy, to ensure that high standards and
'fitness for purpose' are maintained throughout all their activities.
Now its relation to value engineering can be seen. In a sense it is the

consolidation of the results of value engineering into company practice. A comprehensive system of documentation, manuals and instructions is required and when a project is implemented the QA requirements should be defined at the outset. Equipment and material required need to be critically reviewed to determine the level of QA/QC needed, always bearing in mind key factors such as safety, liability, vendor capability and any special standards that have to be complied with. Product performance is now considered a crucial aspect and the strictest internal and external audits are necessary, pursued without fear or favour.

## But not a panacea

Value engineering, quality assurance and quality control are techniques designed to ensure that the client or customer gets 'value for money' and 'fitness for purpose'. Innovation will then be 'cost effective' and the contractor has to provide what he can sell, not try and sell what he has. But nothing is perfect and VE programmes can fail. A VE programme can fail because of insufficient top management involvement, or the wrong emphasis. So VE will never be a panacea for all ills. Similarly QA and QC need to be continuously sustained to achieve the objective in view. Once discipline relaxes – and it does – then poor work and accidents result.

What is the role of the project cost control engineer in all this? He has to watch and to warn. He has to see that the proper balance is maintained between those three key factors – quality, time and cost. His prime concern is cost, and that must never be lost sight of. Failure to keep cost within proper bounds will defeat the basic concept, since the right thing at the wrong price is still a failure.

So far, all that has been said applies largely to equipment and materials used on the project, but hardly at all to the management of the project itself. We have said that a project is well done if it is completed on time and within budget, but is that the end of the matter? Is that completed project the *best* answer, or merely an adquate answer? Surely the project manager and his team should be striving to produce the best possible answer. It is always possible to do better than you did last time and a good project manager realises this: he would never 'rest on his laurels', as the saying goes. Once a project manager and his team cease trying to do their best and become satisfied with 'second best' they are on the road to mediocrity. They must always be asking themselves: 'Have we got the best possible answer?' There is usually more than one solution to a problem and the alternatives should be reviewed, and studied: the philosophy so strongly upheld in value engineering. For instance, Professor Frank Lu of the University of Canterbury (New Zealand) says in his introduction to his book on economic decision making: (5)

> Alternatives are not always obvious, and the search for them can be a difficult task. It is, however, an extremely important task, one demanding skill and creativity. One of the essential attributes of a good engineer and manager is a sensitivity to alternatives and the ability to envisage them. This attribute, natural for some, may be improved upon and added to by others by conscious efforts of learning and vigilance.

This assessment of alternatives should be active not only when a project is initiated, but throughout its life, although the maximum benefits accrue in the early stages and fall away rapidly thereafter. There is a law of diminishing returns, as was demonstrated earlier in Figure 4.2.

Every project manager is inevitably confronted from time to time throughout the life of every project – we are sure that there are no exceptions – with crises that will require resolving. It is the choice of the best alternative for the resolution of such crises that leads on to a successful project. The project cost control engineer can and should be an active participant in such decision making: cost will almost always be a significant factor in relation to any decision reached.

One of the problems in devoting a whole chapter to a specific subject, such as we have just done to value engineering, is that by the time we come to the end of the chapter we may well think that we have the final answer to every problem. But of course this is not so, and never could be. Nothing succeeds like success, they say, but even VE can fail. Some of the reasons for the failure of a VE programme are: (a) overselling, (b) insufficient top management involvement, (c) wrong emphasis (on price rather than value) and (d) novelty wearing off. So you see that VE is *not* a panacea for all ills. Nor is it a cost reduction technique in the normal sense. Normal techniques 'clip costs', whereas VE, when applied with courage and conviction, will 'blast costs'. As we said, earlier, VE is for champions!

Value engineering *must* be a disciplined, organised, teamwork approach, seeking to analyse the functions of a product or process. It becomes a brainstorming session, striving to determine the various alternatives that will meet the function. Basic rethinking of familiar situations and techniques is called for. Only thus will the alternatives come to the surface. Then the alternatives are scrutinised for feasibility and examined for cost, to see which one provides the best value for money. Emphasis is on function and on value, rather than on the item itself, or cost.

In the case of new products or processes, VE introduces the creative concept 'design to cost', rather than the conventional approach of 'costing the design'. When we speak of 'designing to cost', never forget that the cost about which we are talking is the price at which the final product can be sold on the open market. During the course of this chapter, we have described some of the ways in which these fundamentals of VE can be applied to process plants, complex though as they always are.

As is so often the case throughout history, many a valuable concept goes unnoticed either by default or by virtue of the concept being too far ahead of its time. The industrial world has lost much due to such lapses. We are attempting to redress the balance a little and we hope that our enthusiasm will be contagious. Do not be put off by the novelty of this, or other approaches we may bring to your attention. Our subject is cost control *in action*, and we have tried to demonstrate that despite its still limited application worldwide, VE has been successfully in action for many, many years.

## References

1 Zimmerman, L. W., *Value Engineering – A Practical Approach for Owners, Designers and Contractors*, Van Nostrand, 1982.
2 Miles, L. D., *Technique of Value Analysis & Engineering*, McGraw-Hill, New York, 1972, 320 pp. Now in its 2nd edition.
3 O'Brien, J. J., *Value Analysis in Design and Construction*, McGraw-Hill, New York, 1976, 301 pp.
4 Saint, P., 'Value engineering', *The Cost Engineer*, Vol. 24, No. 1, January 1986, pp. 12–14. (Originally Vol. 12, No. 1, January 1973).
5 Lu, F. P. S., *Economic Decision-making for Engineers and Managers*, Whitcombe and Tombs, 1969, 172 pp.

# 5    Forewarned is forearmed

Our purpose here is to learn from past mistakes, and so give life to
the old proverb: 'Once bitten, twice shy'. But do we learn? We shall
pose this question once again when we come to the end of our story,
in Chapter 14 (Will we ever learn?), but let us just say for the
moment: we learn if we want to enough. The choice is most
certainly ours, and there should be no doubt as to the decision we
make after seeing what havoc project delays bring to the two key
parties involved – the owner and the contractor. The havoc wrought
is qualitative as well as quantitative. The quantitative aspect of the
matter has already been brought to your attention: just look at
Figure 2.1 once again. There you see the *direct* loss alone: the
indirect losses are always far greater. The particular illustration
given there shows indirect losses some four times the direct losses,
but this will vary from case to case and more often than not cannot
be fully evaluated. It has been calculated, for instance, that a ten per
cent increase in capital cost can cause a 25 per cent drop in
the return on the investment. This is based on the assumption of a
ten year life and depends to a considerable degree on the industry
we are looking at. With process plants, which is a field of high and
rapidly obsolescent technology, the life may well be only five years
and the drop in the return on the investment will be even more
marked.

The qualitative aspect of overruns has also been discussed in
Chapter 2. This relates especially to the loss of production by the
owner, resulting in lost market opportunities, whilst the contractor's reputation suffers, and his future business is affected. In both
cases the real cost of the delay is incalculable.

**Overruns (unfortunately) are the norm**

Many, many projects overrun in time or cost: mostly both. This is most unfortunate, when we consider that adequate techniques are available to prevent this, or at least minimise it. We have already seen in Chapter 2 that an overrun is basically a *waste* of scarce resources: the resources of time and money. We owe it to ourselves, let alone society, to eliminate waste, for ultimately we always pay for waste, through taxes or other fiscal measures, or the price of the product. Occasionally we hear in the technical press, and even sometimes the popular press, about a major overrun, but such events seldom make news. The contractor has his own interests to protect, and the owner will not wish to make the 'headlines' for such a reason. Their image with their shareholders or the general public can so easily be hurt by that type of publicity.

The major blame for an overrun may well rest on one of the two key parties, owner or contractor, but in the ultimate analysis both should be held equally responsible. Even in the case of a contractor carrying a turnkey contract, where in theory he has it all his own way, the owner seldom abrogates his interest. More often than not he still acts as a 'watchdog' over the activities of the contractor and he has sufficient resources and the authority to act if the 'trend' is unfavourable. But somehow, due perhaps to complacency or the fact that the contractor can be held fully responsible, the owner fails to take timely action: and that despite the fact that he must inevitably suffer as well as, if not more than the contractor. The owner should realise that his ability, contractually, to place responsibility at the door of the contractor in such cases, when a contract is going 'sour', is no help in the long run. A defaulting contractor may well have to pay a penalty for delay in completion, but that is no consolation to the owner, and hardly a deterrent to the erring contractor. The loss to the owner may well be ten times, perhaps a hundred times, the amount of the penalty he exacts, and the loss of reputation by the contractor is usually far more important to him than the direct financial loss.

Quite often, to state a problem clearly is to be halfway to its solution. It is generally accepted that we *know* that overruns are fairly common. But just how frequently they occur is a fact that is not really appreciated. Is it the case in eight projects out of ten? It would, we are sure, be quite instructive to develop detailed documentation on the subject, if only to highlight the problem and so help to resolve – perhaps solve – it.

## But the norm is not desirable

It hardly needs emphasising that overruns, though quite 'normal', are not desirable. They are, indeed, highly detrimental to both owner and contractor. How detrimental? Well, perhaps one real life example may suffice to bring the lesson home. There was once a contract let in the UK for a refinery. The first refinery to be completely designed and built by a wholly UK contractor: not the UK office of an American contractor. Thus, beyond doubt, a prestige project. The year was 1966, and the initial value of the contract, let on a turnkey basis, was some £25 million. The overrun in time was about a year, and the cost overrun some £12 million. The Chairman's report in the annual accounts of the contractor involved for the year ending March 31, 1969 gives a very frank description of the trials and tribulations associated with this particular contract, and details are included later in this chapter. The contractor's total turnover for 1968–69 was £53 million pounds, and this single contract brought a loss of £2.8 million, whereas without it the company would have made a *profit* of £2.8 million. So one contract accounted for roughly 50 per cent of the company's annual turnover, brought a loss of £5.6 million, and transformed the balance sheet.

But do not think that all this was due to lack of experience. In another contract, a USA contractor with an annual turnover of nearly a billion dollars was practically 'wiped out' by the losses on one single LNG (Liquid natural gas) contract in Algeria. The overrun exceeded the initial value of the contract. But more of that particular story later. The points we now want to drive home are: (a) overruns are expensive and can be fatal; and (b) overruns are far too common. But they need not be. The use of strict and efficient cost control procedures will mitigate this state of affairs remarkably. But you have to be convinced of this. Cost control usually receives a lot of 'lip service', but very little else. We hope that the 'how to do it' data we shall be presenting later will be heeded and help to achieve the prime objective, namely to complete a project on time, and within the budget.

### Size has nothing to do with it

Time and cost overruns can occur on any project, large or small, if it is left to itself. Size has nothing whatever to do with it. It is a fact of life that *every* project will overrun if left to itself, and both owner and contractor can then only be silent spectators. At least, they may well be 'silent' to begin with, but at the end of the day, when the position is not only apparent but irretrievable, they may well shout a lot: but by then it is too late.

Small projects can go wrong in this way just as well – just as easily

– as large projects. It is only that the larger the project, the higher the stakes, and the more likely the publicity. You may well think that there are more things to go wrong with a large project. There will be a greater number of suppliers, a bigger workforce on the site, complex coordination problems. But what is a large project? Back in the sixties the refinery we mentioned earlier, costing £25 million (no, £37 million in truth) was considered 'very large': today that order of value would only qualify as a 'run of the mill' project. These days a large project will be more than £200 million, and projects run up to £1,000 million. We will be discussing this question of size and its implications much later (Chapter 13 – Projects come in all sizes), so for the moment let us only recognise that size is an irrelevance when discussing overruns. Small or large, they will all suffer the same fate if the proper approach to project cost control is not adopted.

**The problem is worldwide**

Projects, including process plant projects, come in all sizes, *and* they are being built all over the world. Wherever there is a project there is a strong chance of an overrun. No-one, anywhere in the world, is exempt. No-one is clever enough, wherever they live, whatever their background, to prevent overruns at all times, on *all* their projects. It does seem, however, that the developing and less developed countries are more vulnerable in this respect, and so suffer more from the problem. We have said that overruns are actually the norm, but that they are seldom talked about publicly, and rarely make the headlines. But those 'in the know' are better informed. To take but one example, every senior project manager can undoubtedly list from his own personal experience a dozen projects or more with substantial overruns: never his fault, of course. But this simply indicates the magnitude of the problem. It would be nice if we could produce facts and figures to fully substantiate this basic truth: an overrun is as close as the very next project you undertake.

If this fact is realised and the real seriousness of the situation brought home, then perhaps the subject of project cost control will be taken more seriously and the incidence of overruns reduced, or at least their individual magnitude minimised.

**Some classic overruns**

A classic example of cost overrun in the field of high technology is given to us as we examine the history of the development and construction of Concorde (1). Figure 5.1 illustrates the way in which the estimated total cost of the project grew as time passed, until it was more than *four times* the original estimate. The case for terminating the project along the line must surely have been compelling indeed, but they persisted and as we all know, the plane now flies regular services across the world. The product is a technical success.

| BRITAIN – THE CONCORDE OVERRUN | | |
|---|---|---|
| Original estimate = 100 | | |
| SPENT | COST OF REMAINING WORK | REVISED ESTIMATE |
| 100 | 150 | 250 |
| 150 | 120 | 270 |
| 200 | 140 | 340 |
| 250 | 150 | 400 |
| 300 | 120 | 420 |

**Figure 5.1 The Concorde overrun**
This table demonstrates the way in which the estimate climbed as the work progressed.

As we said earlier, neither owner nor contractor likes to talk about substantial overruns on projects. However, there is one very well documented case history in the UK, the Humberside Refinery referred to earlier. As it so happens, the Chairman of the contracting company issued a very frank and objective history of the entire episode in a statement made on completion of the contract (1969). We would like to quote from this statement extensively since it drives home some of the major reasons for overruns. The italics from time to time are our emphasis, designed to highlight what we consider to be the vital points in the statement. We have also altered the names in the statement to 'owner' and 'contractor' as relevant. The Chairman said:

> The Humber Refinery contract is, by any standard, very large, being of the order of *£25 million*. It had an effective date in July 1966, and the Contractor undertook to use its best endeavours to complete by November 28th, 1986, a period of about *28 months*. At no time was the Contractor responsible for the process design. This had to be furnished by the Owner, who was required to provide the flow sheets (which define the entire complex of sequential and interrelated processes and which are fundamental to the design and to the materials required), the equipment specifications and much other information. Briefly, the Contractor had to convert this information into a going refinery and to that end had to engineer the wide areas of supporting services, generally known as the Utilities. It also had to procure the equipment and arrange for its

erection, all these sub-contracts being subject to the Owner's approval. In the Tender documents, the Owner's requirements were defined in close detail and this justified the Directors of the Contractor in authorising acceptance of the contract on a two-part basis, viz.: *a lump sum price for engineering and management and a Guaranteed Maximum Price for the remainder*, i.e, the equipment and construction costs. As the Contractor began to study the design information supplied to it, it became apparent that the requirements expressed in the documents differed from what the Contractor had contracted to supply. Furthermore, the scrutiny by the Contractor (and one of his major subcontractors) revealed the *need for rectification in parts of the design*. Thus at various times the flow sheets had to be altered, many of them several times and over a period which in fact extended beyond the target completion date. Inevitably the construction fell behind programme. There were other factors too. The *exceptionally bad weather* in the summer of 1968 and during last winter seriously impeded the work. And there was a *serious accident* when a crane being used by a subcontractor to hoist a coke drum into position failed, and this enormous piece of equipment fell, causing loss of life as well as severe damage. While the cost of replacing this coke drum was covered by insurance, the consequential effects were not. This accident caused much delay and disruption in other parts of the site.

An oil refinery consists, basically, of a number of process units, such as heaters, boilers, fractionating towers, heat exchangers, pumps and compressors, connected by literally miles of piping, of different sizes and qualities according to service requirements. The mechanical erection therefore plays an important part in the whole scheme. At the time of signing the main contract, the Contractor had an offer from a sub-contractor to carry out the mechanical erection at a fixed price and this element of risk protection was, indeed, a factor in the decision to undertake the job. However, shortly afterwards, this *subcontractor went into liquidation*. The Contractor subsequently became committed to what proved to be a highly unfavourable and virtually open-ended sub-contract from which stems most of the anguish suffered by the Contractor in recent months. How this came about, and the extent to which the Contractor should bear the whole burden of this situation, is also something we have been and shall be discussing with the Owner and I must ask Shareholders to accept that I cannot say more at the present time.

The engineering, procurement and construction of a refinery of this magnitude called for integrated planning of a high order and all the modern critical path computer aids were employed from the outset. The programme so planned was disrupted by events which the Contractor contends were *largely outside his own responsibility*, and wrecked by the delays these caused. It was the secondary or impact effect of these delays that the Contractor *failed to foresee* and which have been the cause of so much of the expenditure incurred over the past year. Delays or changes in engineering decisions mean delayed drawings, delayed foundations and much scrapped work: delayed drawings mean delayed material purchases and delayed deliveries, so materials arrive late and in the wrong sequence leading to wasteful employment of site labour, with bad effects on morale and productivity. The impact effect of these delays was compounded by the major accident and bad weather. In terms of the time scale, the contract is running *one year late*. In terms of cost, and despite all our efforts to limit it the *overrun may reach £12 million*. In terms of the burden, this at the moment is being borne in its entirety by our Contracting Group with the assistance of the short term finance provided by the Group's bankers, of which Shareholders were recently informed. When the contract is completed we shall continue our efforts by discussion and negotiation to recover the whole or at least a part of the overrun from the Owner.

When one considers the problems which faced this contractor at that time, it is a tribute to their management that they not only survived, but have gone on from strength to strength.

This demonstrates that the company took this 'disaster' to heart and took drastic action (2). We maintain that any problem is well on the way to solution if the problem is recognised to exist. That this was indeed so is demonstrated by a letter we had later from the then chairman of the company, Sir John Buckley. He then said (3):

> I can well understand your interest in this project, but it is now more than 10 years ago since it was completed and it is very much 'old history'. We certainly did not go to the trouble of preparing a case history but I recall that in our annual accounts at the time I summed it up by saying it was a culmination of misfortune, *misjudgment and mismanagement*: a general statement but a categorical comment was that it was a 'splendid refinery'.

The emphasis is ours, and it is refreshing to see the chairman not only taking full responsibility but recognising that it was *management* that was primarily to blame. Whilst the company did not prepare a case history, we think that perhaps that might well have been done, for that is when the lessons are learned. We ourselves thought the lessons sufficiently important to present them to a wider public in our book *How to Learn from Project Disasters*, the chapter heading echoing that final declaration by Sir John, that it was indeed 'a splendid refinery' (2).

The reasons for overruns in cost and time are many and various, but we rarely encounter a situation where the plant cannot be started up. But that is exactly what happened when the Glace Bay Heavy Water Plant was built. What is called 'heavy water', deuterium oxide to the chemist, is used in the Canadian nuclear power plants as the coolant and moderator. The more popular system uses water, but Canada chose heavy water for a combination of technical economic and political reasons. So plants were needed to manufacture heavy water, and the first of these was built at Glace Bay, Nova Scotia. It was not the first of its kind, for similar plants had been built in the US, but the Glace Bay plant was novel in that it used sea water instead of fresh water as the raw material. Construction started in 1963 and the plant was commissioned in 1967, as planned, but it never got into production. It had operating problems and problems due to corrosion. The original scheme was for one 200 ton per annum unit, costing US$33 million, but that was switched to two such units, which had cost in all US$83 million at startup.

The plant was started up and shut down repeatedly. Not only was the sea water used as a raw material, but also as a coolant, and as a result of this intermittent operation corrosion arose due to stagnant water in the coolers. Studies were made, reports were prepared over the next four years, with costs mounting till they reached US$150 million. Then decisions were made. It was decided to have a major redesign, utilising a new process that had been developed in the interim, to use fresh water as coolant, and to reuse as much of the existing equipment as possible. The plant was finally started up in 1976, and produced 70 tons of heavy water in its first year. That was ten years after that first startup! Remember that the original plant was designed to produce 400 tons per year. Since 1976 there have been steady increases in output and it is now of the order of 300 tons per year.

The lessons for both project management and the cost control engineer are many. A proven process failed to work – but a change had been made that had a far more significant effect than had ever been anticipated: the change from fresh water to seawater for cooling. In addition, it seems, there was a lack of consultation, a failure in teamwork, a shortage of resources at a relatively remote site, particularly for operation and maintenance and a complete failure in communications. All this with a project of national significance. The failure of Glace Bay to produce threatened the entire nuclear programme in Canada, since it was entirely based on the heavy water type reactor. The heavy water needed as the nuclear power plants were being started up had to be purchased from the US at much higher prices than had been anticipated. Also, since a sufficient quantity of heavy water was not available internationally, the research and experimental reactors in Canada were shut down for nearly two years in order to give priority in this respect to the startup of the first power plant, Pickering Station, so that it could start up without delay. In retrospect, with all these further consequences of delay, the real cost of Glace Bay must have been far greater than the direct cost of getting the Glace Bay plant on stream through a major redesign and reconstruction effort. The decision finally made could have been made far earlier on these grounds alone.

Of the many reasons for failure, let us just mention one in a little detail: the significant underestimate in the manpower requirements and the personnel facilities required for startup and operation. These deficiencies were identified during that first commissioning phase and have been substantially rectified since. Additional facilities have included: a heavy equipment repair shop, an insulation/sheet metal shop, a carpenter-painter shop, a major expansion of the tradesmen's locker room, a lunchroom-cafeteria and office space for a majority of the plant staff. Overall about

35,000 square feet of permanent enclosed work and storage space was originally provided and these extras added some 75,000 square feet more. Apart from other factors, such as the immediate availability of repair and maintenance facilities, a degree of comfort with respect to working conditions has a substantial impact on morale, productivity and the quality of work, all of which together determine whether the job gets done successfully.

Well, we have brought you a few stories from the past. Are *you* prepared to listen? Will you be forewarned, and so forearmed? Let us not forget that all the cases we have brought to your notice till now have been from what are called the 'developed countries': countries where there is a highly industrialised society with major resources in terms of skill and experience. What happens when we turn to look at the developing countries?

## Developing countries are the most vulnerable

In the developing countries, such as India, the usual problems resulting in delays to project completion are further accentuated by factors such as:

1  Delays in government sanction at various stages.
2  Failure to appreciate the money value of time.
3  Preference for direct departmental execution.

The last factor arises from the fallacy that it proves cheaper. These and other factors peculiar to developing countries result in cost and time overruns that are twice, sometimes three times the original estimates. This is illustrated in Figure 5.2, which gives the relevant details with respect to a series of fertiliser plants which have been built in India over the years. The data on plant capacity and product mix for the same plants is set out in Figure 5.3. As a further illustration of the effect of delays in reaching decisions and the result of changes in those decisions, we can quote the case of the Korba Fertiliser project, the details of which are set out in Figure 5.4. Whilst some of the overrun is undoubtedly due to scope changes, which in their place are right and proper, and escalation also has a significant role to play, the magnitude of the overrun is such that much is left to explain. The need for sound project management and cost control is patent.

Lest we give too sombre a picture of the situation with respect to projects in India as a consequence of the above review, let us say that it seems that there is a 'learning process' going on. These days it is not too difficult to find successful projects handled by Indian

## INDIAN FERTILISER PROJECTS

| Location | Approval | | Completion | | | Overrun | |
|---|---|---|---|---|---|---|---|
| | Date | Budget Rs.m | Sched. | Actual | Cost Rs.m | Time | Cost |
| Barauni | 12-67 | 351 | 11-71 | 1977 | 916 | 2.45 | 2.55 |
| Bhatinda | 8-74 | 1384 | 1-78 | 1979 | 2394 | 1.36 | 1.72 |
| Durgapur | 2-66 | 381 | 12-69 | 1977 | 1022 | 3.00 | 2.65 |
| Gorakhpur | 1972 | 118 | 4-75 | 1976 | 184 | 1.30 | 4.70 |
| Haldia | 11-71 | 880 | 10-76 | 1986 | 4150 | 1.67 | 2.77 |
| Korba | 6-74 | 1183 | 12-77 | – | 221 | See Fig. 5.4 | |
| Namrup expansion | 12-67 | 295 | 1-71 | 1976 | 749 | 2.30 | 2.53 |
| Nangal expansion | 10-72 | 756 | 3-76 | 1978 | 1339 | 1.66 | 1.77 |
| Panipat | 2-75 | 1397 | 5-78 | 1979 | 1876 | 1.38 | 1.34 |
| Ramagundam | 10-69 | 712 | 7-75 | 1980 | 2092 | 1.90 | 3.22 |
| Sindri modernisation | 1-73 | 889 | 2-78 | 1980 | 1990 | 1.50 | 2.45 |
| Sindri rationalisation | 12-67 | 230 | 10-71 | 1980 | 584 | 3.25 | 2.55 |
| Talcher | 10-69 | 705 | 7-75 | 1980 | 2095 | 1.83 | 2.95 |
| Trombay IV | 9-74 | 440 | 4-77 | 1979 | 763 | 1.77 | 1.74 |
| Trombay V | 10-75 | 1114 | 4-78 | 1982 | 1665 | 2.33 | 1.50 |

Rs.m = Million rupees

**Figure 5.2 Indian fertiliser projects**
This table demonstrates that overrun in both cost and time is a constant factor over the years.

## INDIAN FERTILISER PROJECTS – TECHNICAL DETAILS

| Location | Tons/day Ammonia | Tons/day Urea | Feedstock | Main problems in execution |
|---|---|---|---|---|
| Barauni | 600 | 900 | Naphtha | Equipment failures |
| Bhatinda | 900 | 1500 | Fuel oil | Low estimate, scope changes |
| Durgapur | 600 | 900 | Naphtha | Equipment failures |
| Gorakhpur | 200 | 300 | Naphtha | Equipment deliveries, labour problems |
| Haldia | 600 | 500 | Fuel oil | Piling, floods, equipment power |
| Korba | 900 | 1500 | Coal | See Fig. 5.4 |
| Namrup (E) | 600 | 1000 | Gas | Equipment failures |
| Nangal (E) | 900 | 1000 | Fuel oil | Revisions, equipment deliveries, heavy rains |
| Panipat | 900 | 1500 | Fuel oil | Low estimate, scope changes |
| Ramagundam | 900 | 1500 | Coal | Approvals, equipment deliveries |
| Sindri (M) | 900 | 900 (+ AS) | Fuel oil | Equipment deliveries |
| Sindri (R) | – | 1130* | – | Equipment failures, inferior pyrites |
| Talcher | 900 | 1500 | Coal | Approvals, equipment deliveries |
| Trombay IV | 1250 | 1100† | Gas | Revisions to specifications |
| Trombay V | – | 820 | Gas | Engineering, Bombay Port congestion |
| Thal Vaishet | 2 x 1350 | 3 x 1400 | Gas ⎫ | World Bank withdrew support, due to |
| Hazira | 2 x 1350 | 3 x 1400 | Gas ⎭ | change to non-American contractors |

NOTES:   E = expansion; M = modernisation; R = rationalisation; (+ AS) = plus ammonium sulphate;
         * = triple phosphate; † = nitro-phosphate

**Figure 5.3 The problem highlighted**
This table details a number of fertiliser projects built in India, and the main problems encountered during execution.

---

**THE KORBA FERTILISER PLANT, INDIA**

| | |
|---|---|
| 1968 | Feasibility Report |
| 1969 Oct. | Project "approved" |
| 1972 Jan. | "Go-ahead" given by the Government. Estimate Rs. 721 million, including Rs. 202 million in foreign exchange. Target completion date: June 1974. |
| 1973 Apr. | Foundation stone laid by the Prime Minister of India. |
| 1973 Sep. | Agreement made with Techno Export for the Air Separation Plant. |
| 1974 Jan. | Proposals cleared by the Project Investment Board. |
| 1974 Jun. | Project cleared by Central Cabinet. |
| 1974 Nov. | Action on project slowed down. Revised cost estimate Rs. 1183 million, with a completion date of December 1978. |
| 1975 Mar. | Allocation of funds for 1975 reduced to minimum required to meet earlier commitments. No fresh orders to be placed for equipment. |
| 1975 Sep. | First major Indian deliveries made — of electric motors! |
| 1975 Dec. | First shipment of air separation plant received. |
| 1976 | Efforts made to cancel orders already placed. Project to be 'kept in suspense' until after successful commissioning of Talcher & Ramagundam coal-based plants (1979/1980) |
| 1979 Mar. | Total expenditure Rs 221 million. |

**Figure 5.4 The Korba Fertiliser Plant (India)**
This was intended to be a coal-based Fertiliser Plant, but to date it is a non-starter. Rs.221 million have been spent, but nothing has yet been built.

construction companies both at home and abroad. For instance, the Kudremukh iron ore project is said to be one of the largest such projects in the world. Located in the Bhadra river valley, said to be one of the three wettest places on earth, constructed in difficult, hilly terrain, it was nevertheless completed to a very tight schedule indeed: 40 months to mechanical completion. The project cost in all some US$650 million and it is said that the pragmatic and flexible policy adopted by the Indian government helped substantially towards the successful completion of the project. By way of example, the central government provided a blanket foreign exchange release for the project, which left the project team free to make variations within their overall approved estimate and import banned or restricted items provided that it could be justified on the ground of quality or cost. The very heavy equipment, some of it never seen in India before, posed challenges first in transportation and then in operation. Detailed design and construction were carried out in parallel, a calculated risk, but essential for timely completion, and posed a further challenge. Changes and modifications had as a consequence to be made at a very late stage, but that problem too was handled efficiently and costs did not soar. All in all, a difficult project well executed.

The sequel to this particular project is also of interest. The project was planned when the Shah was in power in Iran, to provide raw material for two steel mills there, and the Shah's government was to contribute to the financing of the project. But all that collapsed as a consequence of the revolution that later took place, but that in no way detracts from the Indian achievement. The finance was still found, the Indian government taking over, whilst the plant management have also found alternative markets for their product.

## Third World macroprojects

Having surveyed the scene with respect to fertiliser plants in India in some detail, it is of interest to note that an international agency, the United Nations Industrial Development Organisation (UNIDO) was concerned enough to institute an in-depth study of fertiliser plants in developing countries. This was undertaken by one of us over the years 1981 to 1983, gathering data from a number of major international contractors in this field as well as plant owners. Whilst the study was confined to fertiliser plants, its conclusions are equally valid in relation to process plants in general. The detailed findings were issued towards the end of 1983 and have since been presented at a UNIDO seminar at New Delhi early in 1984 (5).

The background to this particular study is very interesting. It seems that UNIDO were concerned that an impression was abroad in knowledgeable circles in the developing countries that they were 'being taken for a ride' by contractors from the developed world. The subject seemed to come up for discussion at almost every seminar on fertiliser production and related topics. But one major conclusion that could be drawn from the study was that because of the real and intense competition between the several major contractors in the field it was most unlikely that anyone was 'being taken for a ride'. What did however happen was that initial vague, broad enquiries, responded to with tenders that either implicitly or explicitly had a number of exclusions, resulted in the projects executed costing far more than originally expected because of the 'extras' that came along. When the 'extra' is essential the owner has no option to agree, yet he now has no real 'yardstick' to enable him to assess whether he is getting value for money. So this is indeed an area where the owner could and would be very vulnerable. But it is, after all, his own fault: the result of insufficient preparation at the tender stage. Further, the owner is unlikely to be familiar with the proper routine in the handling of scope changes, for that is what the changes are. It was in part the desire to correct this lacuna that we directed our book on the subject of project management at the owner: especially owners in the developing countries (6).

But to come back to the study itself, that directed attention to three critical areas needing attention if the capital cost of future fertiliser – and, of course, other process plants in the developing countries was to be properly controlled and contained:

1  The owner should formulate the project enquiry clearly and precisely
2  The owner should be actively associated with the implementation and monitoring of the project
3  As far as possible, there should be no changes once the contracts had been placed.

The report goes on to make specific suggestions which, if adopted, would result in these objectives being achieved. It was suggested that UNIDO had a role to play, in that it could encourage the training of personnel and lay down guidelines that would assist owners in the effective management of their projects.

## The impact of regulations

The cost control engineer can never forget the impact of government and local regulations on cost, chiefly because many plants take two years or more to build, and they have to meet the regulations in force at the *end* of their period of construction, not the beginning. There is growing concern, for instance, about the impact of new construction on the environment, and this results in a steady flow of new regulations. A few years ago the specific cost of safety and preventive measures to protect the *environment* (not the workers) was estimated at some 5 per cent of the capital investment, with chemical process plants. Today that percentage is probably nearer fifteen and still rising, thanks to the Bhopal disaster and its aftermath (7). Following that incident and then the destruction before the eyes of the whole world of the space shuttle *Challenger*, designers will undoubtedly 'play safe', a policy which will inevitably add to the cost of process plants. Their caution will be matched in the various regulatory bodies, with the result that an ever-growing proportion of the total investment is required to ensure safety. Prior to the Bhopal disaster the chemical industry had been complaining for years about over-regulation, but that has all changed now. The industry is now calling for more strictness: then at least *all* will have to comply with the same standards. However, whichever way it goes, an ever-growing proportion of the total investment is required to meet the regulations that are imposed and are still being imposed. This investment brings no return in terms of reducing product cost: it merely adds to it, and it can be a serious 'unknown' for the cost engineer.

An outstanding example of this is to be found in the nuclear plant industry. It is said that the number of specific regulations relating to the nuclear industry increased some four times over a period of ten years prior to 1980, and their issue was further accelerated by the widely publicised accident in 1979 at Three Mile Island. The construction of nuclear plants, particularly in the US, has been beset by overruns in both cost and time. For instance, if we look at the cost of the 1100 mW Fermi 2 station being built for Detroit Edison in the US, there has been a series of estimates over the years as set out in Figure 5.5. Such a record makes a mockery of cost estimating, cost control and project management, yet it is typical. To what extent it is due to the need to continually revise the design to meet the new regulations, we cannot say, but that must make a contribution to the situation.

Perhaps it is helpful to reinforce this point by looking at a nuclear power plant project, also in the US, that went well. This was the

| THE 1100 MW FERMI 2 UNIT FOR DETROIT EDISON | | |
|---|---|---|
| *Date of Estimate* | *Capital cost US$ million* | *Startup date* |
| 7–1968 | 230 | 2–1974 |
| 9–1972 | 511 | 4–1977 |
| 2–1977 | 894 | 9–1980 |
| 12–1979 | 1,300 | 3–1982 |
| 6–1981 | 2,000 | 11–1983 |
| 3–1984 | 3,100 | 12–1984 |

**Figure 5.5 The mounting cost**
The successive cost estimates for the 1100 mW Fermi 2 nuclear power plant illustrate a very common trend.

Byron Plant for Consolidated Edison and so unusual is that in the nuclear industry that the title of an article on the completion of this particular plant was: 'Man bites dog' (4). The writer went on to proclaim: 'You've heard all those disaster stories. Now harken to this nuclear plant success story'. The plant, installed capacity 1100 mW, was built for a total of US$3.7 billion, or US$1,682 per kilowatt. This is considered to be competitive at the present time: presumably that is why the plant whose dreadful cost history is set out in Figure 5.5 is still being completed. An identical plant, being built at Marble Hill, Indiana, was abandoned after some US$2,500 million had been spent, because the electric supply company concerned said that they did not have the cash resources to complete the project, nor could it ever be profitable, since it would have cost some US$3,000 per kilowatt by the time it was complete, it being abandoned when only some 60 per cent complete.

What is of particular interest to us in relation to the Byron Plant is that whilst the completion of the plant on time and within budget brought its rewards, it also brought penalties. The construction went ahead so fast that the regulatory bodies could not keep pace. The Nuclear Regulatory Commission took its time approving the plant design and issuing a licence. The Atomic Safety and Licence Board delayed the issue of the operating licence on a variety of pretexts. These delays are said to have contributed an extra US$100 million to the capital cost of the project, apart from the cost of delay in plant availability. Such administrative delays can not only be costly, but they are extremely frustrating. So let the cost control engineer always be on the lookout for the cost impact, not only of the regulations themselves, but the routine and possible delay in securing the appropriate permissions and licences.

## Productivity

We have been considering a number of what we might well regard as 'hidden threats' to the successful control of time and cost. There is one last aspect which we believe should be reviewed before we bring this chapter to a close – productivity. This is an abstract concept and a most controversial subject. There is, to begin with, no mathematically correct way in which one can measure productivity. Even its definition projects the bias of the one who defines it. Economist, accountant, engineer, trade union leader: each has their own definition designed to both suit and prove their own point of view.

Productivity, simply expressed, is the ratio between output and input, so that it is also a measure of efficiency. Ideally, therefore, productivity should always be unity. It is obvious that both the output and the input be measured in the same units, for the ratio to be meaningful, but that is easier said than done. It sounds a laudable and worthy goal: increase productivity. This is the same thing as seeking an increasing efficiency of operation, and hence lower costs. Productivity, therefore, is of interest and concern to the cost engineer, and one of the things he should be watching. Developing countries, about whom we have just had something to say, should be particularly interested in it, yet for many of them it is a dirty word, next only to 'profit'! This is very unfortunate and, of course, counter-productive. It is, however, typical: typical of a state of affairs where the simple maintenance of say a plumbing or a telephone installation is considered a tough proposition.

Let us make it clear, however, that despite the innate reluctance of many people to come to grips with productivity for reasons best known to themselves, it is indeed difficult, if not impossible, to measure productivity in explicit terms. Comparative figures such as the tons of steel produced per man per year for a number of countries might be considered, at first sight, a means of comparing the productivity of those several countries in that particular industry, but no. To begin with, this statistic could vary quite considerably from steel plant to steel plant *within* each country and such figures, and the ratios developed, would have to be handled with extreme caution. At best they can only give a qualitative 'feel': never clear cut positive answers.

/ The low productivity of labour on construction sites is notorious, when that is compared with production in a workshop. It is this, in part, that has led to the increasing transfer of work away from the construction site to the workshop by the increasing use of prefabrication and more recently the steady growth of modular design. Modular design allows complete plant units to be fabricated offsite, with interconnecting piping, instrumentation and electrics, all mounted on what is called a 'skid', and set down on prepared foundations at site. All that is then required is that it be connected up.

The reasons for comparatively low productivity at site may be thought to be obvious, but the major factors are *not* poor discipline, hold-ups due to the weather, increased possibility of strikes and the like, although it is these that get the blame. A number of separate studies have confirmed that on the average site the effective, productive time of such workers is not more than some two hours per day. The rest of their time is spent on non-productive activities, as illustrated below:

|                    | %  |
|--------------------|----|
| Constructive work  | 30 |
| Movement           | 10 |
| Miscellaneous      | 25 |
| Not on plot        | 35 |

This is a typical analysis of a working day on a construction site. Data such as this is obtained by what is known as 'activity sampling'. The figures given are representative of the UK, but the relationships would not be all that different in any other European country. Of course, a workman can be 'not on plot' for a number of legitimate reasons, such as visits to the stores, or toilets, or for a 'smoking break' on a restricted site, to a shower before going home, and so on.

There is yet another aspect of productivity from which we can learn something: the so-called 'window'. For planetary probes, an affair of everyday life these days, a certain 'window' is open at very specific and often quite rare times, for the probe to pass through and reach its objective. This window is determined by factors such as closeness to earth of the objective, relative trajectories, and other factors of that type. In just the same way seasonal factors can act as a 'window' with respect to the construction of a project of any size. The Alaskan pipeline, offshore drilling for oil and the more humdrum laying of sewers, are examples where this fact is immediately recognised. A typical 'window' relates to the work on the North Sea oilfields off the shores of the UK. They are in very deep waters, with a hazardous environment, and the offshore construction work has to be carefully planned for execution between May and September of each year. But precisely the same considerations apply to the construction of process plants, if perhaps to a lesser degree. There, in the North Sea, we have a 'weather window' of some five months, but in India the monsoon can be so severe at times that no outdoor work is possible. The west coast of India gets over 100 cm. of rain during one month, July, with an intensity ranging up to 5 cm. per hour. Outdoor construction work must be planned with this in mind. In the UK every attempt is made to get the foundations poured in the summer, to avoid frost, but in the south of France it could be preferable to do the same work in the winter, when it is not so hot, so that the concrete does not dry out too fast.

**More men, less work!**

For each project, and for each site, there is an optimum number of workmen, beyond which the productivity per worker begins to drop. This is a result of the so-called 'Law of Diminishing Returns' and this

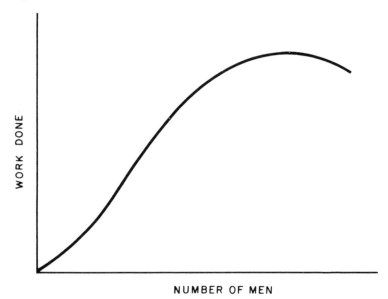

**Figure 5.6 The law of diminishing returns**
Once the optimum workforce is exceeded, productivity falls and completion is delayed.

fact of life is illustrated qualitatively in Figure 5.6. The relationships expressed here have to do with a simple task, such as placing concrete, or erecting steel structures. The diminishing productivity in such cases demonstrates that there are far too many people on the job at any one time, so that they are getting in one another's way. This situation is well expressed in the old proverb: 'Too many cooks spoil the broth'.

Precisely the same considerations apply to a project site as a whole, where hundreds, or perhaps thousands of workmen in various trades are employed in the construction of a major process plant facility. The multiplication of activities, plenty of materials and more and more men will normally lead to more waste and less productivity, unless the project is very well managed indeed and the costs closely monitored. Figure 5.7 is an interesting representation of the actual state of affairs at a process plant project site. The two vital factors, productivity and cost, are plotted against the total workforce. The interesting point that comes out is that the minima of the cost curve do *not* coincide with the maxima of the productivity curve. To seek after a minimum cost for construction may therefore lead to late completion. But, in an effort to rectify the situation, and

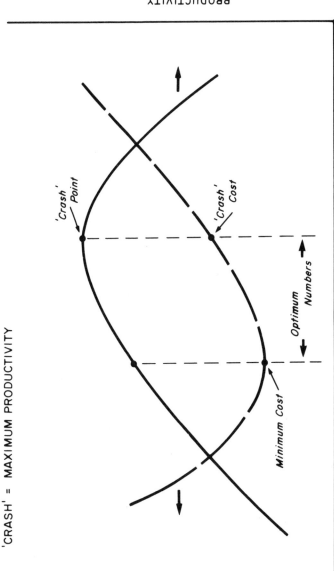

**Figure 5.7 The relationship between productivity and cost**
It is not necessarily advantageous to organise a workforce to achieve minimum cost in the field, since this can lead to delay in completion, which could cost the owner far more than the immediate capital saving.

103

achieve an earlier completion, we can very easily overshoot the optimum region. Then, further pressure by the bringing in of more workpeople will lead to higher costs and lower productivity. Go a step further, and we find that a massive increase in manpower not only brings additional costs, but actually *delays* completion. It just does not achieve the end in view. This may well sound paradoxical, but it *is* a fact of life, borne out by experience on site.

If the project manager is not wise to this particular paradox, then when he gets into the situation where he has gone beyond the optimum area, he may well seek to redeem the situation by bringing still more people on to the site. But this will result in yet a further shift to the right on our graph (Figure 5.7), and so lead to still more disastrous results. A chain reaction builds up: low productivity leads to delay in completion: both add to cost. The project manager, despite all his efforts, is moving ever further away from his cost and time targets.

### References

1   Kharbanda, O. P. and E. A. Stallworthy, *How to Learn from Project Disasters*, Gower, 1983, 273 pp. See Chapter 5, 'Concorde – a technical triumph, but ...'.
2   Kharbanda, O. P. and E. A. Stallworthy, *How to Learn from Project Disasters*, Gower, 1983, 273 pp. See Chapter 6, 'A splendid refinery'.
3   Buckley, Sir John. Letter dated 29 November 1979 to Dr. O. P. Kharbanda.
4   Cook, J., 'Man bites dog', *Forbes*, 134, 3 December 1984, pp. 80+.
5   Report: *Capital Cost of Fertiliser Plants in Developing Countries*, Vol. 1, 133 pp., with Vol. 2, *Annexures*, published by UNIDO, Vienna, December 1983.
6   Stallworthy, E. A. and O. P. Kharbanda, *Total Project Management – from Concept to Completion*, Gower, Aldershot, 1983, 329 pp.
7   Kharbanda, O. P. and E. A. Stallworthy, *Management Disasters and How to Prevent Them*, Gower, Aldershot, 1986, 240 pp.

# Part Two
# COST CONTROL
# IMPLEMENTATION

# 6 Administrative procedures

The approach of a manufacturing company to the problems to be met and overcome in establishing a new manufacturing facility will be governed to a very large extent by the available resources. The fundamental disciplines involved are:

> engineering
> accounting
> purchasing

These are the disciplines directly involved. There are other disciplines, such as sales and marketing, that will have to provide data to establish the nature and viability of the project, but such disciplines as these will continue their normal function. The disciplines outlined above, however, even to the extent that they are available in the manufacturing organisation, will be required to perform tasks radically different from those they normally undertake from day to day once a major capital investment is in view. The larger companies may well employ separate organisations to evaluate and process their plans for such investment, but this book is intended to provide guidance and data to managements who *do not* maintain such resources, usually because the need is only intermittent and it would therefore not be practical or economic to maintain such organisations on a permanent basis. What one then has to do is to examine the resources that *are* available, and consider how to make the best possible use of them, establishing to what extent they need to be supplemented from outside, via a consultant or a managing contractor.

## Management structure

We have to recognise the range of disciplines that will be required in the course of implementing an investment project and then decide how these various disciplines are to be coordinated and organised. The first and most obvious fact is that someone has to be in charge of the new development. Who that will be will vary from case to case, and to some extent will be determined by the size of the project. Within the scope of our interest there are four major categories into which the situation must inevitably fall, namely:

1   *Individual* A single individual, such as a works manager or a works engineer, is confronted with the task of setting up a new development.
2   *Team* A 'project team' is set up, its members being taken away from their routine tasks to develop and progress proposals for, say, a new factory.
3   *Engineering department* An established engineering department, engaged normally on maintenance work (with sometimes minor capital works), or perhaps a section of the department specialising in new works and then continuously involved in the type of work and the problems encountered in new construction.
4   *Consultant/contractor* A consultant, such as an architect, or perhaps a series of consultants, or an engineering contractor, is employed to supervise the works and/or implement them.

The resources of these several categories are clearly vastly different, but once a major project is implemented the resources, to the extent that they are available within the company, will have to be deployed differently. There will be both *direct* and *indirect* involvement. The functions directly involved are:

1   Project management
2   Design
3   Procurement
4   Construction

Other departments provide a service and thus are only indirectly involved. These include:

5   Planning
6   Estimating
7   Cost control
8   Finance and accounts

We have, in effect, expanded our 'engineering' into a number of separate functions, some working directly on the project, some providing support. The effective deployment of these resources, both direct and indirect, is the responsibility of the one appointed to be the project manager or the project engineer. He will have to see, as is usually the case, that the internal resources are supplemented where necessary by external resources. He will have to employ a consultant or a contractor, or both, or a series of contractors, in those areas where his own resources are inadequate to meet the new workload being placed upon them.

We are confining our attention at this time to the support and services, that a project manager, appointed from within the manufacturing organisation to implement the new project, should get from the cost control activity (item 7 above). This means that we shall only be discussing the project management activity insofar as it relates to the project cost control activity. Project management as such is another subject (1). We have shown estimating as a separate function from project cost control. In the early stages of project development, up to the approval of an estimate as a budget item, when authorisation is given to proceed, this is most certainly so. Once a project has been approved, however, estimating comes slowly but surely within the province of the cost control engineer and in the later stages he must be wholly responsible for the estimating of final cost.

### The interrelationship of the project functions

If we try to express things quite simply, those who are directly involved in implementing the project (functions 1 to 4 above) produce first paperwork, and finally a physical entity, which all together cost a certain sum of money. The service activities, more particularly those listed under functions 5 to 8, process the paperwork, build up records and report. If we leave 'estimating' to one side, for the reasons stated above, then we have three service activities working in parallel. They are: planning, project cost control and finance and accounts. How do these three activities coordinate with one another, and support one another? There are three distinct areas of control:

1   Commitments
2   Value of work done
3   Expenditure

These are all controlled in relation to their progress over time. This is portrayed diagrammatically in Figure 6.1, which presents the typical S-curve for 'value of work done'. Similar S-curves develop for both commitments and expenditure. If we now consider the inter-departmental coordination, then planning are primarily

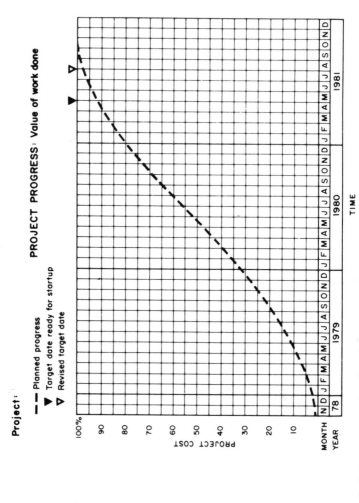

**Figure 6.1 Project progress – value of work done**
Typical S-curve for value of work done. Such curves are normally presented in project progress reports and their use is further discussed in Chapter 7.

110

responsible for establishing the 'time' target, both overall and in detail. Then the primary, although not the only task of project cost control is to establish the exact position of the project from month to month in terms of value of work done, in its 'controllable elements' and compare this with the targets for each month. Lastly, finance will maintain their ordinary expenditure records, but will work in close liaison with project cost control. They will also maintain a record of commitments, since they have to ensure that payments are within and accord with the approved commitments.

Thus, project cost control can comment on the validity of the work of planning, by comparing planned and actual progress on value of work done. The commitment record provides the 'ceiling' at any point in time, if properly maintained. All this involves a lot of paperwork and documentation which has to be properly organised and controlled.

## Document control

We are continually emphasising the importance of good communication, considering it to be a vital element in every successful project (2). An integral part of the communication system within a project is the paperwork, and in particular the wide range of documents that are required. The way in which such documents are handled requires careful management, this beginning with the definition and routing of key documents in the Coordination Procedure to which we refer in more detail in Chapter 11 (see also Appendix C: Typical Coordination Procedure Check List). The management of the paperwork, the so-called 'document control', requires a system to ensure that each document is uniquely identified. It is usual, for instance, to arrange that all letters between say the owner and his managing contractor be numbered in sequence. Steps should also be taken to ensure the prompt delivery of all documents. The necessity for this becomes very obvious when the construction site is in a remote location, but attention should *always* be paid to this aspect.

It is essential that a formalised system is used for document control, which means that a coding system should be used to identify all documents (including, of course drawings and specifications), in association with a registry system, to ensure unique identification and to assist their location when required. The document register will record location, latest version and details of earlier versions. The distribution requirements will be established, through the project manager, via the Coordination Procedure, and

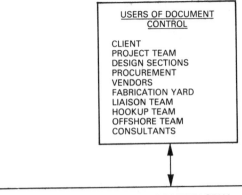

**Figure 6.2 Document control – users, functions and methods**
This outline chart illustrates both the users of document control and the scope of work of the document control team.

it is best to set up distribution routing diagrams and distribution matrix forms to record the detailed requirements. The broad scope of such a document control system is illustrated in Figure 6.2. On the larger projects, all this may well be computerised, the program incoporating an expediting system with particular reference to documents required from vendors and others outside the project organisation. The managing contractor will be well accustomed to such procedures and will have a standard system, to which the specific requirements of his clients are added from project to project. The standard system should therefore be sufficiently flexible to incorporate specific project requirements.

Within the documentation system there should always be a

system of 'cost coding', or a 'code of accounts', since the finance department of the owner of a proposed plant will invariably require that the ultimate cost of the project be broken down, or analysed, into a number of separate costing blocks, or 'accounts'. The primary division will always be between 'plant' and 'buildings', but these two groups will be further subdivided. The project cost engineer has a special interest in the cost codes, since not only are they a very valuable management tool, but the manner of their use is crucial to the successful cost control of a project.

## Cost coding as a management tool

The ideal system of cost coding will be that which it is possible to use at all stages in the development of a project. Such a system would first be adopted in the preparation of the estimate, used for the identification of equipment in the process of drafting, quoted on the requisition and consequent purchase order, and would finally appear on the vendor's invoice. Thus, at all stages, from design through the steps of creating the commitment to the final collection of the cost, a common system of cost allocation and identification is being used. The integration of the coding system adopted in the estimate at the beginning, into all the administrative procedures through to the final accounting is not merely an estimating 'tool' – it is also the basic system for the provision of information to management for the purposes of control.

A variety of systems can be adopted which will achieve this end, but a numeric system is most certainly the best if there is the possibility that the resultant data will be processed by computer at any stage. A typical Code of Accounts for Process Plants, fulfilling the requirements, is presented as Appendix B.

The important principle to be appreciated at this point is that this analysis, or system of cost coding, is not to be pursued as a matter of intellectual satisfaction. It can and only should be pursued because it has value as a management tool. Only if found to be valuable and to have real purpose should it be used, and the degree of detail should match that purpose. This implies that the analysis should only be developed to that degree of detail that is strictly necessary, not merely from the viewpoint of one particular department, but also from a general, managerial point of view. To illustrate this point, it will be seen that the Appendix lists a total of about seventy cost codes from a maximum potential availability of ninety-nine, in the coding system adopted. An alternative system could be used, affording much greater scope, but its value is really questionable.

Care must be exercised if the system is not to negate its usefulness by its very complexity. It is not unknown for a coding system to be of such detail and complexity that it took three weeks to prepare each monthly report, once the figures were available. This made the report up to six weeks behind the state of affairs it portrayed since the monthly accounting figures had to be assessed before the report could be prepared. When a project is in progress on the site, such delays make the report worthless to the project manager, assuming that he had the time to study the report in all its detail when it became available. In addition, the detail in a coding system must be associated with realism. There is no merit, for instance, in analysing an estimate of electrical work between the cost of the cable and the cost of laying that cable, if in practice a contract exists which embraces both aspects in one lump sum, or unit rate. The separate costs *cannot* be analysed, so why break down the estimate? Never forget: the system must be the slave, not the master.

Another aspect of the coding system which is very important, and which can be seen when the Appendix is studied, is that each code requires clear and careful definition. This ensures consistency in the records throughout the life of the project, allows estimate and cost to be compared on a 'like for like' basis, whilst the collected costs, analysed by code, will then provide a sound foundation for estimating data in relation to future projects.

Assuming that we are going to have such a code of accounts, how do we proceed? We divide our project into a number of separate 'units', or 'areas', giving each of these a project number. For instance, each process unit, or perhaps a group of process units can be separately identified in this way, and then the 'offsites', or 'services' given yet other project numbers. A typical breakdown of a project, using this system, is given as Figure 6.3. Then each project is further subdivided in accordance with the 'code of accounts'. So, with a four figure project identification, our cost centres are six digit numbers. Columns in Unit 100 (Figure 6.3) would then be coded: 280120. As simple as that! Do not elaborate further, if you want to keep your fingers on the pulse of your project. Requisitions, whether for each column, or item of equipment, or materials, or site contracts, would be numbered serially – 01 and up. Thus your requisition for a column in Unit 100 would then be an eight digit number: 28012001. If the same number also appears on the order, as part of the order number, so much the better. If not, care has to be taken to ensure that at least the basic code (280120) is quoted as an addendum to the order number, so that it appears yet again on the relevant invoice. This six digit number then becomes the key to all aspects of financial and

| PROJECT NO. | DESCRIPTION |
|---|---|
| 2801 | Unit 100. Primary distillation. |
| 2802 | Unit 200. Reaction section. |
| 2803 | Unit 300. Treating and washing. |
| 2804 | Unit 400. Final distillation |
| 2805 | Unit 500. Tank farm. |
| 2806 | Bulk materials for units 100 to 500 and general inplot facilities. |
| 2807 | General erection contracts, such as civil works, plant erection, piping fabrication and erection, insulation and painting for Units 100 and 500 and the related inplot facilities. |
| 2808 | Design, procurements and construction management for Units 100 to 500 and related inplot facilities. |
| 2809 | Inplot facilities, including Control Room, interconnecting pipework and pipebridges, inplot roads, drains and sewers. |
| 2810 | Administration Building, Plant Laboratory and Warehouse |
| 2811 | Offplot roads, parking areas, with related lighting and drainage. |
| 2812 | Tie in to existing services, including provision of Main substation, steam  gas and water connections and other services outside plot. |

**Figure 6.3 Typical project listing**
It will be noted that this list of projects is divided into two groups, 2801 to 2809 being 'in plot' and 2810 to 2812 being 'outside plot', or 'utilities and general facilities'. Allocation of costs in projects 2806 to 2809 to the several units for asset valuation would be done on completion.

project cost control reporting and is the maximum degree of detail to which such reports should ever go. To ascertain further detail, such as the individual cost of the several columns ordered under cost code 280120 requires scrutiny of the relevant file of orders.

Let us be very clear about this. We are discussing a coding system for use in project cost control and the relationship between the finance activity and the cost control activity in this context. Other

### COST CODING – A TYPICAL DETAILED ANALYSIS

Instrumentation Engineering

50    General instrumentation.
51    Analysers samplers.
52    Flow instruments.
53    Pressure instruments.
54    Level instruments.
55    Temperature instruments.
56    Control valves.
57    Instrument installation materials.
58    Computers and computer related equipment.
59    Instrument erection

**Figure 6.4 Cost code for instrumentation**
This cost code shows the way in which requisitions, and ultimately costs, could be
further analysed. But this analysis would contribute nothing to project cost control
and little to the estimating data.

activities, such as purchasing, may well process their work and
maintain their records in such a way, perhaps via a computer
program, that the information they require for the proper
performance of their function, such as delivery dates, is readily
available, but that is another subject. Further, as we have said
earlier, the project cost control *must* be kept separate from such
other data, whether computerised or not, and not integrated with it.
The coding system can indeed be elaborated in various directions
for a variety of purposes, but if such an elaborated system exists, it
should be condensed for cost control and financial control. Thus,
for example, referring to instrumentation, Figure 6.4 shows the way
in which the instrument engineer, and perhaps also the estimator,
would happily see the various categories of instruments analysed.
But the recommended code of accounts as Appendix B shows only
three codes, and these could well be reduced to two for project cost
control purposes and still be quite adequate. Codes 50 and 51 would
be combined. If this were done, specific instruments would be set
against specific projects (2801 to 2805 in Figure 6.3), the
instrumentation bulk materials (code 52) in project 2806 and
erection of the instrumentation for all the units in project 2807.
This is simple, and it works admirably! Further elaboration only
brings more work, *not* more control.

### Sorting by departments

We have been discussing the analysis of total project cost into 'projects' and 'codes'. But for the purposes of project cost control it is desirable, within any one project, to group the various codes according to purpose. The best grouping is into six, namely:

1 Design
2 Equipment
3 Piping materials
4 Instrumentation and electrical materials
5 Site (erection) contracts
6 Miscellaneous

If we consider the coding system outlined in Appendix B in relation to the above grouping we see that certain 'codes' will always relate to certain 'groups'. This relationship is given in detail in Figure 6.5.

This particular analysis commends itself to project management when progress is being assessed. From the point of view of the cost control engineer there is also merit, since each of these six groups has its own characteristic rate of progress through a project: its own

---

**PROJECT COST ANALYSIS BY DEPARTMENTS**

1. (A) Design
   Cost codes 01 and 02
2. (B) Equipment
   Cost codes 20–28 and 60–75
3. (B) Piping materials
   Cost codes 30–34 and 56–67
4. (B) Electrical and instrumentation materials
   Cost codes 40–47, 50–52 and 68
5. (C) Site (erection) subcontracts
   Cost Codes 10–19 (Civil works)
   29 (plant erection)
   38 (pipework erection)
   39 (erection general)
   48 (electrical erection)
   53 (instrumentation erection)
   71–72 (insulation & painting)
6. (A) Miscellaneous
   Cost Codes 03 (project supervision)
   80–93

---

**Figure 6.5 Listing of 'departments'**
This listing presents a very appropriate way in which to group the cost codes for control purposes, particularly in relation to forecasting. The further groupings A, B and C are the three basic cost streams discussed in detail in Chapter 7.

particular S-curve. This facilitates forecasting and monitoring against the forecast. These characteristic S-curves are illustrated separately in Figure 7.1, where progress per project phase is discussed. Each group above has its own phasing within the project.


## Choosing a managing contractor

We would expect the decisions relating to cost coding to be taken largely by the owner, who should have given serious consideration to the subject when first evaluating the project and preparing the estimates that will have served as a basis for approval of the project. But once the project has been approved, a contractor or contractors will have to be appointed. For the purpose of illustration we wish to consider the appointment of a managing contractor, since this is the most complex situation that can arise. We have already discussed this contractual arrangement in broad outline in Chapter 2, and Figure 2.4 demonstrates the fundamental role played by the managing contractor. In order to appoint a managing contractor what are called 'bid documents' will have to be prepared and issued. The particular approach adopted must depend upon the circumstances, but in Figure 6.6 a logic diagram is presented of the events that could lead to the appointment of a contractor. Great care is needed in the drafting of the bid documents, so that both the project specification and conditions of contract are right in terms of scope. Another aspect of vital importance, which also affects both the project specification and the conditions of contract, is the financial arrangements, which are a specific element in the logic diagram, Figure 6.6. Once the bid documents have been prepared and are ready for issue, they have to be sent out to selected contractors under cover of an enquiry letter.

The primary enclosure with the enquiry letter will be the project specification. It is this document, which can be anything from a few pages to hundreds, even thousands of pages long, that defines the 'work' that the contractor will be required to do, in cooperation with the owner and other third parties. Whilst it is the project specification which is of prime and continuing interest to all those involved in the project, it has to be put into context. That is the function of the conditions of contract. They define the situation – the relationship of the various parties to the work to be done, as described in the project specification, and also to one another, in legalistic terms. The index to a typical project specification is presented as Appendix D.

When the various offers are received in response to the enquiry, a

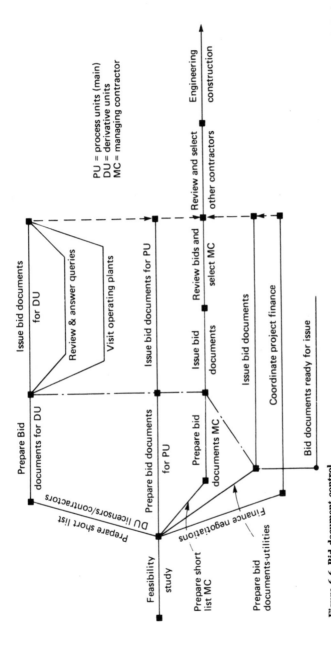

**Figure 6.6 Bid document control**

This logic diagram illustrates a typical plan to get an approved project 'on the way'. (Data provided by Trichem Consultants Limited, London.)

PU = process units (main)
DU = derivative units
MC = managing contractor

119

choice has to be made. The selection criteria include:

(a) Quality of personnel nominated to carry out the project, with special emphasis on the project manager
(b) Cost incentive and liability arrangements proposed
(c) Local currency content of the project cost and the total investment required for the project
(d) Loan terms
(e) Project organisation and relationship with local subcontractors
(f) Workload of office where the design engineering will be carried out
(g) Quality and contents of the technical proposal
(h) Contractor's recent experience in the design and construction of similar projects
(i) Appreciation and knowledge of local conditions at the job site
(j) Ability to provide the owner with technical support services
(k) Schedule for project completion

The above are not in order of importance. Whilst the price is significant (item (c) above) it is only one of three financial considerations. The contractors selected to bid should have been chosen on the basis of past performance, but what now matters is their *present* competence. This means that the specific personnel put forward to form the project team are of crucial importance. Within the project team it is the project manager and his qualifications that need the most careful appraisal, but the presentation made in relation to project cost control should also be studied in detail. In particular the system of cost coding used by the contractor will have to be integrated with that employed by the owner and the cost control engineer should be involved, ensuring that his detailed requirements with regard to the provision and analysis of cost data are fully met. It is always cost effective to specify the detailed requirements *before* the contract is placed: to change later will always be expensive. Amongst those detailed requirements are the methods that will be adopted for commitment control, assessment of value of work done and escalation, use of exchange rates and the compliance with tax requirements. Let us now go on to consider these several key aspects in detail.

## Commitment control

For successful project control good commitment control is vital. In connection with commitments there is one rule that is basic, that is incorporated in the financial rules of practically every company, and yet is just as universally ignored. It may require discipline to follow this rule, but if the rule *is* ignored the project cost control engineer is lost and the project will most surely suffer. The rule is very simple:

### No commitment may be entered into with an outside company without prior WRITTEN AUTHORISATION

A variety of excuses will be offered for inability to obey the rule, and these days there is little that can be done if the rule is ignored. We have yet to hear of someone getting dismissed from his job because he broke this rule, yet the more the rule is ignored, the more control of the project costs will be in jeopardy. The area where the rule is most likely to be widely broken is in relation to site, or erection contracts, where 'extra works' are called for, over and above the original contract. No extra works should be put in hand without prior authorisation by way of an extra work order, but there are always good and seemingly sufficient reasons brought forward for ignoring this. The most common is the need to put the work in hand before the extra work order (EWO) can be processed. Most field cost control procedures include quite extensive instructions on the preparation and control of EWOs, and rightly so. Unfortunately, and of necessity, these procedures include a section on what are often called 'open-ended EWOs'. An open-ended EWO is needed where the nature of the work makes it impossible or impractical to obtain a firm quotation for the work before it is started. Then the work is carried out on a 'unit price' or 'daywork' basis. The rule says, usually, that before an open-ended EWO is issued, an estimated cost of the work must be available, so this is indeed an attempt to bring the matter under a degree of control. If the relationship between estimate and cost is diligently watched, then we have still got our hand on the door. But the real 'open door' is a rule such as this:

> It must be clearly understood that no other means of authorising extra work will be recognised or tolerated. This applies especially to any verbal or written communication outside the EWO procedure. However, in an emergency, the Project Construction Manager has the authority to override this restriction.

But this writer has seen far too many 'emergencies' for his liking!

There is no doubt that this exceptive clause must be there and the only way to avoid abuse is to encourage the members of the project management team to be 'cost conscious'. It is possible to check whether the procedure is in fact being abused and this is discussed when we come to look at our 'early warning signals' in Chapter 8. We can get early warning when they break the rule to any serious extent, since the error in evaluating value of work done then becomes significant.

But first, we have to create our commitment. An essential step in this is the 'bid analysis'. This is a review of the various offers for the supply of either materials or services and a typical bid analysis form is given as Figure 6.7. The form provides for a situation where an outside contractor, or managing contractor is being used to place orders on behalf of the ultimate user of the facility, the owner; but exactly the same procedure should be followed in all cases. It will be seen that the procedure compels comparison between the estimate and the potential commitment.

It will also be noted that the bottom line on the form is the 'estimated total price'. This introduces another very important aspect of commitment control. Every commitment placed *must* have a value placed upon it. If the commitment is open-ended – for instance, use of an engineer at rates for an unspecified period – then an estimate must nevertheless be made and that estimate entered into the record as a commitment. Where there is an 'apparent' commitment – the face value of the order – all the potential costs that will accrue before that commitment is closed must also be evaluated and added in to establish the total commitment, and it is this figure that goes into the commitment record. A typical item in this context is escalation, perhaps covered by a formula in the order. Escalation must be evaluated for the duration of the order, and added into the record: but not, of course, to the order as issued to the supplier. He will invoice in accordance with the formula later.

Commitments will be recorded in accordance with the coding system and a simple approach to this by the use of the form illustrated in Figure 6.8. Always work with cumulative figures: it is much easier to assimilate and check the data if you do. Amendments must be issued to cover all changes in the order and the final amendment could, for instance, cover the claim for escalation in accordance with an agreed formula, as mentioned above. The basic rule is: no invoice is to be paid unless it is covered by the written order or amendments thereto. This compels a proper discipline in relation to the issue of orders and order amendments and ensures that the commitment record is comprehensive.

Yet, in practice, there are still going to be exceptions to this rule. This is where the cost control engineer, working in conjunction with the finance department, can ensure that the commitment record is wholly valid. If you can really ensure this, you know one thing at least: your costs cannot exceed your commitments. Let us assume, as is likely to be the case, that the commitment record is maintained by the finance department. Then one example of costs that do not appear in the commitment record automatically would be 'in house'

**BID ANALYSIS**

Item _____  Tag number _____
Amount allowed in control estimate _____  Clients code of accounts _____
Delivery required by schedule _____  Prepared by _____
Date _____

| | Suppliers | | | |
|---|---|---|---|---|
| Name | | | | |
| Conformity with specification | | | | |
| Quotation details | | | | |
| Price | | | | |
| Duty payable (if any) | | | | |
| Carriage | | | | |
| Terms | | | | |
| Delivery | | | | |
| Other relevant information | | | | |
| Estimated total price | | | | |

For Client's use

Purchasing recommendation

Reasons

Client

Approved for purchasing from

Reason if different from engineering

Engineering recommendation

Reasons

_____  _____  _____  _____
Project Engineer    Date        Project Manager    Date

**Figure 6.7 The bid analysis form**
This form is designed to highlight those aspects of the quotations which are
specially significant in relation to cost control, namely estimated price as well as
actual: delivery: specific item identification (tag number) and the cost code
reference.

| COST CONTROL SHEET | | | UP DATE | |
|---|---|---|---|---|
| | | | DATE | TOTAL VALUE |

DEPARTMENT _ _ _ _ _ _ _ _ _ _ _ _  PROJECT No. _ _ _ _ _ _ _ _ _ _ _ _
COST CODE _ _ _ _ _ _ _ _ _ _ _ _ _  LOCATION _ _ _ _ _ _ _ _ _ _ _ _ _
SECTION _ _ _ _ _ _ _ _ _ _ _ _ _ _  REVIEW ESTIMATE No. _ _ _ _ _ _
ESTIMATED COST _ _ _ _ _ _ _ _ _ _  DATE OF ESTIMATE _ _ _ _ _ _ _ _

| DATE | ORDER No. | SUPPLIER | ORIGINAL VALUE | REVISED VALUE | | | | FINAL VALUE |
|---|---|---|---|---|---|---|---|---|
| | | | | ATO | ATO | ATO | ATO | |
| | | | | | | | | |
| | | | | | | | | |
| | | | | | | | | |
| | | | | | | | | |
| | | | | | | | | |
| | | | | | | | | |
| | | | | | | | | |
| | | | | | | | | |
| | | | | | | | | |
| | | | | | | | | |
| | | | | | | | | |
| | | | | | | | | |
| | | | | | | | | |
| | | | | | | | | |
| | | | | | | | | |
| | | | | | | | | |
| | | | | | | | | |
| | | | | | | | | |
| | | | | | | | | |
| | | | | | | | | |
| | | | | | | | | |
| | | | | | | | | |
| | | | | | | | | |
| | | | | | | | | |
| | | | | | | | | |
| | | | | | | | | |
| | | | | | | | | |
| | | | | | | | | |
| | | | | | | | | |
| | | | | | | | | |

**Figure 6.8 Cost control sheet**
The detailed record of orders placed, sorted per cost code within any one project.

costs. These could be design costs, supervision costs, and the like. They will, however, have been estimated and budgeted, and the cost control engineer should formally advise the finance department of the *total* value of such commitments in relation to the particular project. They will then come into the record. There are other expenses, usually of a relatively minor character, such as insurance premiums, freight costs, which do not normally have 'formal' orders issued to cover them. Invoices are certified and paid as received. To ensure control, the origin and volume of such miscellaneous costs should be identified by the cost engineer. If the total is likely to be relatively insignificant, he can afford to ignore it, in the sense that he only takes note of such monies as they are paid. But the system of administration within the finance department should be such that all such payments are *added* to the commitment record: not only to the record of expenditure.

If, however, the volume of such expenses is substantial, then it begins to be an item to which the cost control engineer will have to pay specific attention, assessing the monthly progress, estimating the potential cost to completion and so estimating the potential commitment. Such expenses are, in our language, already 'committed', since they arise without the need for any further instruction: that is, an order. We will discuss the use to be made of this commitment record for cost control purposes later, in Chapter 8. For the moment, let us content ourselves with ensuring that the commitment record is comprehensive and that *implied* commitments are recorded as well as orders and contracts, and written into the record so that there is nothing left to surprise us later.

### The 'implied commitment'

We have just used the phrase 'implied commitment'. It is very important that this term be fully understood, if the commitment record is to be properly maintained. In addition, the technique of commitment recording needs to be carefully organised to avoid, in particular, the duplication of commitments. We have suggested that the commitment record is best kept by the finance department. This because they handle all payments, and the two – commitments and payments – are directly related. Finance also have a corporate responsibility, which they discharge by checking, before authorising payment, that the commitment has been properly established: that permission, in accordance with the rules of the company, has been given for that payment to be made.

One type of 'implied commitment' is the 'in house' commitment mentioned above. Another, and far more important, is the 'reimbursable contract', such as could be entered into for design.

Here the total commitment *implied* by instructing a contractor to proceed should be assessed and entered into the commitment record. Since it is an estimate, it will need to be reviewed and perhaps later revised, in the light of actual progress made. This is the function of the cost control engineer. A similar function has be exercised in relation, especially, to site contracts let on a 'schedule of rates' basis.

From all this it is clear that an assessment of the commitment over and above the 'face value' as it appears on the order at any time is a matter of estimating, and not only calculation as such. It is therefore something which the finance department cannot generate themselves. So that department has to look to 'project cost control' and the cost engineer, whether in its own organisation or that of the managing contractor, for the data. So the cost engineer develops the information and advises the finance department of the total 'control commitment', which they then compare with the 'face order value'. They only ever pay, of course, up to the face order value. It is the responsibility of the purchasing officer to keep the face order value in line with the status of the order or contract, so that it finally equals the amount that will be paid.

We are concentrating on the cost control function, and have therefore given, in Figure 6.9, a typical set of rules in relation to the calculation of the implied commitment, to be followed in order to set up the control commitment. This illustrates the nature of this particular function of the cost engineer in some detail.

### Value of work done control

Let us be very clear, to begin with, as to what 'value of work done' actually is. It is *not*, and must never be, expenditure as such, although it finally equals expenditure. It is described by the finance man as work in progress (WIP) but it is, most of the time, greater than the expenditure as recorded in the books by the accountant. Figure 6.10 illustrates the relationship between *value of work done* and *expenditure* as recorded over the life of a project. There is normally a considerable time lapse between having a project 'ready for startup' (RFSU) and the final payment of all the bills and 'retentions' so that the project can be closed financially. This time interval is never less than two months and in the closing stages can quite easily be twelve to eighteen months.

What then is *value of work done*? It can be briefly summarised as design and such other 'head office' costs as incurred, together with the value of all materials as they are delivered to, and the value of work as it is done on, the site. This means that payments

## ABSTRACT FROM A TYPICAL COST CONTROL PROCEDURE MANUAL

4.6   *Control commitment*
In the course of awarding each order or erection contract a Control Commitment will be developed.

The control commitment is for Cost Control purposes only and gives no authority to spend up to the amounts stated.

For Unit Price orders or contracts the commitment value will be based on the known scope of work as given in the Form of Contract, but adjusted to include anticipated scope increases/changes. The Unit Prices used in this calculation will be the same as those given in the Form of Contract.

For Lump Sum orders or contracts, the contract amount of the successful tenderer will be used as the basis plus a percentage allowance — derived from experience — for additional work.

On all orders or contracts, the commitment value will include a provision for escalation, to the extent that that is not already included in the Lump Sum price or the Unit Rates. If a formula is incorporated in the order or contract, that formula shall be used: otherwise the agreed escalation forecast shall serve as a basis for the calculation.

The Home Office and the Field Office will work together to establish the allowance to be added to any order or contract.

The difference between the Control Commitment and the Form of Contract or Order value is the contract/order contingency. All contingency information is confidential and MUST NOT be disclosed to the contractor.

4.7   *Form of Contract Up-Date*
The Form of Contract for every erection contract will be updated quarterly. The update will be based on all the latest design information, final quantities, where these are known, plus EWOs approved and completed during the period.

The updated Form of Contract will be the sole basis for amending the erection contract value. It is recognised that such amendments may also be issued to cover the transmission of design information.

**Figure 6.9 The control commitment**
An abstract from a typical cost control procedure manual to illustrate the rules guiding the cost control engineer in this context.

**Project:**

- **– –** Value of work done
- **▬** Payments
- ▶ Target date ready for start - up
- ▽ Revised target date

## PROJECT PROGRESS : Value of work done

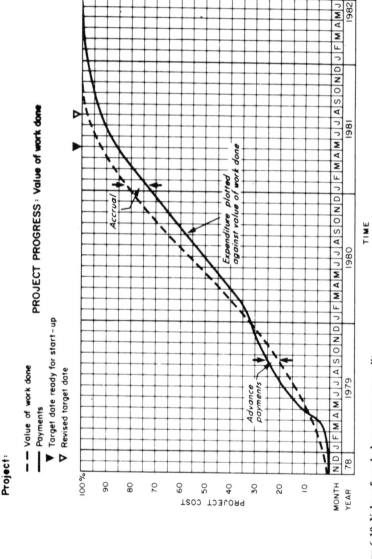

**Figure 6.10 Value of work done versus expenditure**
In the early stages, down payments and progress payments made before equipment and materials arrive in the field may cause expenditure to run ahead of value of work done, but most of the time it will lag two months or more.

128

made in advance of delivery to the site for materials or proposed works on site are not counted as value of work done, although they are money out of pocket at that time and will appear in the defrayed expenditure account.

Value of work done should be assessed with the absolute minimum of reliance on invoices and payments. This can be done by a series of techniques which result in an 'approximation' of the value of work done, this approximation being subject to progressive correction and improvement until, as the project becomes 100 per cent complete, value of work done equals the total of all invoices and charges booked against the project. The important thing to remember is that an approximation advised today is far more useful than an exact figure notified three to five weeks later. The techniques for an approximation of value of work done from month to month can be related to three main areas:

1   Home office effort (off site)
2   Materials deliveries to site
3   Construction contracts (work on site).

The items in this list can be described as follows.

## 1   Home office effort

This deals in essence with the design, procurement and project supervisory activities. The work done can be measured in man-hours. Manhours are usually measured weekly, and data for the last week in the month should be available early the following week. The hours booked can be 'valued' at an average rate per manhour, based on the recent past in the project, and the value of work done assessed. Assuming the work to be costed, the actual cost per manhour will be known later and the earlier assessment can then be corrected. The simple way to do this, and all such corrections as we discuss later, is on a cumulative basis. If the latest cumulative booked cost comes perhaps three weeks later, that is compared with the cumulative including last month's estimate, a correction made and we are in fact only one month behind the fact at any time. This is the 'approximate' approach, which can give figures within a few days of the point of time to which we are assessing value of work done.

## 2   Materials deliveries to site

Materials are delivered against firm orders, so normally an order value is available. Then, as materials arrive on site, the material receipt note can be valued, using the information on the order, and a progressive total maintained. Since the value shown on the order may not be the absolute invoice value, for a variety of reasons (discounts, freight charges, escalation) this approach gives a 'nominal' value, but once again it is a very close approximation and serves the purpose. In the case of bulk materials such as pipe and pipe fittings, it can be very time consuming to value all items on a receipt note from the itemised prices on an order, and it is allowable to use the weighbridge weight, multiplied by the average price per kilo calculated from the order, or orders. This calculation can be done when the orders are being placed, saving time and effort when the flood of materials arrives on site. The figures so recorded for value of work done can be reviewed and revised as the invoices are processed. There can sometimes be a two month lag in the receipt and processing of invoices, so once again the error is minimal, and is continuously corrected, being within some two months of actual.

## 3   Construction contracts

The approach to construction contracts is very similar, but the 'yardstick' this time is erection manhours. Erection manhours, exclusive of site supervision, for all contracts on the site should be faithfully recorded from week to week. This is standard practice where a managing contractor is employed and the figures are always available a few days after the event. Progress in the field on the various construction contracts will be appraised and measured by the cost engineer or specialised teams of quantity surveyors, in accordance with certain standard methods of measurement, to enable progress payments to be made. But such evaluations run two to three weeks late. So for the balance of the time, since the last evaluation, the erection manhours worked are valued, being multiplied by a rate per hour calculated as applicable to the particular site contract. This information will be available as part of the cost control routine, and is discussed in more detail in Chapter 8. Thus we have an immediate approximation whilst we wait on the formal evaluation, but only for the closing week or two of the period.

What has been said above indicates that there are a wide range of possibilities open for an *immediate* evaluation of the value of work done. One would expect the project cost control system to develop specific techniques suited to the standard procedures of a particular managing contractor, the owner and the local situation. The important thing is to make sure that the value of work done is always up-to-date so that it is consistent and the status of the project can be made available to management a few days after the end of the month. Only then is it meaningful.

## The 'measurement balloon'

As has been made clear above, value of work done should be assessed with the absolute minimum of reliance on invoices and payments. If this is done using a series of 'approximation' techniques as suggested, this approximation being subject to successive revision, progressive correction and improvement then, as the project finally becomes 100 per cent complete, value of work done equals the total of all invoices and other charges booked against the project.

If procedures such as have been outlined above are followed, then, as we have said, a report on the status of the project can be made to management a few days after the end of the month. Figure 6.11 illustrates what is required. When data on value of work done is assessed routinely it will become available at various times in the month. The assessments by the quantity surveyors for civil works may well be available some three to six weeks after any particular evaluation, information on deliveries of materials via invoices will relate randomly to materials delivered over the past three months, whilst the cost of design work is usually available within a couple of weeks. This means that the assessment of work done at the end of a month can well relate to a situation spread over some three months. This situation is illustrated by balloon A. However, the objective is to have the value of work done established at a particular *known* point in time, the 'cut-off' date, or report date, as shown in Figure 6.11. This is illustrated by balloon B and this should be achieved if the techniques that have just been discussed are followed. Since most of the assessments within balloon B are estimates, some will be higher than actual and this is suggested by showing balloon B in part *ahead* of the cut-off date.

Balloon A, therefore, represents what happens when assessments of value of work done are used as they become available, without regard to the period they cover, or invoices are used rather than material delivery records. The result is that balloon A no longer represents the position at a precise point in time and when the process is repeated the following month, there is no certainty that the difference represents the value of work done in that month, or even a period of a month. For instance, if a flood of invoices were processed, it might well represent five or six weeks' effort, rather than four. The sudden upsurge would give a false impression: it could be assumed that work was being speeded up when that was not at all the case.

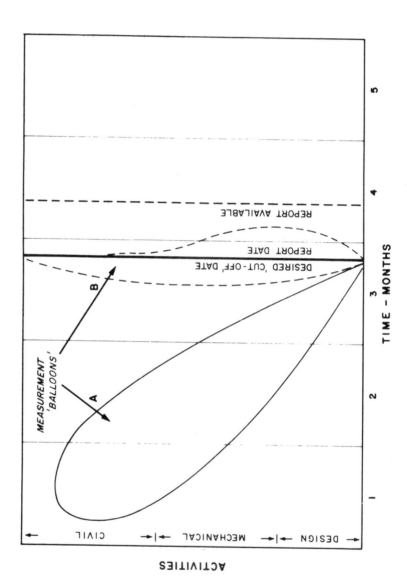

**Figure 6.11 The 'measurement balloon'**
The objective is to evaluate value of work done at the cut-off date. Avoid at all
costs evaluating the various activities at random points within the 'balloon', as
invariably happens when invoices are used to evaluate project progress.

132

## Inflation or escalation

The most apparent, self-evident fact in relation to the dynamism of our times is undoubtedly the movement of prices and costs over the years. A cost spiral that goes ever onward and ever upward, despite all the attempts of governments worlwide to contain it. However, if we are not careful we can be led into a maze of terminology and therefore need to stop for a moment to define our terms. We see inflation as the price movement over time of commodities, salaries, wages and the like. Escalation is the word we shall reserve for the movement in cost of an installation which is the combination of supplied equipment, materials and labour, constructed over a period of time. Escalation therefore reflects and includes inflation, but the movement in escalation is not necessarily parallel to the movement in inflation. Escalation can move faster or slower than inflation, depending upon the circumstances: particularly the market circumstances. For instance, when times are hard, a manufacturer will hold or even reduce his prices by reducing his margins, despite being faced with inflationary increases in the cost of his raw materials or his labour. Or he may be able to hold his prices in the face of inflation because of technological improvements, or an improvement in productivity. On the other hand, a fall in productivity will increase the rate of escalation, as compared with the index of inflation. Another illustration of the type of thing that produces increased escalation, irrespective of inflation, is the need to meet more stringent regulatory provisions.

To demonstrate the way in which escalation has moved over the years, we present a typical graph for the EEC (European Economic Community), excluding the United Kingdom, as developed and used by one of the authors. See Figure 6.12. Escalation within the United Kingdom has been markedly different from the rest of Western Europe and particularly the other members of the EEC over the past decade. It has, therefore, to be assessed and used separately. When, however, costs in the UK are looked at 'from the outside', as it were, so that changes in the rate of exchange for the £ with other currencies can be taken into account, it is then seen that the rate of change, as compared with the other countries in the EEC, is not so different as at first appears. The relationship between the cost of plants built in the UK, as compared with the rest of the EEC (the 'location factor', discussed in more detail later) has remained very close to 1.00 throughout the period, as is demonstrated by the continuing competitiveness of the UK overseas.

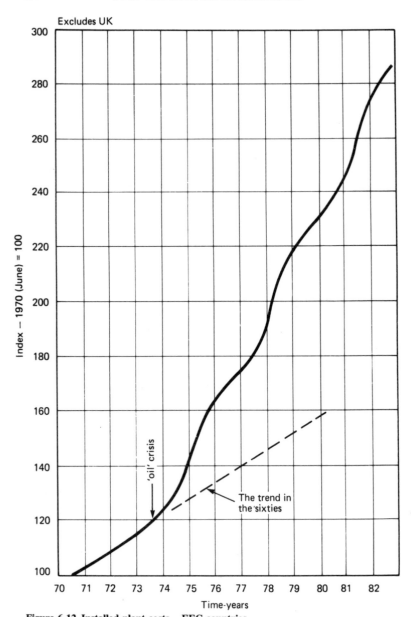

**Figure 6.12 Installed plant costs – EEC countries**
This graph gives the escalation recorded over the past decade for installed plants in the EEC, excluding the UK. It will be seen that the oil crisis of 1973 brought a change in trend that has only recently been reversed.

This effect can be see even more clearly by considering a country such as Brazil, which has been subject to what has been called 'hyper-inflation'. Over the years 1970 to 1976, for instance, the internal inflation rate in Brazil was of the order of 25 per cent per annum (3). But when corrected to US dollars, at which time the movement in the rate of exchange is being taken into account, the actual 'escalation' is seen to be much less than might have been expected: only about 8 per cent per annum and thus no higher than was being experienced by many developed countries at that time. This effect is brought about by frequent devaluations which keep the cruzeiro and the major external currencies in a proper balance. In a wider context such a self-correcting mechanism tends to rationalise the prices of capital items at an international level.

## Escalation

Having seen the difference between inflation and escalation, we should consider how the cost engineer is going to deal with escalation. There is no doubt that this is one of the main problems in project cost control with the acceleration of inflation over the past decade, and it will remain with us although the rate is now no longer what it was. Once the rate rises above some three per cent per annum, it needs to be evaluated and monitored.

But first, let us define our terms. What is five per cent per annum? Escalation can be stated in various ways. An escalation rate of ten per cent per annum can mean that there is a rise of ten per cent from February last year, to February of this year, or it can mean that the average increase over the last year (twelve months divided by 12) is ten per cent higher than the similar figure for the year before. This latter is the preferred approach, a more meaningful statement, and will be used in all our references to rates of escalation.

If we are going to monitor escalation, we must first have a forecast: a target to monitor against. The impact of escalation is not always fully realised. Figure 6.13 shows the effect of various rates of escalation over the years and it will be seen that an average rate of increase of 20 per cent will more than double prices over a period of some four years, and most projects take some three to four years to build these days. But the actual expenditure takes place over time and follows an S-curve. If you study the literature you will find a wide variety of 'cost indices' and there is many more than one index, for instance, for process plants in a particular country. It all depends upon the particular 'build-up' of the content of the index. What are we to do? In a sense we can have too much information. Let us realise that we begin with an estimate and we first have to forecast the possible rate of escalation *as it will apply to our project*. The one index almost always available and publicly discussed, and also forecast by the pundit, is the 'consumer goods' index, 'retail price' index, or 'cost of living' index, as it can be variously called. In the United Kingdom the Retail Price Index aims to measure increased costs by considering the price inflation experienced by an average UK household in purchasing a large basket of goods. The items in the basket of goods are derived from family expenditure surveys, and the index is recalculated monthly.

With this information available to us, the first rule of thumb is to assume that the index for building plants is about two per cent less than the Retail Price Index. That is, if they are talking in the press about the Retail Price Index rising by say ten per cent in the next year, then our plant costs are likely to go up by eight per cent. So we have the basis for a sensible forecast. In the first year costs will rise some eight per cent. In the absence of further information, we can assume that it will continue rising at eight per cent per annum in subsequent years, till our plant is ready to be started up. Now the question is: how much money shall we add to our estimate? Here comes the second rule of thumb. Apply the cost increase estimated two-thirds of the way along the life of our project. You will see this portrayed in Figure 6.13. For an escalation rate of ten per cent per annum, and a three year project, the increase two-thirds along, that is after two years, would be about 20 per cent. So we add 20 per cent to our estimated cost 'as at today', in order to arrive at the final cost. You can make very elaborate forecasts, and many detailed calculations, but you are not likely to improve on the above 'rule of thumb' approach. This is because your basic assumption, the rate of escalation, is so vulnerable. To avoid misunderstanding let us make it very clear that we are giving here a world-wide broad rule of thumb to be used in the absence of more relevant data.

That brings us to the next step. Having added money into the estimate for escalation we have to watch over it, monitor it. In order to monitor escalation as the project proceeds, one has, first of all, to record the actual escalation as it occurs, and then compare that with the forecast. How you approach this depends upon where you are, and what information is readily available to you. If you have nothing better, then once again use the Retail Price Index as a guide, following the assumptions that we have just described in this connection. Plot the corrected rate against the forecast rate made and included in the estimate. All the while the rate is less, you can assume that you are within your estimate in

## ESCALATION

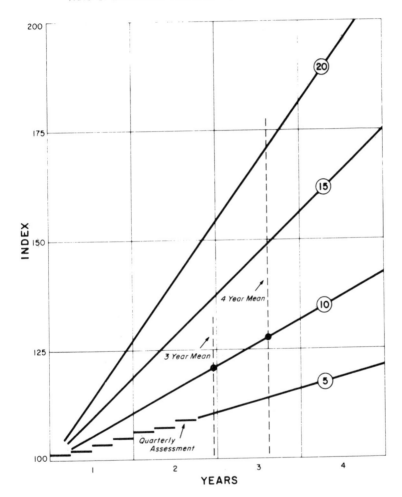

**Figure 6.13 Escalation**
Over four years costs have more than doubled with escalation at 20% per annum. With the normal spread of expenditure over the life of a project, escalation as estimated two-thirds through life is a good average to add to the basic estimate – 27% for a four-year project, or 20% for a three-year project, with escalation at 10% per annum.

this context. If it goes above the estimated rate, then you are in danger of overspending on this account.

Parallel to this overall 'watchdog' approach, detailed monitoring of the escalation fund is required, since our project, and hence our estimate, is dynamic. Everything is changing all the time. We have already said that the commitment as assessed and recorded should include its appropriate escalation. That is the commitment recorded should be the final cost, or estimated final cost where a fixed figure is not available. If we consider the cost control report as published to management (Figure 6.14) the provision for escalation (Column 6) in the latest estimate is reduced each month to the extent that it is taken up in the commitments made in the month.

To calculate the amount (or allowance) for escalation taken up in a commitment, which will not necessarily be discernible as a separate cost in the commitment itself, actual escalation to the date at which the commitment is made is calculated, using the Retail Price Index, plus provision for future escalation as allowed in the estimate, where this is not covered in the price. As the project progresses, and the various review estimates are made, the amount included for escalation will be proportionately less, and the problem of monitoring escalation will steadily diminish, until it finally disappears, *all* escalation being taken up in the commitments.

**Market conditions**

Till now we have been speaking of escalation as if all the costs with which we are concerned are moving in unison, but of course this is not actually so. When we turn from the overall picture to look at the movement in cost of specific terms of equipment, we see that there can be substantial differences in movement from item to item. This is a fact which we think we should highlight, since the various graphs that are published in the journals also tend to give the idea that everything is moving in concert, but this is not so. If we take the Western European equipment market as an example, and take 1970 as our base year, we see that over the period 1970 to 1976 enormous differences in price fluctuation can be observed, as demonstrated by the table in Figure 6.15.

The figures in the table demonstrate, to take but one example, that steelwork fell far behind in terms of price rises as compared with the general trend. This came about because in late 1976 the EEC Commission for Steel in Brussels was formulating emergency plans to protect the EEC steel companies, so desperate was the

## COST CONTROL REPORT

PROJECT :
PROJECT No.:

| PROJECT No. / CODE | DESCRIPTION | VALUE OF WORK DONE 1 | VALUE OF OUTSTANDING COMMITMENTS 2 | VALUE OF WORK DONE AND COMMITMENTS 3 | ESTIMATED TO COMPLETE 4 | LATEST REVIEW ESTIMATE | | | | |
|---|---|---|---|---|---|---|---|---|---|---|
| | | | | | | ANTICIPATED ULTIMATE NET-VALUE OF WORK 4 | ESCALATION REQUIREMENT 5 | CONTINGENCY REQUIREMENT 6 | ESTIMATED COST 7 | CALCULATED PROGRESS % 8 |
| | | | | | | | | | | |

MONTH ENDING:                                                                 CURRENCY

**Figure 6.14 Cost control report**

The estimate, together with the related escalation and contingency is analysed, normally per project, and then per 'department' within a project (see Figure 6.5). Further analysis, to the cost code, is not necessary for such a report as this, normally issued monthly.

Equipment cost indices

| | 1970 A B | 1971 A B | 1972 A B | 1973 A B | 1974 A B | 1975 A B | 1976 A |
|---|---|---|---|---|---|---|---|
| 1 Heat transfer equipment | 100  5 | 105 5 | 110 15 | 126 25 | 157  1 | 158  4 | 165 |
| 2 Compressors | 100 12 | 112 4 | 116  7 | 124 15 | 143 28 | 183  9 | 200 |
| 3 Centrifugal pumps | 100 12 | 112 4 | 116  7 | 124 15 | 143 12 | 160 19 | 191 |
| 4 Instrumentation | 100  8 | 108 6 | 115  6 | 121  7 | 129 20 | 155 17 | 182 |
| 5 Structural steelwork | 100  2 | 102 8 | 110 15 | 127 17 | 148  2 | 151 11 | 168 |
| 6 Electric motors | 100 10 | 110 5 | 115  8 | 124  6 | 131 15 | 151  5 | 159 |
| 7 Switchgear | 100 10 | 110 – | 110  5 | 116 10 | 127 15 | 146 15 | 168 |

A   Price index — midyear point (*not* a yearly average).

B   Percentage change between indices in adjacent columns, in effect the yearly movement.

**Figure 6.15 Equipment cost indices**
Over some six years quite marked differences have emerged in the increase in cost as between various types of equipment. There is no reason to suppose that these differences will later disappear.

situation in that particular industry. At the same time, the US Steel Corporation decided to cancel a proposed price rise of about 5 per cent on cold rolled steel. There is no doubt, seeing these price movements, that the law of supply and demand still continues to operate: when supply exceeds demand, price rises are minimal. However, the key point we wish to make is that price rises are not uniform and the cost engineer should be alive to this fact and consider its impact on his project.

## Exchange rates and currency risks

It is highly probable with any project of substance these days, even if built in Great Britain, certain items of equipment and materials will be purchased abroad. In Great Britain, we talk of purchases 'overseas': elsewhere in the world we are speaking of imported equipment. Indeed, in some countries the design, let alone the equipment, can be imported. Once we cross a national frontier we get involved in the problem of exchange rates and we have to adopt a 'policy' towards exchange rates for effective project cost control. It is taken for granted that all reporting on financial matters, including the project estimates, commitments, value of work done and expenditure will be in the currency of the country where the plant is being built. This is the only logical and sensible approach. The ultimate cost of the plant, as built, where it is built, in the currency of the location, is the one meaningful figure, since that is where all the 'bills' are ultimately paid.

As and when the project is approved it is approved for a certain sum of money, in the currency of the country of its location: this is the budget or appropriation sum. At that time, a set of rates of exchange should be established between the currency of the location and the currencies of any other countries from where the purchase of goods or services is to be expected. These should be the rates of exchange used in the preparation of the estimate, and are usually the published rates of exchange at the time the estimate is made, or the money authorised. These rates of exchange do not have to be precise, in the sense of being the rate of exchange on a certain day, but they should be realistic, and they should be published to the several interested parties, in particular the finance and cost control departments. From then on, these particular rates of exchange are fixed for the life of the project for the purposes of estimating, project cost control and cost reporting. That is, any estimates made will use these same rates of exchange to establish the value in the estimating currency of goods and services purchased abroad, commitments for these goods and services will be translated into the currency of the location in the same way and finally the value of work done relating to such goods and services (the delivered cost) will also be converted and reported using the same fixed rates of exchange. This procedure ensures that all cost control reporting is directly comparable. We can compare commitments and value of work done with the estimate directly, to see where we are going and what is happening in relation to the estimate. Fluctuations in exchange rates that may occur from time to time will not affect our assessment, because they have been excluded.

However, we have to know the absolute cost of our project, so this will require a separate financial procedure. As and when accounts are paid for goods and services purchased from abroad they will be paid for at a certain rate of exchange, usually the rate of exchange prevailing on the day payment is made by the Bank. Each payment so made will result in a 'variance' (either plus or minus) as compared to the payment that would have been made had the 'fixed' rate of exchange been applicable. These variances should be accumulated by the finance department, per project and per cost code. It then becomes possible at any time to adjust value of work done in order to establish the potential expenditure or final cost. When reestimates are made account can be taken of this variance, outside the estimate as such, in reporting to management and in order to determine whether or not more funds are required.

| YEAR | US DOLLAR | GERMAN MARK | FRENCH FRANC | ITALIAN LIRE | JAPANESE YEN |
|------|-----------|-------------|--------------|--------------|--------------|
| 1970 | 2.40 | 8.75 | 13.25 | 1,500 | 860 |
| 1972 | 2.50 | 8.00 | 13.50 | 1,510 | 845 |
| 1974 | 2.35 | 6.05 | 11.25 | 1,520 | 750 |
| 1976 | 1.80 | 4.55 | 8.60 | 1,500 | 535 |
| 1978 | 1.90 | 3.85 | 8.65 | 1,630 | 400 |
| 1980 | 2.35 | 4.25 | 9.80 | 1,990 | 525 |
| 1981 | 2.05 | 4.55 | 10.95 | 2,300 | 445 |
| 1982 | 1.75 | 4.25 | 11.45 | 2,360 | 435 |
| 1983 | 1.50 | 3.85 | 11.55 | 2,300 | 360 |
| 1984 | 1.30 | 3.80 | 11.65 | 2,330 | 320 |
| 1985 | 1.30 | 4.00 | 11.90 | 2,600 | 320 |
| 1986 | 1.40 | 3.80 | 11.65 | 2,500 | 300 |

**Figure 6.16 Movement in exchange rates**
The above table illustrates the comparative movement in the major currencies, as related to the pound sterling, over the past sixteen years. The figures are yearly averages and thus indicative only. For accurate data refer to your bank.

In conclusion, one should mention that certain financial risks are involved in relation to the movement of exchange rates. Figure 6.16 illustrates the relative movement in the major currencies over the past sixteen years, just to give some appreciation of the wide fluctuations that can take place. Since it is not unusual for the contracts for international projects to specify various levels of purchase of equipment and materials from various countries, together with milestone dates for payment, continuous monitoring and analysis of currency movement is essential if the risk of an adverse movement in the exchange rate is to be minimised. In times of widely fluctuating exchange rates, such as occurred between the US$ and the £ sterling in 1985, the buying or selling of currency in the 'futures' market may be one way of limiting the risk, but this involves speculation. We would therefore recommend a policy whereby no attempt is made to profit from possible movement. Then the appropriate amounts of currency can be purchased forward at the known rate of exchange to cover purchases in the various countries. Whilst advantage cannot be taken of any fall, at least the cost of the project is protected against any rise. But all this is very much a matter for the experts and we only mention it since the cost engineer should be aware of the possibilities in this context. The handling of the currency will incur costs, for there will be commissions and other charges to be paid. But once again these should be separately accounted for. But there is no doubt that when it comes to dealing with multi-currency payments and the related contractual conditions cost control really *must* be 'in action'. The timing is often crucial.

## Grants, taxes and other burdens

Perhaps it is just as well, whilst we are discussing the administrative procedures required to facilitate effective project cost control, to discuss the importance and impact of the various government schemes designed to encourage the construction of factories and similar facilities. Most countries these days have development grants and investment support designed to encourage development in certain areas. The UK, for instance, in addition to various types of grant, has what are called 'enterprise zones', where certain continuing financial advantages are available to firms setting up business within the zone. The EEC has schemes whereby development is encouraged by financial support in distressed areas throughout the community.

The manner in which the grant is applied can have considerable impact upon the cost control function: in particular, the development of the cost codes. For instance, in the UK and some other countries, Regional Development Grants (RDG) are currently available for approved projects. Once a project has been approved for RDG, the grant payable is calculated as the higher of either:

(a) 15 per cent of the eligible capital expenditure towards new buildings, plant and machinery (the Capital Grant), or
(b) £3,000 for each new job created (the Job Grant).

The calculation of applicable grant is further complicated by the fact that certain costs and activities do not qualify when the RDG is being calculated. For instance, the cost of the site has to be excluded, and individual assets costing less than £1,000. It is therefore essential that the project cost is broken down in such a way that the various elements of cost that qualify for the calculation of grant can be easily identified. The vehicle for this is the code of accounts, which will have to be modified as appropriate. The cost engineer will not only have to be closely involved in establishing the appropriate coding structure, which demands intimate knowledge of the regulations, but will have to monitor costs to ensure that the rules are being obeyed.

The number of schemes available is continually growing and in all cases government departments will be involved. This means that a knowledge of the protocol is essential to ensure that the grant is eventually received. If the detailed criteria demanded are not met, then the grant will not be paid.

The impact of taxes, such as value added tax, import duties and the like must also be considered. First and foremost, one has to be very clear as to the scope of the estimate in this context. The estimate used for authorisation (the budget estimate), which later becomes the basis of project cost control, should exclude all such costs. That is, value added tax (VAT) should be excluded (it is usually recoverable), together with import duties and other similar costs. Neither should credit be taken in the estimate for grants that may ultimately be paid. Of course, the evaluation which is prepared when the project is being assessed and approved will take account of such matters, but the best and simplest course, particularly from a cost control point of view, is to exclude them all from the project control estimate and from day to day reporting on project progress. Treat them as purely financial matters. The project control estimate will then present the basic cost of the project, and 'work in progress' as recorded should be on the same basis. If grants are made, for instance, to encourage investment, then the impact of these will have been taken into account when assessing the profitability of the project, and the finance department will have the responsibility of securing the necessary grants, and recording the final net cost of the project to the company. Similarly, if value added tax (VAT) is recoverable, finance will have a separate booking system to achieve this. In some countries it is common for import duties paid to be recoverable for particular types of investment projects, so once again these should be excluded from the estimate and handled separately as a financial transaction outside the province of project cost control as such. The typical Code of Accounts presented in Appendix B shows a code where, for instance, import duties can be collected (code 93) and similar codes can be created when necessary to facilitate the control of VAT payments, or the financial impact of the changes in rates of exchange. What is important is that it should be recognised that all these matters are far better handled by the finance department, for whom they would be normal routine, and the interface between that department and project cost control should be set up so that this is clearly recognised and the data processed accordingly. Part of the function of cost control, however, is to make sure that these aspects are not overlooked and that *all* costs, and credits, however they arise, are finally accounted for.

## Expenditure: the finance function

So we come to the end of the line: expenditure. At the end of the day commitments will equal expenditure and value of work done will also equal expenditure. Whilst the expenditure records will be the responsibility of the finance function, the cost control engineer should not ignore them completely, just as he should never rely on them completely. Cash flow and credit control, for instance, whilst primarily financial matters, are of interest to the cost engineer, since inefficient money management will always affect project cost. Contractors and vendors should always be paid promptly. We have indicated in our discussion on commitments earlier in this chapter, the way in which certain items of expenditure can be incurred without prior commitment, and care must be taken to see that the total commitment is actually the sum of expenditure and outstanding commitments at all times. Whilst the total commitment should be the basic record, a separate record should be maintained by finance of 'outstanding commitments'. As the project nears its end, this record of outstanding commitments should be scrutinised for validity. With the approach we have outlined, there is always the possibility of over or under valuation of commitments which will be disclosed as orders are finalised, contracts closed and claims settled.

Finally, throughout the life of the project, the cost engineer should watch the relationship between expenditure and value of work done, as illustrated in Figure 6.10. Finance should separately record and control 'advance payments' – expenditure incurred on down payments or progress payments made prior to delivery or prior to commencing work on the site. Excluding these payments, expenditure will normally run at least two months behind value of work done at any time. That is, at any time, the difference between the two is the value of work done for the last two months. This is the normal lag in the presentation and payment of invoices and progress payment claims. If this is not so, it is a matter deserving investigation. Delay in payment can result in frustrated contractors and so affect the progress of the project.

## References

1   Stallworthy, E. A. and O. P. Kharbanda, *Total Project Management – from Concept to Completion*, Gower, 1983, 329 pp.
2   Kharbanda, O. P. and E. A. Stallworthy, *Successful Projects – All with a Moral for Management*, Gower, 1986.
3   Thorne, H. C., 'Impact of inflation on international ventures', *The Cost Engineer*, Vol. 17, No. 5, September 1978, pp. 13–20.

# 7 Establishing proper targets

Each process plant, even when no new technology is involved, differs to some degree from its predecessors. This means that there is never a standard available which can be considered reliable when we review the steps to be taken with respect to project cost control. It is assumed that we are at the stage when the project has been approved, and this means that the two prime targets have already been established. The total project cost has been assessed and authorised, and the total time to the plant being commercially available (or 'ready for startup') will have been estimated and become part of the basis for authorisation.

Capital cost estimating and planning are the two skills called for here. The result of this preliminary work is to create two key targets: *time* and *money*. The next step is to build the project in the time, for the money. In other words, those two key targets now have to be met. Effective project cost control occurs, then, when the project is completed at a cost close to that predicted when the decision to go ahead was taken, *and* also within the time then estimated. Conversely, poor cost control is considered to occur when these primary targets are not met, although that is not always the case. There are reasons other than poor project cost control that result in overruns.

But there is a human aspect involved. We usually expect – even after years of experience – that a task will be simpler to achieve than it ever actually is. Our vision of the task ahead always leaves out the unexpected and the unpredictable: yet they occur. Not always, but very often. This is well illustrated when we consider the estimate that will have been prepared for the authorisation of our project and that is now the target we have to match. This human weakness, this inability to envisage the expected, is one of the reasons why estimates of cost are more often low than high, and why project costs tend to overrun rather than underrun. This has always been so. That is why contingency allowances are added to estimates. It is an attempt to counteract this weakness. If cost estimates were not almost invariably optimistically biased, contingency would be unnecessary. The weakness is not quite so apparent with time estimates: estimates of project duration tend, on the whole, to be more realistic than the estimates of cost, although when estimates of cost are sadly in error, the estimates of time can hardly help being seriously at fault as well, since cost represents the assessed volume of work that has to be done in the time.

We are laying the emphasis here on project cost control and we must assume that the estimates of cost and time, prepared by the estimating engineer and the planning engineer, and now the prime 'targets' are realistic. Without that assumption we are lost: we are completely in the dark, for we are saying that we do not believe in our targets. And if we do not believe in them, why were they ever accepted and submitted to the board for authorisation? In the following chapter, which discusses 'early warning signals', details are given of certain techniques which help to assess the validity of these targets of time and cost before it is too late, but some time has always to pass, and some progress has always to be made on the project, before the cost engineer can begin to play his role. He has to have some project history behind him before he can look into the future with any degree of certainty. So, when we begin a project, we begin with the acceptance of the given targets of cost and time. Let us now see how the project engineer starts to develop his own targets within the basic framework thus provided.

## Cost control and planning

The interrelationship between the two targets of time and money must also be recognised. A low cost estimate almost invariably leads to an underestimate of the time required to complete the project, which in itself will bring additional costs. Experience is always a great help, but can also be a hindrance. It is easy to be over-confident and complacent and think, for instance, that project cost control is easier than it is. Whilst, as we have said, one usually does not plan for the unexpected, yet the unexpected occurs surprisingly often. What is known as 'Murphy's Law' is indeed a law, even though it is often taken as a joke: 'If something can go wrong, it will!' Such considerations are often completely ignored when the early estimates for a project are being prepared and it is assumed that all will go well. But it doesn't!

It also has to be realised when 'targets' are under discussion that the immediate target is *not* the final target. There is a route to the final cost target, an S-curve, and the shape of this curve is as much a target as the final cost. The plot gives a continuing target, and an increment month by month. This is, in effect, a much more important target than the final cost, since it is close at hand and a month later one knows whether that particular target has been met or not.

The same approach applies when we come to planning, which relates essentially to the 'time targets' established for the project. There are a wide range of systems available, but any system should have the versatility to cater for multi-level reporting and should report against what are called 'milestones'. These are the immediate targets. Harrison discusses the art and science of planning in detail in his book on project management (1). Whilst he has much to say in favour of bar charting and is very critical of CPM methods, such as CPM, CPA and PERT, there is no doubt that on all major projects a system of network analysis will be used. Our concern, since the cost control engineer has to work closely with the planning engineer, is that the system adopted shall be straightforward, not relying too heavily on computer facilities. Lester presents what amounts to a unique practical approach to planning, with continuing emphasis on control, which is therefore less liable to failure than the more complex and inflexible computerised methods that are so often adopted (2).

With major projects, control is much simplified if the project is divided into a number of work packages. The logical sequence to carry out the work, the work package manhour estimates and the durations are analysed by the planning engineers using precedence network techniques. The engineering personnel review the logic to ensure that the sequence of tasks and their interrelationships are correct. Finally a plan is produced in which the several work packages are scheduled and from which the manpower resources and manhour histograms are obtained. Throughout the project this plan, which is integrated with the work measurement system, is used as the basis of assessing the actual progress of the work. The cost engineer, meanwhile, will have the estimated cost of each work package, and will be translating work done into cost and comparing that with *his* targets.

**The basic targets**

When a project is implemented there are a number of cost

generating activities which can be grouped into three broad streams
in terms of percentage of total project cost, thus:

A   Design, engineering, project management
    and site supervision                                   25%
B   Equipment and materials                                40%
C   Site construction                                      35%

In passing, this is a United Kingdom cost analysis, so far as the
percentages are concerned. For Western European conditions
generally, the figures might well be more of the order of 25–45–30.
This analysis gives us three basic targets, each with their related
targets in terms of time. This time/cost relationship forms an
S-curve in total, as already demonstrated in the previous chapter,
Figure 6.1. But each of these three separate activities has its own
time/cost relationship, which is also an S-curve, as demonstrated
in Figure 7.1. It will be seen that the target for the cost engineer is a
flowing combination of time and money. He is concerned with his
position relative to the forecast S-curve.

These curves are the basic tools of the cost engineer. They tell
him where he should be in terms of work done at any point in time
during the life of the project, they tell him what should be achieved
in the coming month and, if he can look that far ahead, the coming
three months. But that is as far as the S-curve can be relied upon for
detailed month by month forecasting. The trend tells the cost
engineer the direction, and hence the probable end result. If we are
to maintain effective monitoring, we have to clearly understand the
scope of the several separate money targets that are now being set
up. This has been discussed in some detail in Chapter 6 and if we are
to establish our position on any one of these three S-curves, we have
to avoid the 'balloon' type of measurement of value of work done
(Figure 6.11) against which we have warned.


### Trend analysis

In order to establish a trend, one has to measure actual progress,
and then compare it with forecast progress. Since the forecast
progress depends, in essence, upon our end targets in terms of time
and money, these also need to be reviewed from time to time as our
project progresses. This should be done at regular intervals,
probably at least every three months. Revised targets in terms of
either cost or time will, of course, influence the progress to be made
per month to meet the revised targets. Targets should always be
realistic when handled and processed by the cost engineer. There is

## PROGRESS PER PROJECT PHASE

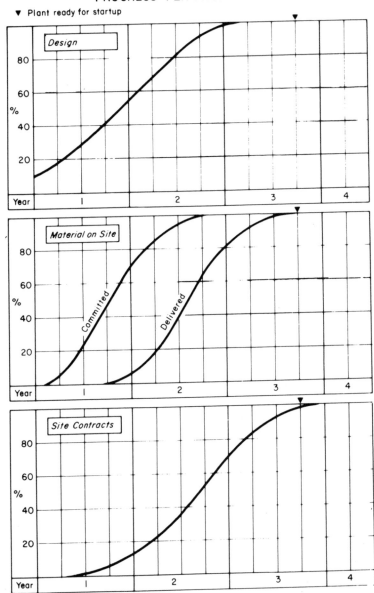

**Figure 7.1 Progress per project phase**
Typical progress in terms of value for work done for the three basic phases into
which every project can and should be subdivided.

never any merit in 'hiding one's head in the sand'. Once it becomes evident, for instance, that a project is going to cost more, or less, than the original (or earlier) estimate, then the targets should be revised and the potential influence on monthly progress evaluated and accepted as the new target. At what point in these successive revaluations the project manager, for instance, decides that he must ask for more money because the estimate shows an upward trend, may well be a difficult decision – even a political decision – but the cost engineer must use his new targets as they become known to him. In fact, this movement of what is often called the *site current estimate*, or the *review estimate* against the original board authorisation has in itself a characteristic trend, illustrated in Figure 7.2. This experience is so universal that it has become the subject of caustic comment – surely we should know better. But we never do!

There are a number of possible pitfalls ahead of us in the life of a project that lead to the result portrayed in Figure 7.2. They include:

1  Inadequacy in scope definition
2  Changes made in the scope of the project
3  Influence of external conditions, such as escalation and fluctuations in exchange rates.

Whatever they are, they are always what some people delight in calling the 'unmeasurables'. Inadequacy in scope definition results in underestimation, or allows work to be done on the project that was not in the 'real' scope, which amounts to the same thing. Formal changes in scope are more manageable, in the sense that they can be defined, estimated and approved. Unfortunately, the end result is still the same, since scope changes are not going to be made unless they are essential to the successful completion of the project, or the proper operation of the plant. So they too remain an inevitable and unavoidable increase in cost as compared with the original estimate. So, for better or worse, we have the cost/time target, and the S-curve gives us the route to that target. But where do these S-curves come from?

### The law of the S-curve

Now we come to a very, very important principle, proven in practice: an empirical law. This principle has long been well known to engineers and it is interesting to quote from a book written by a founder member who later became one of the

# CAPITAL COST ESTIMATES – TREND

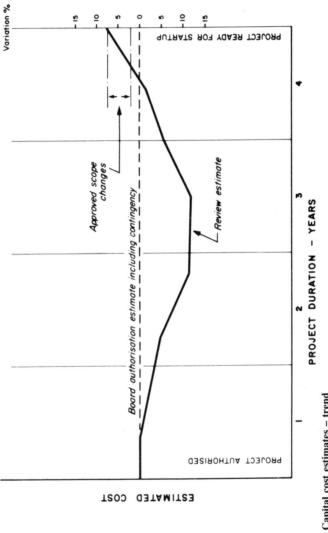

**Figure 7.2 Capital cost estimates – trend**
This graph illustrates the characteristic movement of the review estimate as compared with the amount originally authorised, during the life of the project.

Presidents of the Institution of Chemical Engineers in London. He says (3):

> More often than not, as 'nature does not proceed by leaps and bounds', the various functions involved in chemical engineering calculations are continuous, and when plotted on squared paper give smooth curves. Plotting on logarithmic paper of such relations will generally give something near a straight line, and substantial accuracy can be secured, at any rate over a restricted range of conditions, by expressing the results as though they gave a true straight line on log paper, *i.e.* expressing them in the form of an equation of the type: $Y = Ax^b$.
>
> Such formulae have the merit of being generally applicable, and they also lend themselves to quick calculations on a slide rule. The great merit of 'monomial' formulae of this kind is that although they are purely empirical, they can be very useful as a means of summarising observations. Very frequently quite complicated phenomena can be concentrated into a useful formula of the type $Y = Ax^b y^c z^d$, *etc.*, where the various variables are indicated by the letters $x$, $y$, $z$.

This quotation is clearly dated by its reference to the use of a slide rule – everyone uses pocket calculators these days – but the comment remains as true as ever. In fact, the concept outlined is the basis of the well known 'six-tenths' law, used in estimating. This law goes:

$$C = C_1 \times \left(\frac{V}{V_1}\right)^{0.6}$$

and is used for scaling up the cost of complete plants and items of equipment, where $V$ and $V_1$ are the relative sizes or capacities, and $C_1$ the known cost. But the important point at this moment, however, is that things – and particularly chemical construction projects – *do not* proceed by 'leaps and bounds'. As a result, we have the classic cost control tool, the S-curve: and especially the S-curve for the value of work done. On the background of the above empirical law we have been able to develop another: the law of the S-curve. Once again, this is an empirical fact and it finds its fullest expression in the plot of value of work done for a construction project. Figures 6.1 and 7.1 illustrate typical S-curves of this type.

With any and every investment in new manufacturing facilities all the efforts involved in process and detailed design and engineering, procurement, expediting, and the supervision of construction in the field find their ultimate reflection in a mounting complexity of worked materials on the site. It is the end result, when measured in terms of monetary value, that produces the S-curve for value of work done. For any particular area of capital investment, and for a particular project development and management approach, the

S-curve is essentially always the same and it is this fact – an empirical fact – that enables a sound forecast to be made of the progress of value of work done over time. Whilst the detailed experience in this context relates to petrochemical plants, there is no doubt that the same principles apply to all major investment projects. A pharmaceutical plant is very different to a food factory, and both are different to the petrochemical plants which brought the law to light, but all are subject to the same external economic forces, all benefit from about the same degree of management expertise and each group will have its characteristic S-curves, very little different from the ones discussed here. The significance of this statement will be more fully appreciated if our remarks on the *real constraints* in Chapter 3 are borne in mind. However, for the law to be seen in action, value of work done must be clearly and consistently defined, and recorded as defined. The techniques to achieve this have already been set out in some detail in Chapter 6.

On this background, the S-curve for value of work done *always* follows the same path when expressed in percentage terms. This is an empirical statement, based on the analysis of a substantial number of completed installations of a similar type. Radically different types of installation can well have different S-curves, but the difference will never be significant. The margin of error in this statement is never more than plus or minus ten per cent and within this it can most certainly be taken as a law. For chemical and petrochemical plants the limits are more probably plus or minus six per cent, and the implications of this can be seen when studying Figure 7.3.

### Definition of the parameters

It has to be remembered that the form of the S-curve is determined by the 'start date', the 'end date' and the manner in which value of work done is assessed. Value of work done has been defined in detail in Chapter 6, but let us emphasise once again that in order to ensure comparability of the data the manner in which it is measured must be consistent. This is because value of work done is only meaningful in terms of the assessment of a trend if it is measured over a known specific period of time, such as a month, rather than on a purely cumulative basis.

With respect to the other two parameters which determine the shape of the S-curve, namely 'start date' and 'end date'; the 'end date' is the date by which all the work on site in relation to the project is complete. It can be referred to as 'mechanical comple-

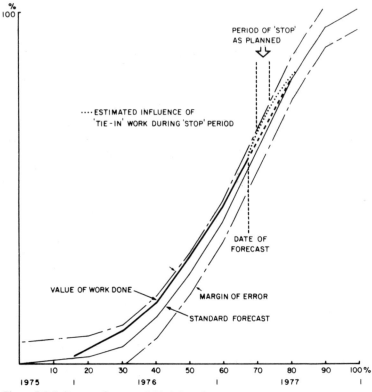

**Figure 7.3 Influence of proposed 'tie-in' work**
A practical demonstration of the 'solidarity' of the law of the S-curve, once the volume of work, and hence the 'constraints', is substantial.

tion', or 'ready for start-up', but it should not include commissioning activities. The 'start date', however, can be more difficult to define and hence to determine. It should not be related to the vote of monies, as such, but preferably be that point in time at which the project moves over from the 'study phase' to project implementation, in the design offices.

## Application of the law

Once a consistent approach has been established and the historical data analysed, there are only three significant variables to be considered: time, money and the route (shape of the S-curve). The law says that the route is fixed, so two significant variables are then left. Thus, if the actual curve as plotted deviates from the standard then one or the other, or both, of these two variables, time and money, must be wrongly estimated. It then becomes the task of the cost control engineer to review the situation in order to establish the position and to set new targets. The manner in which this is done in practice can be seen by reference to Chapter 8 (section on 'The monthly trend').

The strength of the law can be seen if we consider the influence of potential disruptions, such as strikes, trade holidays, shortage of labour and the like. To take a rather extreme example, one group of utility projects in a major development required more than 200 'tie-ins' to the existing plant, all to be accomplished in a 'shut-down' period of some five weeks. This demanded intensive planning and intensive working on the site for a short period, relative to total project duration. The average manpower on the site for that group of projects at the time was some 350, and it was estimated that this had to be increased for this short period to some 750 in order to cope with the completion of the tie-ins, with all the other work proceeding as planned. The influence on the related S-curve for value of work done for this projected increase in effort is shown in Figure 7.3. It will be noted that despite the intensity of the effort relative to the normal flow of work at that time, the 'distorted' S-curve still remains within plus or minus six per cent of the standard. The strength of the law is further emphasised when it was later seen that this total projected increase in effort on site was never achieved. External forces, such as the limited availability of labour in the area, took over, mitigating the planning, so that the work had to be done at the expense of progress in the other projects associated with the utilities on the site. The result of all this was that the 'actual' value of work done ran even closer to the standard than had been forecast.


**The erection subcontract**

The third and in some respects the most significant of the cost generating activities are the site (or erection) contracts executed in the field. We assume – indeed we recommend – that the work in the field is let out to what we might call 'specialist' subcontractors, under the control of the owner, if he has the resources: or under the control of an appointed managing contractor. The role of the managing contractor acting on behalf of, and cooperating with, the owner is expounded in some detail in Chapter 11 (Proper project management). For the moment, we want to think about the specific subcontracts for packets of work let out in this way in terms of the targets they create.

Erection subcontracts deserve special consideration because they are the most difficult aspect of the work on the project to control. As has been said earlier, the assumption is made that work on the site is handled by a series of separate erection subcontracts. If maintenance labour is utilised because the plant is being built on an operating site, then cost control will be more difficult, but such use of existing labour is not usual these days. Most factories are run on very tight schedules, with the result that labour cannot be spared from the routine work.

It must be realised that erection subcontracts, whether let directly by the owner or through a managing contractor, can take many forms. These contracts will be let one by one over a substantial period of time: probably over a period of at least two years with a major project. As the contracts are let, their work content becomes gradually more predictable and this allows for a change in the form of contract. The earlier contracts may well have to be let on the basis of a schedule of rates since quantities are not known, but later contracts may well be 'fixed price' contracts. Every effort should be made to achieve this development, whilst recognising that the 'fixed price' contract is not always the best type of contract. The success of the fixed price contract depends very much on the completeness of the design and the drawings when they are handed over for tendering purposes. Increased effort from the design team can sometimes result in earlier finalisation of drawings, but this could bring extra design and management costs and the lower beneficial cost may be minimal. The change to the fixed price contract should be made when the benefit to the project in terms of the greater control in scope and work content afforded by the cost reimbursement type of contract, with a schedule of rates, becomes less than the benefit to be gained by the greater competition between contractors that becomes possible with more precise scope definition, associated with the reduced administrative load on the project team when they have a 'fixed price' contract to manage.

The relationship between these several forms of contract and the effort required for their control is well illustrated by Figure 7.4. The diagram is simple enough, yet the manner of presentation means that the implications of change in the form of contract can be clearly seen, together with the demand then made on detail. It should be realised that this variety of choice does not affect the need for cost control: only as the triangle is climbed the work of cost control is made easier. It therefore becomes important to assess the potential number and size of what are called 'cost reimbursement' contracts,

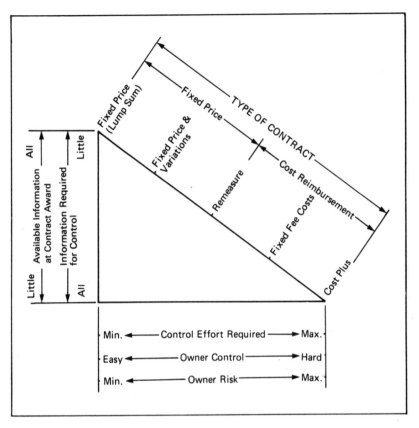

**Figure 7.4 Which type of contract?**
This diagram illustrates the relationship between the type of contract that is employed and the control effort required, the choice of contract usually being determined by the information available.

since these demand the most effort in terms of control, so that the staff made available can cope. Many of these contracts are handled, costwise, by quantity surveyors in the UK.

Irrespective of the type of contract being used, care should be taken to ensure that a proper record is kept of the manhours worked on the contract and valuations made of the cost of work as done. With lump sum contracts this may only be available from the contract in terms of a percentage of the total value of the contract, but it should nevertheless be demanded and the figures incorporated in 'value of work done'. This means that there will then be two separate views of erection subcontract progress: (a) via the value of work done for the contracts individually and in total; and (b) via the erection manhours recorded from week to week for each contract. If we assume that the project team decide to make bulk purchases of piping, electrical and instrumentation materials, which is both good project engineering and sound commercial practice, then the piping, electrical and instrumentation erection on site may well be largely labour, but tankage and structural steel, insulation contracts and the like will still be let as complete contracts. That is, the contract price and hence the value of work done will include detailed design by the contractor and the supply of materials as well as erection. Similarly civil and building works will also bring their quota of materials and supplies.

Whether the tender from the subcontractor is on a lump sum basis or based on a schedule of rates, each contractor, as part of his tender is required to submit his plan for the progress of the works being tendered to completion. This plan must include an estimate of the time required from receipt of instructions to proceed and an estimate of the manning, or related erection manhours. This information is essential in relation to planning of the field activities as a whole, but it also gives useful information for project cost control. The result is that each subcontract let has its individual time and money target, and also an 'effort' target, expressed in manhours. The S-curve followed by each subcontract is almost identical in normal circumstances and it has been found in practice that the progression given in Figure 7.5 is a very satisfactory target for value of work done in relation to erection subcontracts.

The erection manhours worked on the site have a direct relationship to value of work done. This relationship will vary from subcontract to subcontract and will also vary within each subcontract over the life of the contract as well. We discuss this relationship between value of work done and erection manhours in more detail in the next chapter (Chapter 8: see Figures 8.2 and 8.3), since this relationship is a valuable tool in cost control. However, when we sum all our subcontracts, over the life of the project, we get two S-curves: one for value of work done and the other for erection manhours. They relate to one another as illustrated by Figure 7.6. So, once again, we have S-curves as a target to follow: a basis for comparison as the work proceeds.

### It's a moving target

The various S-curves which we have used as illustrations (Figures 6.1, 7.1, 7.3 and 7.6) all measure progress in monetary terms, and

| SUBCONTRACTS |
| --- |

PROGRESS OF VALUE OF WORK DONE

| Time elapsed<br>% | Progress<br>% |
| --- | --- |
| 0 | 0 |
| 10 | 1 |
| 20 | 3 |
| 30 | 10 |
| 40 | 25 |
| 50 | 44 |
| 60 | 59 |
| 70 | 73 |
| 80 | 88 |
| 90 | 96 |
| 100 | 100 |

A CHARACTERISTIC S-CURVE

**Figure 7.5 Construction subcontract progress**
Typical progress for the value of work done. This is measured from the date of contract award to the date that particular contract is complete.

progress is expressed as a percentage. A percentage of what? Our estimate is the sum of today's values, plus escalation and contingency. First of all, progress should always be measured against the final estimated cost exclusive of contingency. As review estimates are made from time to time through the life of the project, and assuming that the original provisions for contingency are progressively being taken up, the estimate, and hence the 'target', will steadily increase. The review estimate can change for a number of reasons apart from under/over estimating as such. Escalation can move at a rate different to that first allowed. Scope changes can be introduced. As this information becomes firm, the estimate of project cost is reviewed and revised.

In the early stages of a project, reestimates have no value if done too frequently. The usual approach is to reestimate when certain 'milestones' in the life of a project have been reached. Typical 'milestones' are:

1   As soon as possible after contract award, when a managing contractor is being employed
2   On virtual completion of the placement of orders for plant and equipment

# PROGRESS ON SITE

— ERECTION MANHOURS

— VALUE OF WORK DONE

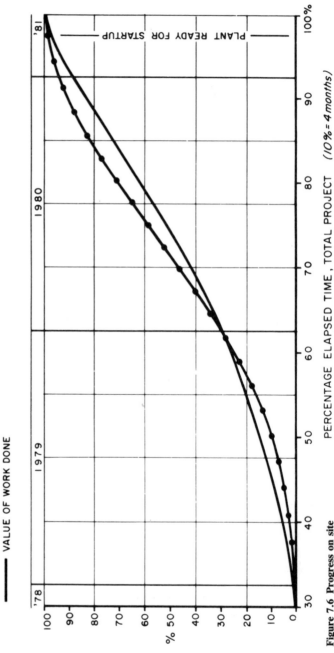

PERCENTAGE ELAPSED TIME, TOTAL PROJECT   *(10% = 4 months)*

**Figure 7.6 Progress on site**
The S-curves for value of work done and erection manhours, in relation to the construction subcontracts as a whole, during the erection phase of a project.

162

3 On substantial completion of the detailed engineering
4 At an advanced stage in the placement of the subcontracts for work in the field
5 As the project is being closed out.

But, as orders are being placed and commitments established, particularly in the area of plant and equipment (cost codes 20 to 27, Appendix B) specific cost codes will become fully committed, one by one. As a code becomes fully committed, the cost engineer should compare the committed cost with the provision in the cost control estimate at that time and revise his estimate – and hence his target – as appropriate.

If this principle of approach is followed then, as the project develops, progress, expressed as a percentage in monetary terms (value of work done), is always a percentage of the very latest estimate, which estimate, of course, is also incorporated in the reporting of the cost control engineer. Figure 6.14 (see Chapter 6) showed the cost control report, where this should be done. It will be seen that this report makes no mention of any board appropriation, or authorised budget. Obviously, the amount authorised for a project is significant – indeed fundamental – but it is *not* the immediate target of the cost control engineer, nor indeed of project management. It is *not* involved in the exercise of cost control at such. The cost engineer is concerned, in the first instance, with the status of the project as compared with his latest estimate. *That* is *his* target. It is another step to compare that estimate with the amount authorised, with a view to discussion on under/over expenditure. Action in the area of the budget, or authorisation, tends to be political rather than practical, in any event. Indeed, there is real danger to the proper exercise of the cost control function if the cost engineer is pressurised (or commanded) to suppress his latest review or control estimate because there is a substantial variance between that and the amount authorised. This pressure is the more likely to happen, actually, if the review estimate is *lower* than the amount authorised. But to give in to such pressures or desires is, quite simply, very bad project management. But it happens all too often!

Revision of the estimate will automatically revise the shape and course of the target S-curve, in its time/money relationship. But when expressed as a 100/100 relationship, as in Figure 7.3, the shape will remain the same if we accept and apply the law of the S-curve. Acceptance of this law, therefore, not only simplifies our forecasting technique, but also presents us with an approach which lends itself to computerisation.

### Scope changes, extra works and claims

Having realised that we have a 'moving target', with both time and cost liable to change, let us now examine some of the major reasons for those changes. These are: scope changes, extra works and claims. The scope of the project will have been defined at the outset and the difference between scope changes and extra works needs to be clearly recognised. A procedure for dealing with changes made is therefore required, both to ensure that they are properly controlled and that their full impact on project cost and plan are evaluated in advance, so that approval of worthwhile changes may be given prior to implementation and unnecessary changes rejected. The project cost control engineer should be responsible for change control procedures and he will have to differentiate between the several types of change with which he may be confronted. There are three major groups: scope changes, extra works and claims. Let us look at extra works first.

Extra works are works done *within* the scope as originally defined, but not recognised as necessary when the original instructions were issued to a contractor. Extra works can arise in two major ways. Firstly, a contract may have been awarded before all the works required have been fully detailed or defined. Then, as design progresses, further information is provided to the contractor as he is thereby called upon to carry out 'extra works'. The other major cause of extra works is the unexpected. For instance, ground conditions call for extra excavation, errors on drawings have to be rectified, or one contractor makes a mistake that results in another contractor having to do work he otherwise would not have to do. This latter is a very common occurrence when delays take place in the completion of drawings, delivery of equipment and the like.

Scope changes need special and very detailed treatment and the cost control engineer must always be involved. A scope change is usually initiated by the owner, but they can in certain circumstances be initiated by a contractor. However they arise, the contractor involved will call them 'client changes' or 'contract changes', since they become, when approved, changes made in his contract by the owner. There must be a complete system within the contractor's organisation for their record, their estimation and their evaluation in terms of their effect upon the contract. A contract change is not necessarily a scope change, either for the contractor or the owner, since it is quite possible to add further work to a contract which is within the original scope of the project. What must be realised and accepted is that scope changes *will* come. This means that not only the contractor but the project team running the project for the owner must *also* have a sound system for the registration and control of scope changes.

The approach of the contractor to a contract change is straightforward enough. On receiving a request from the owner, he assesses for himself:

1  Cost
2  Effect on the engineering schedule
3  Effect on construction completion

He registers:

4  Acceptance of items 1–3 above by the owner
5  Authorisation by the project manager for the owner

But how should the owner approach this same problem. Well, ideally he should not make any changes. But seeing that he will, he too must recognise *from the very beginning* the potential impact of his pending scope changes on his basic cost and time targets. This demands rigorous control and discipline. The manner in which that control is exercised will of course vary from case to case, but a form should be prepared that has to be completed and circulated before a scope change is authorised and passed forward to the managing contractor for action. The form will usually be initiated by a member of the project team, but the request can come from anyone involved in the project – most often from the process design engineers. That form should demand:

(a)  Description of the change. This should include the equipment estimated to be involved and the design/construction work involved.
(b)  Descriptive data, such as drawings, sketches, flow schemes, equipment lists.
(c)  Justification for the change. This should be something such as easier or cheaper operation or maintenance, safety, technical requirement, or marketing requirement.
(d)  Estimated yearly saving. This is the financial benefit to be expected, if any.
(e)  Required start and finish dates for the work involved.

Answers should also be required to the following key questions:

(f)  Can the plant operate at full capacity even if the change is not made?
(g)  Will the plant be forbidden to operate by any outside authority if the change is not made?

Once this form has been completed it should be approved by the interested parties within the owner organisation, until it finally reaches the owner's project manager for acceptance or rejection. He *must* have the authority to decide, giving his reasons, of course, if the change is rejected.

Every effort should be made to resist major scope changes because of their inevitable and often unexpected impact on time and cost. Even when the cost is recognised and accepted, such changes will still have a disproportionate effect on the time taken to completion, in view of their disruptive effect. It is far better, therefore, where technically possible, to delay major scope changes until, for instance, the first major shut-down of the new installation. They can then be treated as a completely separate project or projects, to be progressed and planned as necessary – perhaps alongside the main project, if need be, until they are finally tied in. Any limitations on output, for instance, are then accepted until such time as the changes can be incorporated.

Let us, to conclude our review of the changes that can influence project cost, consider the impact of 'claims'. It is almost inevitable that, as a project proceeds, various contractors engaged on the project will make 'claims' for a variety of reasons. What is a 'claim'? A claim is a request for payment for costs incurred in completing a contract, where the basis for payment is not precisely defined within the terms and conditions of the contract. The amount involved is therefore the subject of negotiation between the parties. Because the subject of a claim is not precisely defined within the contract, its actual existence, as well as the amount involved, can be challenged by the other party. Because it is the subject of negotiation and can vary from the frivolous to the serious, much time can be consumed in the assessment and analysis of claims and their eventual agreement between the various parties involved.

A typical example of a 'sound' claim would be where a piping erection contractor, doing his work under a schedule of rates, made his offer of those rates under a plan proposed to him, starting in the February and finishing by the October of the same year. But in the event the necessary isometric drawings of that pipework are not produced on time and construction is therefore delayed through no fault of the piping erection contractor. The work actually takes longer, going forward at a slower tempo than was originally planned. Also, the work now extends into the winter period. So the contractor has a 'claim'. He claims for increased costs due to the extension of his time on the site (increased site and home office overheads): he claims for loss of productivity due to having to work at a slower tempo: he claims for increased costs due to escalation: and so on.

Some of these items can be measured fairly accurately, such as the increased overheads and the impact of escalation, but the impact of 'loss of productivity' could well lead to prolonged debate. You will realise that there is no dispute over the basic fact. The contractor was given a programme to work to: he *has* been delayed through no fault of his own, but the dispute arises in relation to the cost impact of that fact. What did it really cost him? How much of the extra costs were occasioned by his own dilatory approach to the developing situation?

The best defence against unjustified claims and the best possible investment is to have a very detailed historical record of the project, contract by contract, to refer to. We have already mentioned a project where this routine was *not* followed, with disastrous results – the construction of the Humberside Refinery, dealt with in some detail in Chapter 5. One very useful procedure in this context is to make sure that the site manning is on record week by week, for all the contractors. It is surprising the way in which such detailed records (provided by the claimant, for the most part!) will enable many such claims to be evaluated and often refuted very quickly indeed. Care must also be taken to see that the people directly involved in the project, and particularly those involved in project cost control and site supervision do not disappear elsewhere, to another project, too quickly, for there is nothing to replace personal memory and involvement when disputes arise. To be able to say 'I saw it' has tremendous strength in argument. It should also be remembered that this matter of 'claims' is quite big business and often, for the contractor, success or failure with a claim will make all the difference between profit and loss on a contract.

All projects, even the best of them, end with the settlement of claims. There never was a project built where there was not, at the end of the day, some financial dispute that needed resolving before the project could be considered closed. It is therefore important that all those involved in a project recognise what is likely to happen and take steps beforehand to mitigate against the effects. The best way to minimise disputes is to resolve them as you go: not defer them until the end of the day. It will always be far easier to resolve such matters immediately after the event since everybody's memory is then fresh. Also, to accumulate disputes is to build up discontent and amicable settlement becomes ever more difficult. So all such matters should be taken up as they arise, remembering that the best defence against claims is *facts* – and that demands careful and comprehensive records.

## Computerisation

The method of analysis of empirical data to provide the necessary target S-curves and the plotting of the data so developed has to be done on a 100/100 basis. That is, both the time and money axes are measured in terms of percentage, not actual money or actual time. This has to be so, since this is the only way we can compare one project with another in terms of time or money. Each project is different, both in terms of project duration and project cost, and we have to reduce our data to percentage terms in order to compare it.

Once we have set up our target curves for the various sections and phases of our project, including each erection subcontract, we next have to plot actual against the target. This can be very tedious when it is being done by hand, particularly when the forecast has to be rephased in terms of either time or money. The work is largely repetitive and can be related to 'standard' curves. It has been established by experience that perhaps a total of 16 different curves is all that is needed to provide suitable target curves for both the placing of commitments and value of work done. Remember, if you find this surprising, that we reduce each curve to 100/100, and we are happy if we are within six to ten per cent of our target curve. Try it for yourself: that is far better than us providing you with an illustration that would be a dense black square with two white corners. Take a piece of squared paper, marked off 100%/100%, and draw a number of S-curves which you consider reasonable for commitments, and for the various phases of value of work done – material deliveries, subcontract progress, and so on. Now widen each curve to cover the margin of error we are prepared to accept. Be mean, and make it plus or minus five per cent. Having done all that, and drawn say ten or twelve curves, how much space is left, that *could* be covered by further curves. Practically none!

So then, we have a fact of life that lends itself to computerisation. We can have a data bank of 12, 16 or perhaps 20 target curves, choose the most applicable from the data bank for each aspect we wish to monitor, and the computer will do the rest. This aspect is discussed in some detail in Chapter 10 (Use of the computer) so all we need to do at this point is to remind ourselves that the computer does *nothing* that cannot be done by hand. We can remember the time, perhaps a quarter of a century ago now, when one wall of the project manager's office on site was covered with a series of perhaps fifty S-curves, each one different. All had to be drawn by hand, and were carefully updated from month to month. The computer is a time saver, but not a miracle worker.

## References

1 Harrison, F. L., *Advanced Project Management*, Gower, 2nd Ed., 1985, 374 pp.
2 Lester, A., *Project Planning and Control*, Butterworth, 1982, 195 pp. This book has a very extensive bibliography, with over 200 references.
3 Griffiths, H., *The General Principles of Chemical Engineering Design*, Benn Brothers, London, 1922. (Mr. Hugh Griffiths was a past President of the Institution of Chemical Engineers and this reference is of historical interest only. The book has been out of print for 40 years.)

# 8 Early warning signals

When we were discussing 'Why control cost?' in Chapter 2, we said: 'No sudden shocks, please!' We said then, and repeat once again now, that whilst the final cost may not be within the first budget, and perhaps only rarely is, how much better it would be if we could but *know* in good time what was going to happen, rather than just *watch* it happen. We quote once again, because they are words that come from the heart of every owner (1):

> Great is the grief of one who is deeply entrenched in a capital spending programme and *suddenly learns* [our emphasis] that the cost will exceed expectations.

It is quite obvious from all this that the most meaningful of all the information that can become available in relation to cost is the *trend* – where we are going. Management never likes to suddenly learn that the budget is going to be exceeded. Much, much better to know ahead of time if that is indeed going to be the case. Data that contributes to the early assessment of the cost trend is therefore very valuable indeed, since it can provide an 'early warning system' to management in relation to the estimates of both time and cost.

All estimating techniques, and many cost control techniques, depend to a greater or lesser extent upon the analysis of historical data for their validity. Over the years the most valuable and flexible technique which has been developed, relevant to both estimating and cost control, is what is often described in the literature as 'factor estimating', or sometimes, in its more detailed form, 'module estimating'. The 'factor estimate' begins with an assessment of the estimated cost of the plant and equipment, and then establishes factors to determine the total erected cost. The 'module' estimating technique goes a step further, in that it applies separate cost factors to each separate cost code, such as columns, heat exchangers, pumps and so on. Of course, all these factors are, in effect, cost relationships, derived from the analysis of completed plants built in the past.

It will almost invariably be the case that the first estimate available for cost control, which has served as the basis for board authorisation, will have been prepared in some such manner as this. In other words, it is a 'statistical' estimate, the total estimate being a function of the estimate for plant and equipment. It is only the plant and equipment itself which has been specifically estimated for the plant that is going to be built, from the flowsheet details. One effect of this approach is that the first cost control estimate available as a 'target', or as a 'yardstick' is subject, so far as accuracy is concerned, to the validity of the relationships chosen: but this is the best estimate that can be prepared at that time. If the appropriate analysed data is available, considerable detail can be made available in connection with this statistical estimate. The estimate can be broken down into cost codes, the length of pipe and its weight can be stated: even the anticipated average line size of that pipe.

It has to be remembered, however, that such estimates have what many feel to be a disadvantage, but which we can now turn to advantage from a cost control point of view. We can use it to the advantage of the project, saving money, and giving direction to the early phases of cost control. This disadvantage is that since this estimate has been prepared largely by the use of estimating methods and techniques, and data, rather than by using preliminary quotations and takeoffs specific to the project, it does *not* include data on the actual project being developed, other than the specific equipment items. The estimate therefore reflects the performance on previous projects, probably the average of a number of previous projects, and hence the average performance to be expected.

In effect then, such an estimate mirrors what an average project manager can achieve with an average managing contractor. If the performance on the current project is better than average, the estimate will be underrun: if worse than average, then there will be an overrun. This fact can be put to good use, as we shall see. The variances disclosed should not be used to criticise the estimate: they should rather be used to assess current performance.

One major owner has made his analysis of historic data and its subsequent use as a basis for an internal cost control estimate, which then becomes a tool for the analysis of the design as it is being developed, in order to see whether it is above, below, or at the average of past performance, and on that basis to initiate action. This analysis will never become out-of-date, and is well worth seeking out in the library. The philosophy in relation to cost control is well expressed and examples are given where better cost control could have cut construction costs (2). But whether the average owner has sufficiently detailed and sufficiently reliable historic data to react in a similar fashion is very much open to question. However, the principle remains: use the estimate as a measure of efficiency rather than to say that it is wrong. The example is there to be followed by those who believe that they have sufficient historic data, and the paper on the subject is well worth reading.

### The equipment commitment

The first major purchasing exercise, once a project moves into detailed design, is the writing of the requisitions and the placing on order of all the major plant and equipment. This usually proceeds fairly rapidly, and all the equipment is usually placed on order by the time we are some 30 per cent through the total life of our project. At this point, or even a little earlier, it should be possible to draw a major conclusion as to the validity of our total cost target, since it has been a principle that all the further costs we shall incur are related to, and contingent upon, the cost of the plant and equipment we have just placed on order. If we are saving against our target on plant and equipment, then we shall expect to save *to the same degree* on the rest of our costs.

Taking the analysis given in Chapter 7 (The basic targets) where the cost of procurement of equipment and materials is given as 35 per cent of total project cost, the equipment alone is probably some 50 per cent of this, or say some 15 per cent of total project cost. The rest of the materials (20 per cent) and the site construction (40 per cent) are directly dependent upon the assessment of the cost of the equipment. So, having placed 15 per cent of our total commitment we are in a position to reassess a further 60 per cent of the total project cost. An increase of 10 per cent, for instance, in the cost of equipment will give us, in effect, an increase of 7.5 per cent in our total estimate.

It is very important, of course, in making comparison between 'commitments' and the estimate, that the commitments be properly assessed. Never forget that final cost, which is of course, the basis for the estimate, and which includes *all* extras, is the commitment that should be used, not the immediate face value of the order, which can be subject to a number of extras for good and proper reasons. We have, of course, discussed this aspect of the subject in detail in Chapter 6, in the section on commitment control.

So then, the potential commitment for plant and equipment is our first early warning signal, telling us the way things are going. This should be the first review of the estimate, and the total estimate should be revised, if necessary, at that time, not merely the sections of the estimate covering plant and equipment.

## The monthly trend

If we take care to measure the value of work done from month to month with precision, in the manner described in Chapter 6, we can then compare movement from month to month both with the target (movement along the S-curve) and with the previous month, or previous two months, and have a really valid assessment of the trend. It is then possible to review the implications, for instance in relation to the forecast end date and ascertain by discussion with planning whether they are prepared to support the indications being developed from the progress of value of work done. Figure 8.1 illustrates a study made in Month 11, when construction in the field had just began. It was obvious that progress, as expressed in value of work done, was falling behind the forecast. At Month 10 there was a lag of about £1,159,000. This is roughly one month's progress at that time in the project, and so indicates a delay of about one month in completion. But, of course, progress is not going to pick up overnight – things do not proceed by 'leaps and bounds' – and from that point on a reduced level of progress must be anticipated for some while. Redraw the S-curve, and you will see what this means. If you have a computer program (see Chapter 10) the program will do it for you. In fact, at this point, to see where we were going, the S-curve was reset with a three month delay and this gave a reforecast for the following month, Month 11, as indicated in Figure 8.1. The actual for Month 11 was £1,100,000, so this was a first indication – and an *immediate* indication – that the reforecast was realistic. Of course, planning had been consulted and they could highlight certain events which, in their judgment, could well result in a two to three month delay in completion. But the progress of value of work done, as illustrated in Figure 8.1, gives a very clear picture of the potential of the situation to the cost engineer. We see the early warning signal which he has received and the use he can make of it in his report to management.

## Piping: another trend indicator

Piping, particularly in process plants, is a very significant cost item and, since it is a bulk item, most difficult to evaluate, particularly in

| MONTH | FORECAST | | ACTUAL | |
|---|---|---|---|---|
| | In month | Cumulative | In month | Cumulative |
| 7 | 900 | 3800 | 794 | 4533 |
| 8 | 900 | 4700 | 495 | 5028 |
| 9 | 900 | 5600 | 402 | 5430 |
| 10 | 1630 | 7230 | 641 | 6071 |
| | | | REFORECAST | |
| 11 | 1630 | 8860 | 1000 | 7071 |
| 12 | 1630 | 10490 | 1360 | 8431 |
| 13 | 2000 | 12490 | 1410 | 9841 |
| 14 | 2000 | 14490 | 1410 | 11251 |
| 15 | 2000 | 16490 | 1410 | 12661 |

PROJECT PROGRESS

VALUE OF WORK DONE

All figures are expressed in £ x 1000.

Actual lag in value of work done is about one month's work at month 10.

Reforecast is on the basis of a 3-month delay in the completion date.

**Figure 8.1 Progress of value of work done**
Forecasts are compared with the actual progress. The reforecast assumes a three-month delay as compared with the original forecast. The actual value of work done for Month 11 was £1,100,000, which supports the reforecast.

the early stages of project development. Piping materials are normally some 10 per cent of project cost, and 60 per cent of plant and equipment cost. If we add to the basic cost of the piping materials, the cost of fabrication and erection of that piping, some 170 per cent of the basic material cost, then the total cost of piping is one and a half times the cost of the plant and equipment, and some 27 per cent of the total project cost.

Seeing that piping plays such a significant role in total project cost, it most certainly deserves the closest attention. There are three interrelated activities:

1   Piping material purchase
2   Piping fabrication
3   Piping erection in the field

The progress of insulation work is also very dependent upon the progress being made in the erection of the piping. Probably the most important decision that has to be made in this context is the point in time at which piping fabrication and piping erection are to begin. This work must *not* begin until some 70 per cent of the total piping materials are available in store. Management must therefore have the courage to delay the start of fabrication and erection until that point is reached. If they do not, they will have to meet a series of claims from the contractors doing that work for delays due to the non-availability of specific items of piping material. The 'roll-on' effects of mis-timing in this area can also be disastrous. The insulation contract should also start at the proper time if a good flow of work is to be achieved, and this is determined by the date from the start of erection of piping in the field. If the delivery of piping materials – and more specifically, the 70 per cent point – is not reached by the planned date, then delays will result in all these follow-on activities. The delay in completion will be of the same order as the delay in reaching the 70 per cent point and the planning should be revised accordingly. If the planning is not revised, and the attempt is made to start the other contractors on time, then the final delay will probably be even worse – certainly not better.

Perhaps this is the place to mention another trend indicator. It is related to piping, but comes very late in the day, when the piping erection is nearly complete. It is, however, quite significant because we are then at a point in time when the project as a whole, in terms of value of work done, is about 90 per cent complete. Everyone thinks that the worst is now behind them. We have reached the stage of finalisation. But it is a significant fact that, in terms of time, for any major project, we *still* have some six to nine months to go! That last ten per cent will take that long! So check, and if the time estimated to elapse is less than six months at that point, then think again. Check and recheck, because it always takes longer than you think to *finalise* things: to reach the point where you can say, hand on heart, that we are 100 per cent complete. Never forget that 'operations' are not going to be seriously interested in taking over the plant until it is indeed 100 per cent complete.

## Construction contracts

We have dealt elsewhere with the basic division of a project into six groups, one of which is 'construction contracts'. The construction contracts will be coded, and belong to a range of cost codes that we treat as one in relation to our S-curve forecasting. So we can monitor construction contracts in total, and also one by one.

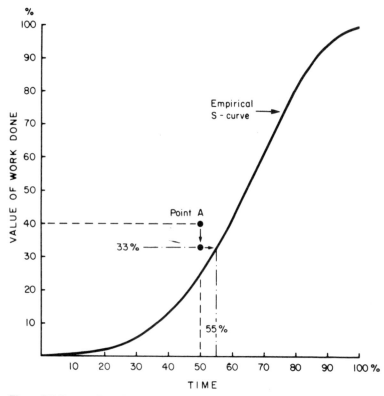

**Figure 8.2 S-curve for value of work done**
This illustrates the empirical curve, with an actual Point A indicated, which is used as the basis for the case study.

Parallel with the cost evaluation of progress, the value of work done, as generally indicated in Figure 8.2, a record is being kept of the progress in erection manhours for each contract, and in total. It is thus possible to analyse, and then compare, value of work done and erection manhours in terms of progress to date. A typical analysis of this type is presented as Figure 8.3. The illustrative projects include one, 4826, where only some 10 per cent of the work has been done to date. The initial works include piling, costing some Nfl. 300 per manhour (1976 values) and this results in the difference in rate seen as compared with the average for the total project shown against the estimate (ADJ EST). Then, as the project progresses, the cumulative rate will steadily fall, and approach the average assessed for the total project of Nfl. 80.70 per manhour.

```
                    ABSTRACT - COMPUTER PRINTOUT

   GIVE PROJECT NUMBER
   >4819
```

| PROJECT | SUB GROUP | VALUE OF WORK DONE CONTRACTS | ERECTION MANHOURS | RATE IN FLORINS PER MANHOUR |
|---|---|---|---|---|
| TOTAL OF PROJECT: 4819 ROADS AND PIPE TRENCHES | | | | |
| TARGET PERIOD | | 7560000 | 46150 | |
| CUMULATIVE | | 7472027 | 62334 | 119.9 |
| ADJ EST | | 7560000 | 63285 | 119.5 |

```
   GIVE PROJECT NUMBER
   >4822
```

| PROJECT | SUB GROUP | VALUE OF WORK DONE CONTRACTS | ERECTION MANHOURS | RATE IN FLORINS PER MANHOUR |
|---|---|---|---|---|
| TOTAL OF PROJECT: 4822 TELECOMMUNICATIONS | | | | |
| TARGET PERIOD | | 870000 | 11350 | |
| CUMULATIVE | | 439628 | 5906 | 74.4 |
| ADJ EST | | 870000 | 11600 | 75.0 |

```
   GIVE PROJECT NUMBER
   >4826
```

| PROJECT | SUB GROUP | VALUE OF WORK DONE CONTRACTS | ERECTION MANHOURS | RATE IN FLORINS PER MANHOUR |
|---|---|---|---|---|
| TOTAL OF PROJECT: 4826 SERVICE CENTRE | | | | |
| TARGET PERIOD | | 2400000 | 41000 | 153.3 |
| CUMULATIVE | | 527426 | 3441 | 153.3 |
| ADJ EST | | 6070000 | 75200 | 80.7 |

**Figure 8.3 Assessing the rate of progress**
Three typical projects. We examine the way in which the various rates per manhour can be used to evaluate the status of the project and the trend. Such data could be presented on a VDU at the cost engineer's desk. (See Chapter 10.)

We have just seen that the costs, in terms of commitment and later in terms of value of work done, for construction contracts are directly and intimately related to the parallel accumulating data on erection manhours. When the project is completed these relationships, amongst many others, will be utilised to provide estimating data for future projects, but during the life of 'our project' these relationships are progressively changing. The changing relationships, and the rate of change, are of great value for project cost control. Let us see how we can put this fluid situation to use for cost control purposes.

### The moving relationship

Before considering in some detail the way in which the various relationships between value of work done and erection manhours change during the life of a project, perhaps it is as well to define once again the terms which we are using. The term 'erection manhours' is fairly self-evident, but what is meant by 'direct' manhours are manhours used in the field (inside the fence), usually up to the level of foreman. Site supervisory staff and local administration hours are not included. These erection manhours can be directly recorded from day to day and give an immediate picture of the progress being made. They are normally summated per four or five week period to give the monthly movement. The measurement of the value of work done should relate directly to these erection manhours, period by period. For the purposes of demonstrating the use that can be made of this progress to provide early warning signals, consideration is being given to that portion of the total value of work done that relates to the construction contracts.

On this background, let us consider the unit rate, already discussed above: that is, the amount of value of work done per erection manhour worked. This is money per manhour. For a site where the first works to be carried out are piling, followed by buildings and other civil works, then later mechanical works such as plant and pipework erection, this rate, expressed in cumulative terms, will commence at a high level and then fall over time to finally reach the average unit rate for the project. If we express the cumulative unit rate at any point in time as a factor of the final average rate then we get a ratio that falls over the life of the project to unity, as illustrated in Figure 8.4. The time scale is the value of work done on construction contracts. That is, the duration of construction in the field, not the total duration of value of work done as a whole, which is a much longer period. The 100 per cent point comes when the plant is ready for startup.

Another relationship in this context that can be readily plotted, and so presented graphically, is that between the progress of value of work done on construction contracts and the parallel progress in erection manhours, but now expressed as a percentage of the totals for these two items. This gives the graph shown as Figure 8.5. Of what use are these two graphs?

First of all, of course, similar graphs will have been developed from the empirical data on previous projects for the particular country or site, since the contractual procedures, the way in which the works in the field are developed, and the consequential cost-time relationships will certainly vary from place to place. Their shape will not necessarily be the same as those presented in Figures 8.4 and 8.5. But assuming that such an empirical average is available, then when, as is illustrated in Figure 8.4, the plotted curve runs away from the standard, the value of work done has been incorrectly assessed, or the productivity (value of work done per erection manhour) is different. When it is below the standard curve, for instance, productivity is falling and relatively poor, or the estimate of the value of work done for those hours is low, and wrong. In our experience, the first thing to review is indeed the estimate of value of work done. If you are the owner, and monitoring the activities of the managing contractor and his cost control department, this is most certainly the first thing you will do. The estimate of value of work done can be low for a variety of reasons, including the possibility, in the case of lump sum contracts, that a lot of work has been done that has not as yet been measured or reported.

Departure from the standard curve shown in Figure 8.5 is a warning that there is an error in the assessment of the completion date (100 per cent value of work done). When the actual ratio is below that indicated, for instance, the probability is that the project will be completed earlier than is presently being estimated.

It must be remembered that we are suggesting that these graphs be used to provide an early warning signal. They are trend indicators, and do not give absolute answers. They are 'yardsticks', but they do not stand alone. They are not the only data available on which to form judgments at this point in time. They provide information in conjunction with a variety of other data coming from within the cost control department, and also from outside, such as from the planning department. The prime role of the cost engineer, using these 'tools', is to give early warning that something may well be going wrong. Detailed study will finally be the basis of cost control action under the direction of the project manager.

## A case study

Probably the best way in which to demonstrate the manner in which this movement and the status of costs, in particular the value of work done, and the related erection manhours can be utilised to

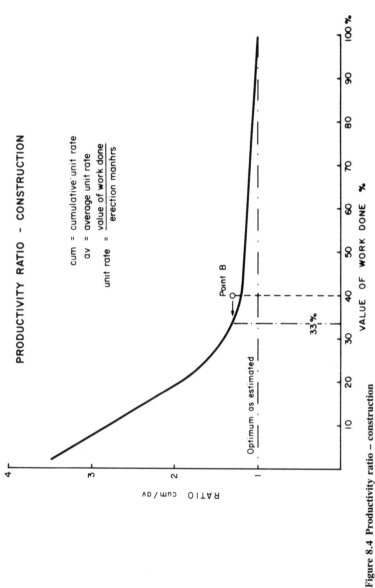

**Figure 8.4 Productivity ratio – construction**
This is a plot of the ratio between progress in terms of value of work done and progress in terms of erection manhours, over time, with case study data added.

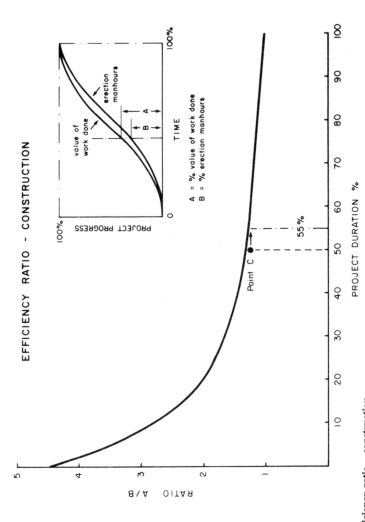

**Figure 8.5 Efficiency ratio – construction**

This is a plot of the ratio between progress in terms of value of work done, and the progress in terms of erection manhours, again with case study data added.

ascertain the trend and hence the ultimate outcome, is by the use of a specific example. Let us then consider a project where, at a particular point in time:

1  Value of work done is 40 per cent of the estimated cost, exclusive of contingency:
2  Erection manhours are 31 per cent of the estimated erection manhours required for the project:
3  Progress in time is 50 per cent of the total estimated time to completion.

The status of this project is set out in detail in Figure 8.6 and the relevant data has also been imposed on Figures 8.2, 8.4 and 8.5. Value of work done has therefore reached the point A in Figure 8.2, as compared with the empirical S-curve for value of work done. The productivity ratio has been calculated, and appears as point B on Figure 8.4, whilst the efficiency ratio is plotted as Point C on Figure 8.5.

Accepting the law of the S-curve, as discussed in Chapter 7 (see the section: 'The law of the S-curve'), point A should of course lie on the curve, but it does not. Thus our estimates of total cost or time, or both, are at the moment in error. But *not* the curve, remember, for we are accepting the law. When we study the productivity ratio, Figure 8.4, we see that that is also off the curve.

| | |
|---|---|
| **ESTIMATES:** | |
| Net estimate: | Nfl 6070,000 |
| Contingency: | 530,000 |
| Total: | Nfl 6600,000 |
| Erection manhours: | 67,444 |
| Hence average unit rate: | 90 fl/hour |
| **PRESENT STATUS** | |
| Value of work done: | Nfl 2428,000 |
| | (40%) |
| Erection manhours spent: | 20,907 |
| | (31%) |
| Cumulative unit rate: | 116 fl/hour |
| Productivity ratio: | 116/90 = 1.28 |
| Efficiency ratio: | 40/31  = 1.29 |

**Figure 8.6 Case study data**
Data relating to a typical project, serving as a basis for the case study discussed in the text.

If we bring it on the curve, as indicated, then the value of work done would be 33 per cent, rather than the 40 per cent which we have said that it is. But if value of work done were 33 per cent, we are still not back on the S-curve shown in Figure 8.2, as you will see. What else remains? Let us look at the efficiency ratio, which relates to time, as shown in Figure 8.5. This, we see, is too low, and for it to come on the curve the time elapsed should be 55 per cent, and not 50 per cent. If we make this further correction in relation to the value of work done, as shown on Figure 8.2 again, we are back on the empirical S-curve.

The conclusions to be drawn from this exercise are:

1  The value of work done is in fact 33 per cent and the final project cost will therefore be Nfl. 7,350,000.

2  The project will be completed somewhat earlier than presently planned, since 50/55 gives 90 per cent of the originally estimated duration.

Thus the cost engineer is in a position to advise management, subject to consultation with planning, that the project will cost Nfl. 7,350,000 rather than the Nfl. 6,600,000 estimated earlier, but that it can still be completed on time.

## Conclusion

This chapter has presented certain techniques in broad outline, that have been developed and used over the years as a supporting tool for management in relation to cost control, that are able to give early warning as to the way in which a project is going, and in particular whether it is likely to meet its prime targets in relation to cost and time. These techniques are largely based upon an analysis of empirical data in relation to past projects and it will be seen that one of the principles of the approach recommended is that past experience is accepted as a valid guide as to what to expect in the future, even to the extent, in one case, of calling it a law.

The essence of this particular approach lies in the ability, on the basis of the status of a project at a particular point in time, to assess the trend and evaluate its implications in relation to project duration and final project cost. It is far more important to look forward than to look back. But let us never forget that the cost control engineer is not in a position to *control* cost. He can but advise management, and in particular the project manager, in the hope that the right influence can be exerted if things are going wrong, or the information used to best advantage if things are going right.

It is our sincere hope that this proposed analysis of data coming on the desk of the cost engineer, if the recommended procedures are followed – data that is dynamic, ever changing through the life of the project – will provide a few more 'yardsticks' that will assist the cost control engineer to 'see into the future' with a certain degree of confidence. It has to be realised, of course, and we say it yet again at the risk of repeating ourselves once too often: these particular suggestions are only a few of many, and the cost engineer is only one man in a team. The information from a wide range of disciplines will always have to be weighed up before decisions are taken. However, that said, experience has shown that the approach we have suggested is quite powerful when used in conjunction with the other data that is available.

In the context of project management the most meaningful of all the information that can become available is the trend – where are we going? Data that contributes to the assessment of the trend, particularly in the early stages of construction, is very valuable indeed and we believe that the analytical approach we have described in this chapter can make a substantial contribution to such assessments.

## References

1   Miller, W. B., 'Fundamentals of project management', *Jnl. of Systems Management*, vol. 29, 22–29 November 1978.
2   Paper: 'A new look at cost control for contracted construction', *Oil & Gas Jnl.*, 2 October 1967, pp. 85–89.

# 9   Simple is beautiful

There is a contemporary ethos 'that technology can do virtually anything'. The result of this is that when technology encounters problems, or creates problems, the solution is sought in more and better technology. This is rather like saying: 'the cure for bad management is more management'.

This situation can be seen at the present time in the field of project management and project cost control. A symposium is held, papers are presented. We are told how to interrelate project estimates and CPM Schedules: we are told we can have computerised two-dimensional progress reports – once a week if we please! Yet, at the very same time one paper dares to have as its title: 'Can we really control multi-million projects?' We are told that 'the advancement in technology, in scientific management ... has reached a peak in the entire history of mankind. We have had a glorious past and a glamorous present.' Yet, only six months later – the peak must have passed – one of the specialised software companies offering some of these wonderful systems issues a brochure in which their systems are offered as an alternative to 'shoddy project planning, slipped schedules, overrun budgets, sloppy coordination ...' It would seem that, in their opinion at least, the situation is grim indeed, and that there is enormous scope for improvement: with their systems, of course.

They are not alone in that opinion. Another six months passes by, another summer is reached, and we have *another* symposium. Still more papers are presented. What are they saying this year? Just listen, and learn:

> the project network method is the most powerful technique yet developed for PLANNING and SCHEDULING a project. But ... it has not proved as useful for MONITORING and CONTROLLING a project.

And again:

> whilst remarkable advancement has been achieved in the area of networking techniques and sophisticated reporting, the rate of SUCCESSFUL UTILISA-TION of such systems has not attained a comparable growth.

Why not? What is the problem?

### The underlying problem

There is no doubt at all, of course, that the need for effective project cost control, in its turn the primary result of good project management, grows by the year. The plants that are being built get bigger, more sophisticated and ever more complex. Over the past ten years or so, costs have practically trebled and the average size of plant built in the process industries has also trebled in many cases. This leads to a proliferation of joint ventures. Then, in the developing countries in particular, the local government is also involved as a partner, which makes the need for effective project management ever more pressing. All this makes every aspect of the project ever more complex. There are more parties to be consulted, more design constraints to remember, more cost items to control. The end result of all this is, to use a well-known proverb, that one 'cannot see the wood for the trees'. What is to be done?

Let us stand back for a moment and try to take what in management circles is called the 'helicopter view'. Managers who take this approach to their work are much sought after in industry we hear: they must be quite rare 'birds'. Catch phrases can help us to approach this problem and deal with it – they help us to remember what we ought to be doing. The phrase we want to keep in mind now, and all the time, that we must *KISS* our project – *K*eep *I*t *S*tupid *S*imple. Unfortunately, that is a very very difficult thing to do, and you will find a great many people who have no faith whatever in simplicity. They just do not trust it. Indeed, they think it dangerous. Perhaps even more, they are afraid of it! They want to know everything, and to do everything, in the greatest detail. With such people you will have to be very firm. You have to twist this *kiss* principle slightly, and say to them: 'Keep it simple, *stupid*!'

### Leadership is all important

The first person who has to accept, apply and deploy the *kiss* principle wholeheartedly is the project manager himself. If he is not convinced of the merits of such an approach, then his team have little chance, for he will spend his time asking for unnecessary information, demanding detailed reports, which they, in their turn, will have to spend their time preparing. This leads to overstaffing. There is no doubt at all that many projects suffer from this disease, and overstaffing brings in its train a whole series of problems, particularly in the project team. So this is the first place where the principle must be recognised and applied. The project manager must make sure that his own house is in order. In Chapter 11 we discuss the role of the project manager in some detail and we stress very heavily the crucial importance of the role he plays. If he is surrounded by a large team, providing voluminous paperwork, this may well impress the owner, for whom he is working. But the owner will in fact have quite a false impression as to what is going on, and a false sense of security. He will actually be doubly in jeopardy. Not only is he being deprived of effective project management, but a cumbersome and bureaucratic organisation is inevitably inefficient: it deadens and dampens its own efforts.

It is with the leadership, then, that keeping it simple begins. The best engineers, contractors and construction labour in the world will never make up for poor leadership. On the other hand, at a time when poor standards of workmanship are multiplying, good project management will often redeem the situation, seeking the essentials and exerting pressure where it will be most effective. But this will only be possible if we have kept it simple. Leadership will inevitably rest in the hands of the few, and they are but human. If they are flooded with irrelevant detail they too will be unable to 'see the wood for the trees'. But let us turn from what is perhaps philosophy, to some practical detail.

### The work cycle

What goes on in any and every project? We have attempted to illustrate this in a simple manner, diagrammatically, in Figure 9.1. The project is initiated by the owner. He seeks the assistance of a managing contractor, and so work is generated, each field of effort leading on to the next, until finally the plant is built and paid for. Throughout the life of the project two key activities have to run in parallel. All the other activities come to an end, one by one, but these two *have* to continue: planning almost to the end, and cost control most certainly to the very end. Not until every claim is settled, every invoice paid, can the role of the cost engineer be said to be over, and his work done.

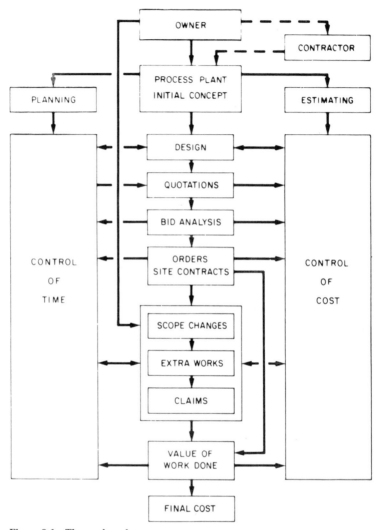

**Figure 9.1 The work cycle**
A diagrammatic representation of the work flow through the life of a project. The control of cost and time are seen as a continuing function throughout.

Each of the several activities set out in Figure 9.1 will have its own complexities. You will get the feel of this when you are reading Chapter 11, and we take a look at 'proper project management'. Meanwhile, let us look at that 'lump of lead' in the middle – scope changes, leading to extra works and claims. If we want to keep things simple, here is one area indeed that can make a great contribution. Minimise, even if you cannot eliminate changes once you have approved the project and set it on the road. We do not include in this the 'involuntary' changes that will have to be made as the plant is erected, and errors in process or engineering design are disclosed and have to be corrected. These are usually called 'field changes' and since nothing is perfect, they will always occur.

The real cost and impact of scope changes is rarely realised. The underlying cause of most of the problems in project management is the failure to do the right thing at the right time. It is a well-known saying that 'time is money', but during the life of a project, from inception to completion, time costs more and more money. We have already made reference to this aspect more than once. First, Chapter 4: look, once again, for instance, at Figure 4.8, which demonstrates the way in which the cost of change moves. Then in Chapter 7, since they are part and parcel of every project, and have a serious impact on both the time and cost targets, we discuss their administration in some detail.

Looking now on the effect of scope changes on the capital investment as such we can say that, roughly speaking, project time itself is at least five times more costly as a project nears completion than at the start. Therefore, the time to make changes is quite obviously at the beginning of the project, and most certainly *not* at the end. To quote Mr. King himself (1):

> One must take the time to do a proper job of basic design while the project is still pliable and capable of change at a low cost while time is still cheap. On the other hand, in the engineering and construction phase, every effort must be made to move fast and expeditiously. People work better under some pressure: this is the time for production, not deliberation.
>
> At this stage, the Owner is locked into an irreversible position, and every day the fixed charges are mounting higher and higher. Too often, too little time is taken to do a thorough job in the basic design phase. Too often, too much time is taken to do the detailed engineering and construction work. Such disregard for priorities may prove disastrous.

Time is cheap at the beginning of the project, and dear at the end because of the impact of the fixed charges, the growing investment in plant and equipment, together with the growth in numbers of people employed on the project, whose time is wasted if there is prolongation. The impact of this basic fact, that the cost of time climbs as the project progresses, is tremendous. It means that virtually all engineering studies should be made in the design phase, before firm orders for major equipment are placed, or big volume detailed engineering is committed.

So then, here is at least one area where we can and should keep it simple – simply do not change your mind! Clean decision making is most productive, even if second best is accepted as a more immediate solution to a problem. The recycling of work that goes on in a contractor's organisation once changes are being made just clogs the system, slows it down, and costs a lot of money.

### What degree of detail?

What degree of detail is really necessary for effective project cost control? Remember that we are not talking about the degree of detail necessary for effective control of design, *or* procurement, *or* construction. Much detail will be available: how much of that detail should be accepted, considered, processed, scrutinised, by the cost control engineer for the effective performance of his function?

Once again, let us 'keep it stupid simple' – and it is not so stupid as it looks, because it works. Appendix B details a cost code which is considered to be completely adequate for project management, including cost control. The cost engineer should never cost or control in units smaller than a cost code, as illustrated in Appendix B. Where construction work in the field is subcontracted, he will tend to control construction work per subcontract, which will usually be pretty much the same thing. But in certain areas, such as temporary facilities, a large number of small contracts are likely to be placed, and here he should group them and watch the whole: not the detail. This means that the cost engineer is content with summarised reports on commitments, value of work done and erection manhours from month to month. He accepts and processes movements in the month per cost code in each project only.

One area where the cost engineer can waste a lot of time is in relation to miscellaneous costs. Miscellaneous costs will vary in their nature and content from project to project and depend to some extent upon the type of administration involved in relation to materials for engineering purposes in force with the owner. For instance, piping materials on any major project wil normally be bought for *that* project, and so we have first a commitment, and later value of work done in relation to the specific project, processed throughout the project accounts (WIP). But, and particularly in the later stages of construction, materials can be drawn from the owner's works stores, if available, and these costs can well mature as charges against the project months later, after they have worked their way through the 'system'. The significant difference about such costs is that we have no prior commitment.

There are other costs that can be set against a project without prior commitment: perhaps the facilities in the works are used for offloading materials as they arrive. Freight and insurance charges can also fall into this category. The best way to monitor costs accruing to the project without prior commitment is to consider them in bulk, as a recurring expense. Review of past projects may give some idea of the order of magnitude of such costs, and their progress from month to month should give a trend indication, which can be projected into the future. But they must remain a small proportion of the total cost. If the system is such that they form more than one or two per cent of the value of work done in any month, then special administrative steps *must* be taken to control them.

### Reports from the managing contractor

We come to examine the activities of the managing contractor in some detail in Chapter 11. As will be seen, the project manager employed by the managing contractor, as compared with the project manager employed by the owner, will require a range of information to keep his finger on the pulse of the project, and the wide range of disciplines involved. But let us look at it from the point of view of the owner – and more particularly, from the point of view of the cost engineer working for the owner. What reports should *he* expect from the managing contractor in order to be kept in the picture? The temptation is to ask for far too much. But such reporting should be kept simple, and limited to:

1 *Contract changes* This details and costs scope changes affecting the contract between owner and managing contractor.
2 *Procurement report* This lists orders for materials, including plant and equipment, with 'face' values and estimated final values (this latter per cost code only), summated per cost code and per project.
3 *Subcontract schedule* This lists each subcontract, giving for each subcontract authorised contract value, value of work done to date, movement in month, and estimated final cost of contract. Contracts would be sorted and summated per cost code and project.
4 *Value of work done, materials* This details, per cost code only, the value of materials received at the site.
5 *Managing contractor's effort* Progress/performance of the

managing contractor, from month to month. The detail will depend to some extent on the nature of the contract with the managing contractor.

6  *Erection manhours* A weekly report, based on the daily 'force report', of the hours worked at site, for both direct labour and supervision, separately.

Six sets of data only, which vary in significance to the cost engineer as the project progresses. From this information the cost engineer for the owner can distil the progress on commitments, value of work done and erection manhours, to use as progress markers and to forecast trends. At the same time he can monitor the statements of the managing contractor in this context and discourage optimism.

### The progress markers

What does he watch? There are three 'keys' to project progress: (a) commitments, (b) value of work done, and (c) erection manhours. We will assume that these records are kept in the manner outlined in some detail earlier, in Chapter 6. A lot of intensive work may well be involved in maintaining these records in a proper manner, but it is well worth while, since they then become reliable 'markers' for the cost engineer. In the early stages of a project, it is the progress being made with commitments that is all important. We follow the commitment for equipment and bulk materials with special interest. The commitment in relation to design, and the volume of design work, is not the point: that is reflected in the commitment record anyway. This is separately monitored, as shown, for instance in the second graph in Figure 7.1. The actual movement tends to be stepwise, rather than the smooth graph shown, so a lag (step) of a month or so is not too significant in itself. But commitments *must* be placed at the rate indicated in the early phases of a project if the programme is to be maintained. Delay in placing orders inevitably delays completion, with all the consequences of increased costs.

Once the value of work done passes the 15 per cent mark, and starts its steady linear progress at 4.5 to 5 per cent per month (and it is fantastically difficult to improve on this rate) then value of work done becomes the key indicator of progress. The progress on erection manhours is monitored in parallel, since comparison between these two is a sound check on the validity of the data being followed. The manner in which this is done has already been set out in the 'Case study' presented in Chapter 8. What does one watch? The progress being made each month against the forecast. A lag in progress indicates, in general, that completion will inevitably be delayed. It could just possibly mean that the target is overestimated in terms of money, but that does not happen very often, especially if the target estimate (site current estimate) is being reviewed regularly in the light of the commitments being placed.

As our project approaches completion, and value of work done climbs to the 90 per cent mark, the level of commitments becomes once again the key marker in relation to potential total, final cost. At this point the only significant *moving* commitment is in relation to erection subcontracts. All materials will have been committed and largely delivered. That is why the rigorous discipline regarding the estimated final cost of subcontracts recommended in Chapter 6 is so important. The monitoring, progressing and evaluation of extra works in the field subcontracts is crucial at this stage, together with the assessment of potential claims before they are even presented. Here, once again, the comparison being made between value of work done and erection manhours is all important, with the significant lead role now being taken by erection manhours. These are a fact of life, and if comparison with value of work done indicates falling productivity, then the first assumption is that value of work done is being undervalued, in all probability along with the commitment. At this stage, the percentage completion in terms of erection manhours must never exceed the percentage completion in terms of value of work done. These are simple, but most important markers. If it is so, then value of work done is being underestimated, the usual reason being a backlog of extra work orders and claims. This underestimate leads directly to an underestimate of the final cost of the project. Costs missing at this stage are missing from the estimate as well.

Let us *really* keep it simple, in every respect. We will stop right here. If you can approach project cost control in this simplistic fashion, keeping your eye on what, in another context, might be called 'the main chance' at any time, but applying a lot of effort to getting the data up-to-date at all times, then you will be successful. Not necessarily successful in keeping costs within budget, but certainly successful in giving management due and proper warning as to what is going on.

Management will *know* where they are going: how long it will take, and what it will cost.

## Reference

1 King, R. A., 'How to achieve effective project control'. *Chem. Eng.*, July 1977, pp. 117–121.

# 10  Use of the computer

There is no doubt at all that the automatic processing of data has moved at a revolutionary pace during the past few years. Advances in technology and the ever-growing scale of production, with the consequent dramatic fall in hardware prices, have brought us to the stage where everyone can have a pocket calculator for a few pounds, personal computer for less than £100 and every office can readily afford its own computerised system (1). Project cost control is just one area where full advantage can now be taken of the available facilities. The ready availability of low-cost hardware and software packages means that quite small organisations can still find such facilities both valuable and economic in use. But the relationship between a project team and the computer, be it a PC or a mainframe, must be clearly understood. Simply expressed, it is the relationship between man and machine. The project team still has certain resources completely lacking in the computer system, namely:

- Initiative
- Originality and creative ability
- Experience
- Judgment

although that last item is being intensively worked on. By contrast, the computer system has certain capabilities which the project team find very valuable, such as:

- Speed of data processing
- Accuracy
- Memory capacity
- Reliability
- Facile data reproduction and presentation

194

These qualities are continually being improved and increased, particularly speed and memory capacity. The project team should therefore seek to delegate to the computer system only those tasks which the system can perform better than the team.

It is very necessary for the significance of this relationship between man and machine to be properly appreciated, keeping one's 'feet on the ground'. Because a machine appears to think, that does not constitute proof that it does think, although we may be approaching the day when machines become commercially available that have some sort of thinking facility. But at the moment the machine operates in obedience to a program, and incorporates the thinking of those who built the machine and designed the program. This means that it is essential, if such systems are to process cost control data in a useful fashion, that they have been designed in cooperation with experienced cost control engineers. Only *then* can they be an effective management tool for them.

### The impact of information technology

Communications is the key to information technology. Without adequate means of passing the data between terminals, work-stations, offices and countries the power and sophistication of the systems would be limited indeed. The communications industry is however developing in such a way that it has revolutionised every aspect of our lives – at least in the Western world. Computers tell robots how to build cars, they regulate traffic flow and guide ships and planes from continent to continent. Telefax machines swap vital information across the globe in seconds. The high street banks, shops and offices are experiencing a revolution in their daily routine, with computerised tills, fax machines, electronic printing and word processing. As the industry moves towards the one million bit chip, the four million bit chip is said to be around the corner and the Japanese are said to have asked for government support to design a 100 million bit chip!

To come to aspects of more immediate interest, the demand for information about engineering standards is so great that the British Standards Institution (BSI) has launched BSI *Standardline*: a massive bibliographic data base available on-line through a host computer. *Nexis* is another world-wide electronic data base that can quickly search the full text of over 200 periodicals for precise information and data. In the modern office Local Area Networks (LANS) are gradually appearing. The LANS is designed to move a large volume of data around a comparatively small area, such as a single building or an office complex. All the principal elements in the office – telephones, word processors, personal computers, electronic file stores, fax machines, printers and copiers are interconnected.

The board room has not escaped this information revolution. Let us see how that works. The board have two key tasks: they make decisions and they have to monitor the organisation they control. So immediately they are in the midst of the 'what if' and the 'what is' scenarios. With the help of a good software package individual board members can easily access the data on budgets, actuals, forecasts, sales, margins and other vital corporate information on the company and its subsidiaries and even the latest data on its competitors. Clearly a board adopting such techniques is very much 'in action' and in a much better position to make sound decisions than a board relying upon what is now the old-fashioned approach: written reports. Such a software package, called *Resolve*, is on the market in the UK (2).

A similar approach to their task can be adopted by the project team and in particular the cost control engineer. He too, can apply such technology to make his cost control procedures ever more effective, but he must be careful. There is a hidden paradox: ignorance about the potential of information technology, coupled with an almost insane desire to use it (3). We therefore exhort our readers once again to always keep in mind the acronym presented in Chapter 9: *KISS* –*K*eep *I*t *S*imple, *S*tupid! The cost benefit of any proposed system must always be very carefully assessed, so that the full power of the resource is effectively deployed and the user not snowed under and bogged down in piles of paper that he will never assimilate.

### Terminology and definitions

We have been using a number of words, such as hardware, software, mainframe, PC and the like which may or may not already be familiar to our readers. Perhaps an outline description of some of the normally accepted definitions in relation to computers and the relevant terminology as met with in normal industrial practice will not be out of place. The glossary at the end of this chapter presents a classification of the various types of computer currently available, together with a glossary of the terms in common use.

### Personal computers and software packages

The principal data processing tool in most companies of any size is the general purpose computer (GPC), often referred to as a mainframe computer. This machine provides a full on-line service to the several production areas within the company throughout the working day and is usually switched over to a batch mode for shift working. It is used for design programs, control systems, materials monitoring, payroll processing, statutory and management accounting. A typical computer in this classification is the IBM 4381 Model 2, with sixteen megabytes of memory, linked to a communications and other peripheral systems. A company using such a system will employ 2,000 or more people. We shall discuss later the way in which the cost control engineer can utilise the facilities offered and the data available within such a system.

However, the personal computer (PC) is probably of more direct interest and service to the cost control engineer. This is the fastest-growing area in the computer market, it being estimated that by 1990 more than a million personal computers will be sold in the UK: more than three times as many as in 1985 (4). At the present time IBM is a clear leader in the 16-bit sector of this field, with some 40 per cent of total sales, followed by Apricot with some 15 per cent. It is the software which is more significant and presents the user with the greatest risk, because of the extremely wide choice available. Whilst the market is dominated by a limited number of well-known products – trade names such as *Lotus 1–2–3*, *Visicalc*, *Supercalc* and *Wordstar* are familiar to most people – there are over a thousand different programs on offer in accounting alone. This wide choice means that selection should be made most carefully. It is important to bear in mind that the real cost of software lies not in the package itself but in its use: the cost of operation and inserting data into the system. This is an ongoing cost. But before one starts it is necessary to understand the instruction manuals and this can be very time-consuming. If the operator has to read parts of the manual before using the keyboard it is hopeless. In fact, lawsuits have been started and won by companies who were sold the wrong system. These additional costs can soon outstrip the original investment, so once again we advise careful selection of both hardware and software (5). We ourselves recommend most strongly that the selection process start with the software, *not* the hardware.

The method of approach can be briefly defined as follows:

1  Define your problem: the need you have which you believe a computer could satisfy.
2  Decide whether your computer is going to be 'in house': or whether you will use a service bureau. Costs have dropped so sharply that quite small companies can now justify the use of their own computer.

3   Evaluate the volume of work. This dictates the type of hardware to be purchased. In doing this, have an eye to the future.

With respect to that last point, the basic choice these days is between microcomputers, which use floppy disks and mini and mainframe computers, that employ hard disks. Hard disk systems can cater for much more data and can be connected to many more terminals.

## Project control systems

Where does the cost control engineer fit into all this? We come back once again to the two basic features – control of cost and control of time, as set out earlier in Figure 9.1. Within the framework of a contracting organisation wide use will be made of a computerised integrated project control system, covering such matters as network analysis, work measurement, cost control, document control and material tracking. Some of these systems, particularly bulk material control systems, have a 'spin-off' for project cost control, but we are concerned particularly with the cost control activity as exercised within the organisation of the contractor, and particularly the managing contractor. In this case the cost control engineer can be looking two ways at once. If the contractor is working for a fixed fee, then the cost control engineer is concerned with the relation-ship between actual costs, progress and the fixed fee. At the same time he performs a cost control function for the owner, in relation to the reimbursable elements in the contract with the owner.

The planning engineer on the project team is normally the focus of the several control mechanisms. He will liaise with the lead engineers in the various disciplines involved in the project to produce a feasible plan in relation to the numerous activities. We recommend that the cost control system is to some extent divorced from the computerised company system, somewhat in the manner indicated in Figure 10.1. Where the full system outlined in the diagram is not available, the cost engineer will utilise what *is* available, but always divorced from the main system in the manner indicated.

The systems surrounding the cost engineer are many and various. In the field of accounting the *Pegasus* integrated package is a market leader (6). A somewhat different approach is offered by *Application Systems* (AS), an IBM package. One advantage of AS is that it is a single, integrated system covering eight functional areas: information retrieval and analysis, information manage-

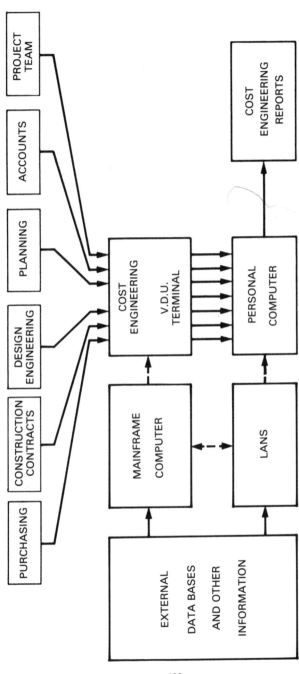

**Figure 10.1 Data access and distribution systems**
Information is available to the cost control engineer by VDU. He takes that which is relevant to himself and then processes it via his own PC in order to develop his own data bank and reports, also using LANS wherever possible.

199

ment, formal reports, business graphics, business communications, business planning, specialised analysis and project control. The integrated nature of AS means that these areas are not independent: applications will typically utilise many components from several areas (7). More than one contractor uses AS as an aid to its project control activities.

Another powerful software package is called *Symphony* and is a development from the *Lotus 1–2–3* package now so widely known (8). The program offers spreadsheet, word processing and data base facilities that can be used independently. Used in conjunction with the graphics and communications facilities also available, one can enter information into a data base, move to a spreadsheet and calculate the latest numeric information, graph it in any one of a number of different graphic formats, change to word processing to write the appropriate memo, and then use communications to send the finished report anywhere in the world. Since the program can be handled adequately on a PC which would sit by our cost control engineer's desk, he has all the facilities he needs, once the system has been set up to suit his own particular requirements. In project control reports graphic displays are being used more and more, since they are often able to communicate information more clearly than rows and columns of numbers. For instance, *Symphony*'s graphic capabilities enable one to draw graphs from the data in a spreadsheet, graphs being previewed as they are created and then modified as necessary. Once a graph is finished, it can be printed out on a printer or plotted on a graphics plotter (the latter gives a better presentation). As with spreadsheet data, a graph is automatically updated whenever a value is changed on the spreadsheet, so one has to enter the relevant information once only.

As we have said, there is a wide range of such programs, of which the ones we are mentioning are but typical. To conclude this brief review of the possibilities, let us mention a leading self-contained project management control and reporting system: the *Artemis* system offered by Metier (9). This is in use worldwide and versions are available to run on micro, mini and mainframe computers. The system can be used for a wide range of applications, including planning and scheduling, cost control and cost management, maintenance planning and control and records management.

With *Artemis* a project is broken down into a logical sequence of steps and then, using critical path analysis techniques, a plan can be modified at any time, taking account of progress or changes. An integral component of *Artemis* is the Cost Management System (CMS). This is structured in a modular fashion, starting with a base costing product and this contains seven sub-systems: organisation, budget, work measurement, cost collection, forecast, estimate and analysis, all leading to a formidable multi-level reporting and controlling system. The *Artemis* system comes in a range of sizes and therefore a selection can be made to suit the project in hand.

## Getting down to detail

But how is all this, or any of it, to be used? This brings us to the electronic spreadsheet. The first electronic spreadsheet, *Visicalc*, arrived on the scene in 1978. Since that time the system has been integrated into a variety of work environments, such as the *Symphony* and *Artemis* systems mentioned above.

An electronic spreadsheet is a structure for carrying out numeric or financial calculations working through a matrix of columns and rows that intersect to form a pattern of boxes, called cells, each separately identified and stored in the computer (10). The original *Visicalc* contained 63 columns and 254 rows. The *Lotus 1–2–3* package, developed in 1983, has 256 columns and 2048 rows, whilst *Symphony* is very large, having 256 columns and 8192 rows. There are two kinds of spreadsheet entries, labels and values. In most cases labels are letters or words: titles or captions to describe what is in a column or a row. Values are the actual data: numbers or formulae used in the various calculations. Once in place, all the interrelated calculations work automatically as new material is entered. Individual cells can be easily erased, moved, copied or printed as required. Whilst the electronic spreadsheet's immediate beauty is its automatic recalculation facility, its ability to answer 'what if' scenarios in minutes is the key to better decision making and a most valuable facility for the project cost control engineer. A change in one cell is immediately reflected in all relevant cells, allowing for the rapid evaluation of alternatives.

The project cost control engineer can now use the spreadsheet format on his PC in his day-to-day tasks of trend forecasting, reporting, modelling, and controlling. Having the ability to rapidly integrate with other aspects of the project, as illustrated in Figure 10.1, he has a highly sophisticated management tool at his fingertips, allowing him both to receive and give up-to-the-minute information in a most professional manner.

We do not want to reproduce computer output sheets here – they are more liable to confuse than help – so what we have done is to present, in Figure 10.2 the 'description' that runs down one page of a computer printout that serves as the basis for a 'Project Cost Summary Report'. Each line would have data under a series of

| CAT | COSTCODE | DESCRIPTION |
|-----|----------|-------------|
| 01A | 0600 | FURNACES |
| 01B | 0605 | FIRED HEATERS |
| 01C | 0606 | STEAM DRUMS |
| 01D | 0801 | HEAT EXCHANGERS (NOT S&T) |
| 01E | 0802 | HEAT EXCHANGERS (S&T) |
| 01F | 1100 | COMPRESSORS/BLOWERS/FANS |
| 01G | 1301 | DRYERS & MIXERS |
| 01H | 1302 | LIFTS & CRANES |
| 01J | 1303 | LUBS/PORT FIRE EXTINGS. |
| 01K | 1600 | PUMPS |
| 01L | 1701 | DRIVERS (NOT MOTORS) |
| 01M | 1702 | WORKSHOP EQUIPMENT (NOT CRANE) |
| 01N | 1703 | MOBILE FIRE EQUIPMENT |
| 01P | 1704 | LOCOS & ROAD VEHICLES |
| 01Q | 2001 | TANKS |
| 01R | 2107 | NAMEPLATES |
| 01S | 2200 | VESSELS |
| 01T | 1014 | INSTRUMENT AIR DRYERS |
| 011 | ****** | TOTAL EQUIPMENT |
| 02A | 0202 | HEATING/AIR CONDITIONING |
| 02B | 0500 | ELECTRICAL MATERIALS |
| 02C | 1000 | INSTRUMENT MATERIALS |
| 02D | 1200 | PIPING MATERIALS |
| 02E | 1900 | STEELWORK |
| 02F | 2401 | CATALYST |
| 02G | 2402 | CHEMICALS |
| 02H | 2403 | LABORATORY EQUIPMENT |
| 02J | 2501 | FREIGHT & PACKING |
| 021 | ****** | TOTAL BULK ITEMS |
| 03A | 0701 | PROP. PLANTS—SUPPLY&ERECT |
| 031 | ****** | TOTAL PROP. PLANTS |
| 032 | ****** | TOTAL MATERIAL |
| 04A | 0100 | CIVILS |
| 04B | 0200 | BUILDINGS |
| 04C | 0803 | COOLING TOWERS |
| 04D | 1900 | PLANT STEELWORK |
| 04E | 2003 | TANKS |
| 04F | 2100 | INSULATION |
| 04G | 2106 | PAINTING |
| 04H | 2204 | VESSELS |
| 04J | 0508 | ELECTRICAL |
| 04K | 0600 | FURNACES |
| 041 | ****** | TOTAL SUB/CON SUPY+ERECT |

**Figure 10.2 Computer listing**
A listing of the various headings appearing in a typical computer printout for a Project Cost Report.

| COLUMN NO. | DESCRIPTION |
|---|---|
| 1 | ORIGINAL ESTIMATE |
| 2 | ESTIMATE CHANGES |
| 3 | REVISED ESTIMATE |
| 4 | COMMITMENT TO DATE |
| 5 | EXPENDITURE TO DATE |
| 6 | COST TO COMPLETE |
| 7 (= 4 + 6) | FORECAST FINAL COST |
| 8 (= 7 − 3) | OVERRUN (+) UNDERRUN (−) |
| 10 (= 8 − P8) | OVERRUN/UNDERRUN DIFFERENCE (+/−) |

**Figure 10.3 Computer output detail**
A listing of the several columns under which cost could be presented for each of the
headings detailed in Figure 10.2.

headings which we list in Figure 10.3. The pattern of the printout
can be seen by reference to Chapter 12, where the format can be
seen in a typical report – Figures 12.6 and 12.12. As figures in the
body of the report are changed, so do the totals. If we may
categorise the listing in Figure 10.2 as a level 2 report, made to the
project engineer, and the report in Figure 12.6 as a level 1 report,
made to management, then once the format has been established,
the summary report (Figure 12.6) would be reproduced at the
same time as the detailed report, with no further work on the part of
the project cost control engineer.

The underlying principle with such a system is that all costs are
itemised and given a unique identity, consisting of project number,
cost code, area code and item code. The cost engineer will collect
the relevant data verbally, manually, via other system users, LANS
and computer printouts, such as those being used by the accounts
department for invoices or the construction department for
manhours and then collate the whole in such a manner that the data
can be transferred to his system, as data for the cost control
reporting. This procedure is very quick and a complete project can
be updated and a report produced in a few hours once the data is
available, say at the end of the month.

## Cost reporting

Having once checked and approved the computer reports with the
project manager, the cost engineer will issue the reports as part of

the documentation for the weekly or monthly project reports to the project team, his own management and the owner. The data available from such a system is used by the cost engineer to:

1 Validate and process the cost control data, which has been either manually or electronically input to his system.
2 Use the input in a logical and auditable fashion to produce cost reports in the appropriate detail.
3 Produce those reports 'on request' in a common internal format as required by the owner on any particular project.
4 Provide the facility to accumulate the costs of several projects into one, providing consolidated summary reports of variable format and at various levels of detail as necessary.
5 Enable items of cost and their associated details to be transferred from one classification to another.

With such a system, where all the elements of cost in a project are itemised and stored electronically, the cost engineer can both store and retrieve data very rapidly. With that further invaluable aid, and his own PC at his desk, he can quickly bring himself up-to-date with respect to the material and manhour commitments and status, deliveries, vendor order loading, estimate over or underruns and other costing data, which all form part of the necessary feedback for the tight control of projects in progress and the development of estimating data for future projects.

### Estimating

Whilst the cost control engineer is responsible for the continual updating of the estimate of final cost as time passes, to maintain the 'Forecast final cost' mentioned in Figure 10.3, the computer does not assist the estimating function in quite the same way as it does the cost control function as such. There are many estimating programs available (11) but estimating is absolutely dependent upon experience and judgment, the very qualities we said earlier the computer lacked. An estimating program relies on its data bank and one task of the cost control engineer, as already mentioned above, is to develop estimating data for future projects, which can then be fed into that data bank and so update it. He therefore needs some knowledge of such programs and in particular the program available to him, if any, within his own company. Should he be involved in a major scope change he might well find such a program useful, but it would not be needed for updating his cost control estimate.

It is perhaps appropriate to mention, by way of example, two such programs that are commercially available and are likely to be of practical help to the cost control engineer. Many major companies have developed their own estimating programs, but these are not made public. There is the *Economist* program, developed by the Computer Aided Design Centre at Cambridge for estimating the capital and operating costs of process plants and carrying out profitability and sensitivity analyses (12). The central feature of the package is the cost estimating module which consists of a large data bank of equipment costs accessed via subroutines correlating process design information. The program then uses a range of factorial methods to arrive at total plant cost. It is the data bank that could be of use to the cost engineer in certain circumstances. The other program is called *Cost* and has been developed by the Icarus Corporation (13). The *Cost* system builds a comprehensive cost estimate for a proposed project similar to that produced by a definitive quantity takeoff. The *Cost* system contains computer models for simulating fabrication, design engineering, construction methods for developing manhours, equipment and material costs and engineering costs. The data held is therefore very different to that held in the *Economist* system, but the approach has value for the cost engineer, if he has to develop an estimate from limited information

### Future trends

The progress that has been made in the development of computer facilities over the past twenty years compels one to consider what the future holds in this context for project management and the project cost engineer. There is much development work going on: processing chips working in parallel, fibre optics, lasers, optical storage, flat screen displays, speech recognition – the rate of progress is limited only by limitations in terms of finance and more importantly, the human resource.

In the immediate future we shall very likely see the emergence of the 32-bit system as the norm in personal computing along with 1Mb of memory as a minimum, together with improved displays, an increase in portability and multi-user operation via LANS. What does this mean to cost engineering in particular? Not too much, since the best solution is already within our grasp, the cost engineer using his own programs and administering his own data. Too many 'fingers in the pie' must be avoided at all costs. To be effective, the cost engineer needs to have simple input and straightforward

## GLOSSARY OF TERMS

### General purpose computer (GPC)
Often referred to as a mainframe computer and built by one of the major manufacturers such as IBM, ICL, Burroughs and Sperry. The user site probably employs more than 500 people and in such a context these machines usually provide a full on-line service to the production areas of the company.

### Mini computer
General purpose in design but sold as a tool rather than as a solution. Manufacturers include DEC, LSI, PDP and VAX. The larger user will have from 100–500 employees and the small mini computer user less than 200.

### Small business systems (SBS)
General purpose computers aimed at the small business and first time users and sold with at least one software package, often an accounting program. The systems available include IBM's System 34, Philips P330, the TA1100, and the Wang, Olivetti, Nixdorf and NCR systems. Once again, the larger users of such systems can employ up to 500 people.

### Personal computers
These range from the simple home computer costing less than £100 to the 16-bit business/professional machine. Main manufacturers include IBM, Acorn, Commodore, Apple, Sanyo, Sinclair and Compaq, but there are many others.

### Operating systems
This term describes the software system necessary for working a computer. It does not do anything directly for the user, being a system for the handling of input and output. Common systems include MS/DOS, CP/M80, the IBM PC-DOS, GEM, UNI/XENIX, the MP/M.862, Apple and CP/M86.

### Computer aided design (CAD)
Now generally understood to be a computer software package that provides two- and three-dimensional design and modelling facilities. Two well-known systems are Computervision and Plant Design Management Systems (PDMS).

### Micro computer (micro processor)
A very small computer, usually dedicated to one task and often built into a piece of machinery (for example, a washing machine).

**Program**
In order to solve a problem, its solution must be specified in terms of a sequence of steps recognised by the computer. The specification of these steps is a program.

**Central processing unit (CPU)**
The heart of the computer. This carries out the manipulation of data and the control of the other parts of the computer.

**Terminal**
A device that allows the user to submit data to, and obtain output from the computer. Types of terminals include card readers, printers, video screens and teletypes. These may either be adjacent to the CPU or remotely located and connected by cable.

**Storage device**
Used for the long-term storage of data and programs. Examples include cards, magnetic tapes (including the cassette tape), floppy disks, hard disks and drums.

**Memory**
The memory of a computer is formed by a large number of basic units called memory cells. Each cell is an electronic or magnetic device that can be used to store information.

**Hardware**
The physical components of the computer and other related mechanical devices.

**Software**
General term for the programs needed to make computers and related devices perform their intended tasks.

**On-line system**
A system in which the user has immediate access to the computer. A response can be made within a few seconds of a request being received.

output, best achieved by the concept already demonstrated in Figure 10.1 above.

Finally, the importance and influence of computer-based systems and information cannot be in dispute. It is patently transforming the nature of products, processes, industries and even competition itself (14). The skill now is to understand the broad effects and implications of the new technology that has either arrived or is on the doorstep and harness it in such a way that we do not die of information indigestion. The cost engineer will still need to exercise judgment, creative ability, objectivity and initiative, however fast the calculations are made.

## References

1 Oakley, B., 'The computer – its existing and future possibilities', *Management Accounting*, December 1985.

2 Harper, W., 'Make way for the computer in the board room', *Accountancy*, November 1985.

3 Noble, A., 'The best of times, the worst of times, in a time of change', *Management Accounting*, December 1985.

4 Article: 'Data management', by the International Data Corporation, *Management Today*, December 1985.

5 Morrison, S., 'Selecting a personal computer', *Chemical Engineering*, September 1985.

6 Brochures and data: '*Pegasus* software', issued by Pegasus Software Limited, Kettering, Northants.

7 Brochures and data: 'Application systems', issued by IBM UK Limited, South Bank, London SE1.

8 Brochures and data: 'The *Symphony* package', issued by Lotus Development (UK) Limited, Consort House, Consort Street, Windsor, Berks.

9 Brochures and data: '*Artemis*', issued by Metier Management Systems Limited, Metier House, Hayes, Middlesex.

10 Rounds, S. L., 'The electronic spreadsheet', *Cost Engineering*, Vol. 26, No. 6, December 1984.

11 Williams, L. F. and A. M. Gerrard, 'Computer-aided cost estimation – a survey', *Process Economics International*, November 1984.

12 Williams, L.F. *et al*, 'Using the new *Economist* package', *Process Economics International*, November 1983.

13 Blecker, H. G. and D. Smithson, 'Detailed cost estimating during the process engineering phase of a project', *Process Economics International*, July 1985.

14 Porter, E. N. and V. E. Millar, 'How information gives you competitive advantage', *Harvard Business Review*, August 1985.

## Part Three
# THE PRINCIPLES APPLIED

# 11 Proper project management

The manner in which project management is implemented can vary enormously from project to project. The most important thing is to use the available resources to best advantage, whether that be a contractor, consultant or managing contractor. Money spent on good advice regarding project management and control is money well spent. If the owner, wanting the plant built, has not got the available resources in his own organisation, then it is essential that he gets a 'watchdog': someone on his side to protect his interests.

The scope of work let out can vary from the front-end design package to the fully turnkey responsibility for the complete project. This latter is usually done for major investments, when large numbers of people have to be employed in the planning, design, procurement and construction phases, all involved in a complex network of decisions and subsequent activities. The first and essential objective of project management, if we assume that a contractor has been selected to fulfil this role, is to provide a professional service to enable the owner, who is then also a partner, to engineer and construct the plant to the latest safety and quality standards and within acceptable time-cost limits. The project management and control methodology illustrated in this chapter have been developed and proved in practice as achieving management objectives together with the overriding paramount aim of providing a professional coordinated service meeting the owner's specific requirements.

## Project organisation and definition

Projects requiring part, or all, of a contractor's services will be managed by an experienced project manager who usually reports at board level in his company. The normal practice these days is to have a project management team, and this team embraces all the personnel reporting directly to the project manager/The team thus includes project engineers and senior engineers representing process, planning, cost estimating, construction and procurement coordination. The numbers involved will depend upon the scope and requirements of the specific project/Figure 11.1 illustrates a typical project organisation. The owner, if he has the resources, may well provide a matching team to work alongside the project team in order to achieve effective project coordination. Then the owner invests in his team the responsibility for decision making on his behalf. The project management team will be supported by the process, design, procurement and construction departments of the contractor and there will be other back-up service departments such as accounts, contract finance and legal, who will cooperate as required. A computer is normally available for data processing.

In setting up the project organisation, the contractor must work closely with the owner in order to define the requirements of the project and its boundaries. This involves process decisions, fixing design standards, material supply, financing, transport and shipping, site conditions, subcontract services, and the parameters of performance and reliability. At this stage of project definition, and as soon as the plot layout philosophy has been determined and an equipment list written, the overall master project programme has to be drafted, covering engineering, procurement, construction and commissioning. The project should from then on be controlled by this single master programme, which is under the direction of the project manager. Any other programmes that are prepared are expansions of this basic programme and are subsidiary to it: they must in all cases conform to the main key dates and milestones laid down in the master project programme.

Another key task of the project manager at this stage, in addition to cooperating with the owner to define the project requirements will be to set down and issue procedures generally called project coordination procedures. These procedures will give all the information relevant to the administration and management of the project including the organisation, planning and control procedures to be used in order to achieve the basic objectives. A typical check list as would be used for the development of such a coordination procedure is presented as Appendix C. This check list has been relegated to an Appendix not because it is relatively unimportant, but because we had no wish to condense it. Every item is of importance and they should be reviewed one by one, the necessary information being written up and agreed with all the interested parties.

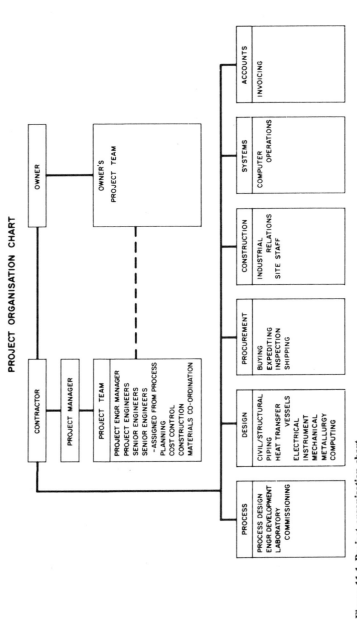

**Figure 11.1 Project organisation chart**
Typical organisation built around the project team, when a contractor is being employed.

213

This definition of the organisation and procedures for the project are essential right at the outset. The personnel necessary both to carry out the work and to manage it should be precisely identified and the terms of reference of each team member involved need to be clearly established. The project team, or task force as we might call it, must be clearly instructed so that they understand the contribution required of them. Project plans are useless unless they are adequately communicated and agreed. But are we not preaching to the converted? All good contracting organisations will have had experience in this field, and will know what they ought to do. But we are writing more particularly for the uninitiated, for the owner who has to feel his way, and not only has he to do something of this sort in his own organisation, but he must understand and appreciate the tasks that the project team are putting in hand at this time, if he is to cooperate with understanding.

## The project manager

The success of a project depends on many things and many individuals. A project is a dynamic thing and the plant that is finally built is not always the one that was first envisaged. A dynamic situation demands a dynamic project manager and team, and communication tools that can quickly react to meet the everchanging situation. It is very desirable for the project manager and the senior members of his team to have had previous experience in the type of project that they are going to manage. Each member of the team should have a good working knowledge of each other member's job, needs and responsibilities. Each should be able to understand the major control documents produced by the others and above all, be fully aware of, and follow, the requirements set down in the coordination procedure. When receiving information, they should invariably ask: 'Who else needs to know?' Good and effective communication is of paramount importance if success is to be achieved.

The project manager should be concerned with all matters within the project and his influence should be seen to begin at the very start. It is not necessary that a project manager be a specialist in any of the fields with which the job is concerned, but he should certainly be a man of broad background, preferably experienced in the type of project being managed, fully informed of the general nature of the specialities and various disciplines involved, able to communicate well with each and every one of the people who work on his project and to produce results from their efforts as a team. It would not normally be expected that the project manager would overrule a specialist in the specialist's own field. Nevertheless, occasions might well arise when, by virtue of the particular experience of an individual project manager, or simply on the ground of common sense, there is concern that the solution to a particular problem may not be optimum or even correct. Although this could be confined entirely within the specialist field, the project manager is entitled to challenge the solution with his top management who are, of course, in the end answerable for it and all other similar issues.

More often than not in project work, the problems that do arise are not confined to a single specialist role. They exist in the conflicts and interactions which occur between, for instance, the search for technical excellence, the programme requirements for the job, the cost and the individuals involved. It is in these boundary areas, where a precise definition as to the way that the project should proceed is difficult, that the judgment and authority of the project manager is particularly important. He is the person empowered to decide matters where conflicting interests compete with each other, although – as he sees fit – he may well enlist the advice of his seniors. For example, it is often possible to short-circuit the selection process for a particular piece of equipment and so make more rapid progress with the engineering design and produce results beneficial to the project as a whole, whilst that individual piece of equipment thus selected is marginally more expensive. This is the province of the project manager, and this is where his judgement must prevail.

## Project control – the elements for success

Technical control of the project must lie with the contractor's top technical management, who exercise this through the managers of the various disciplines. For example, the lead process engineer and the lead project engineer in a project team coordinate the process and mechanical aspects of the technical design of a project, in consultation with the company's specialists. They are responsible for ensuring that the technical policies laid down in company procedures and standards are followed, taking into account the specific requirements of the owner. Technical problems requiring solution will be discussed with the managers of the relevant disciplines, who will liaise with the project manager to establish acceptable solutions. It is important that the technical supervision, no matter how administered from the top, must act in such a way that the project manager retains control over all the major aspects of the work and is not hindered or delayed in achieving the objectives laid down for the project.

### Document control

There is no doubt that for the project manager to retain effective control over the project he must have an efficient system of document control. This involves both the documentation itself and document indexes, which have to be kept up to date and issued periodically to publicise the current issue status. There should be a document control section responsible both for filing and distribution, together with indexing and the expediting of vendor drawings. Where mainframe computer facilities are available the system will be programmed, with a data base containing information relating to document registration, document movement, document distribution and facilities to report by exception and so highlight the necessary expediting of the documentation. Such a system will cover both in-house, vendor and subcontractor produced documents and a typical flow chart is presented as Figure 11.2. An outline listing of some of the documents involved is given in Figure 11.3. The reader is also referred to Chapter 6, where the administrative procedures in relation to document control are discussed in a section with that heading.

With respect to document indexing, there are two basic types of report, the document status report and the document expediting report. The document status report will provide the current status of each document, and would be sorted to suit the user. A typical report would contain document number, issue, title, issue date, status and remarks, and be sorted by discipline, module and document type. Document expediting reports, on the other hand, contain the status of outstanding actions instigated by the transmittal of the documents. A typical report could list documents awaiting approval by a certifying authority, documents required to be re-submitted by vendors, comments awaited on documents circulating in-house, and so on.

### Cost control and planning

When it comes to project costs, the prime responsibility rests directly with the project manager. Cost control *must* start at the top (1). Cost engineers appointed to the project team report directly to the project manager. Through these cost engineers and the reports

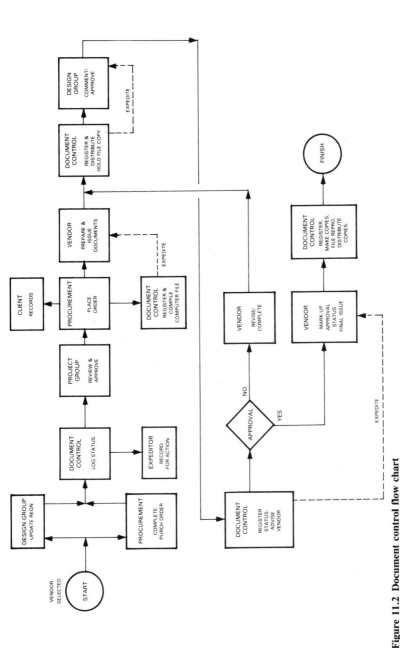

**Figure 11.2 Document control flow chart**
This flow chart outlines the movement of documents, such as the purchase order, expediting and inspection reports, drawings, erection and maintenance manuals, that will be created once a vendor has been selected for an item of equipment.

217

CONTROL DOCUMENTATION

*Project*
a) Coordination procedure (issued as necessary)
b) Overall master project programme (network)
c) Cost control reports
d) Change notice report

*Engineering*
a) Master task bar chart
b) Control schedule
c) Variance highlight, action due and actions overdue report
d) Manpower loading — planned/actual per discipline
e) Requisition status report
f) Outstanding vendor information report
g) Spares status and progress report

*Procurement*
a) Master task bar chart
b) Variance highlight, action due and actions overdue report
c) Manpower loading — planned/action report
d) Requisition and bid status report
e) Vendor expediting report
f) Inspection reports
g) Committed expenditure of material and equipment curve —
   planned/actual
h) Order status report

*Construction*
a) Master task bar chart
b) Subcontract status report
c) Manpower loading — planned/actual
d) Variance highlight, action due and actions overdue report
e) Shortage/damage on site report
f) Field status summary

**Figure 11.3 Control documentation**
This documentation is fundamental for departmental guidance. Each department
and discipline must keep its own house in order.

they prepare, with the advice they give, the project manager is able to review costs and potential costs, give the necessary directives and take corrective action as necessary.

Planning is the related key function and the planning engineer on the project team, also reporting directly to the project manager, is responsible for all aspects of planning, including construction. He prepares the overall master project programme and any other subsidiary programmes, agrees these with the project manager and issues them for use to all key personnel working on the project. He collects the variance reports from each discipline and prepares the necessary highlight reports, updating the master and any other programmes or charts as necessary. These documents, together with the manpower curves are the project manager's major control documents and he uses these to assess progress, measure the effective use of resources and so decide on the appropriate action as needed. The highlight reports will form part of the agenda for the project manager's progress meeting.

Cost engineering and planning thus work continuously in parallel, providing the basic tools for project control. This parallelism of effort is illustrated graphically in Figure 11.4, which is an extension of two of the activity blocks seen in Figure 11.1.

### Procurement

Procurement as such will be the function of the procurement department, but the project team should have a procurement coordinator. He will ensure that the owner's specific procurement policies are followed as laid down in the contract. The typical responsibilities of a procurement coordinator could include the following:

1   Issue a procurement coordination procedure, which would form part of the overall project coordination procedure (see Appendix C). This would give all the information relevant to the procurement department's activities and policies neces- sary to achieve the objectives laid down by the project manager.
2   Liaise with the purchasing manager, checking the timing of the activities of the purchasing group busy on the project.
3   Watch over the procurement plan, which is part of the overall project master plan, checking adherence to the specified activities.

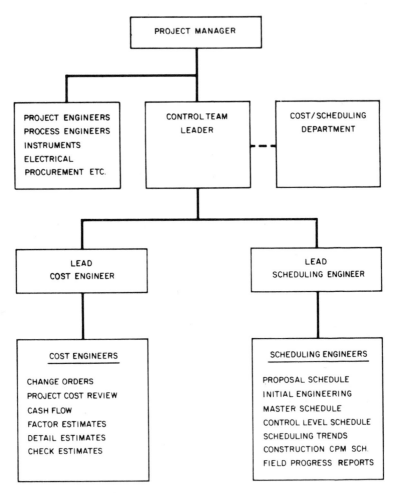

**Figure 11.4 The cost/scheduling control team**
Cost control and planning (scheduling) are key functions for overall project
management and control.

4  Liaise with the group heads within the procurement department, to ensure that suitable staff are deployed at the right
   times.
5  Ensure that reporting dates are met and that reports are
   complete and explicit.
6  Issue variance and highlight reports, summarising the activities of the procurement department in relation to programme
   and costs, at the agreed frequency.
7  Check the documentation issued by the procurement department, such as the orders and schedules, to ensure compliance
   with the contractual requirements.
8  Attend critical meetings with vendors.
9  Ensure that all critical points are both highlighted and then
   actioned.

## Construction

The construction engineer in the project team advises the project
manager on all site matters, including site organisation, staffing,
labour relations, site agreements where applicable, construction
planning and cost control activities, quality control and performance. The construction engineer assists design with advice on
methods of erection and installation of plant and equipment.
During the initial phase of the work he will be resident with the
project team at head office, but transfers to site at the appropriate
time.

## Subcontracts

With the 'managing contractor' concept, which is the basis of our
approach to proper project management, the degree to which work
will be subcontracted to other contractors, rather than by directly
hired labour, will vary from case to case. It can well be that *all* work
on site is subcontracted, and this has some real advantages.

However that may be, it is essential that all subcontracts be
placed by the appropriate procurement specialists, after selection of
the successful subcontractor by the project manager, in consultation with the owner. This is an area where the owner may well have
very specific and limiting requirements, but the specialist must
ensure that all contractual matters are properly covered. Every
subcontractor must be subject to the same cost and progress
reporting system as has been developed for the project as a whole.

Each contractor must therefore prepare his own detailed programme, within the milestone dates for the overall master project programme, report on manhours weekly, and report on any failure immediately. Techniques for the monitoring of the activities of subcontractors on site were discussed in some detail in Chapter 8, where we sought to recognise the early warning signals for later failure to meet the stated targets.

Having surveyed the activities of the project team, in broad outline, let us now look at two key elements, cost control and planning, in some detail.

## Cost control – in detail

The major functions of the cost engineer are to establish the cost targets, maintain a control estimate throughout the life of the project, monitor performance relative to the targets and to predict the final cost of all materials and services provided. He must receive all the relevant project documentation for evalution and he must maintain regular and frequent contact with all the key personnel in all disciplines who are working on the project and discuss all cost changes and any other event or decision that has a significant cost impact before they take effect with the project manager. Project cost reports and other relevant forecasts would be issued and updated at monthly intervals while a project is in its active phase.

### Cost targets

At the commencement of the project the estimate prepared by the owner or perhaps the successful contractor, if sufficiently detailed, would be taken as the project control estimate. If this estimate is not detailed enough, then a control estimate would have to be prepared. In this case the earlier estimate is used as a control estimate, perhaps broken down into cost codes on a statistical basis, until such time as the detailed control estimate is to hand. This may be some three to four months after contract award.

With the agreement of the project manager, the control estimate is issued to all key personnel working on the project, with estimate detail sheets so that all knowledge on potential cost which is then available is before those who are starting to implement the project. The fact that, for instance, because of the lack of detailed estimating, certain elements of the estimate may have quite a wide margin of error should not deter the project manager from making the information available. The cost analysis, summarised per cost code (see Appendix B) would be presented on the project cost control report and form the base against which final expected costs would be compared. The estimate thus serves to control all subsequent purchasing and construction activities. Where the nature of the contract with the owner is such that these costs agree with his own estimate, the report system must then accommodate this. However, as review estimates are prepared as more information becomes available, these become *the* target for the cost control engineer when making forecasts and assessing trends.

*Estimate updating*

This brings us to estimate updating, a key function of the cost engineer throughout the life of the project. If, following bid comparison, an acceptable technical and commercial quotation becomes an order (commitment), then this potential cost is entered into the estimate, with all the related oncosts, such as packing, transport, escalation and allowance for the 'cost trend' on that particular order. The latter is very much a matter of experience. The designers are preparing bulk material take-offs for piping, instrument and electrical materials at planned stages during the design phase. These, too, are costed, taking into account probable sources of supply and current market prices. The potential accuracy of such take-offs has to be assessed against previous achievement within the company and other statistical data.

When we come to implementation of work on the site, the cost engineer located there, working in conjunction with the construction engineer, prepares a statement showing the commitments being entered into, and forecasts all construction costs. It is the construction engineer's responsibility to predict and report construction trends to the project manager. The measurement and costing of uncompleted construction work is undertaken at site and agreed by the construction engineer and the site cost engineer, and then incorporated in the review estimates and the project cost report.

In this way the costs in the control estimate, amended where necessary, and detailed per cost code, are reported in the project cost report as the 'estimated final cost'. Details of changes to the original scope of the project, having been estimated and authorised, and which lead in part to these revised review estimates, are also given in the report. The report compares the estimate with the commitment to date, value of work done to date, but variances between the final expected cost and the authorised estimates, which should include scope changes, are better the subject of a separate comparison. The format of a typical presentation of this comparison of progress with the review estimate (the cost engineer's target) is to be seen in Figure 6.14.

### Planning – in detail

On project award the contractor would prepare a programme of activities in chart form to show the so-called 'front-end' schedule. This would be used to monitor progress until the overall master project programme is prepared using such information as is available. This would include:

1   Planning studies by the owner
2   Equipment list
3   Preliminary layout
4   Drawing schedules
5   Input from all the separate disciplines.

This information would be analysed by network methods, and in sufficient depth to enable the owner and the contractor to agree that the result is feasible and can form the basis for detailed planning. These detailed plans would show manpower resource by discipline, to meet the nominated milestone dates.

From the overall master project programme specific master task charts are then prepared, together with histograms of the manpower requirements and the related S-curves for the separate design disciplines, and related departmental activities. Figure 11.5 illustrates one such chart as prepared for the procurement activity. These master task charts define tasks and give the relationship between tasks and milestone dates as first indicated on the overall master project programme. Each of the tasks presented on the master bar chart is numbered and this numbering enables these tasks to be readily identified in the various communications systems that exist in the organisation, such as from the contractor's home office to the owner, from home office to site, and also within the home office itself.

The next step is to see what happens as compared with the master plan. Task control schedules would be prepared by the lead engineers in each discipline, and these would be reviewed and updated every two weeks, in cooperation with the planning engineer. Variances would then be highlighted and reported. The planning engineer analyses these variances, assesses their signific-

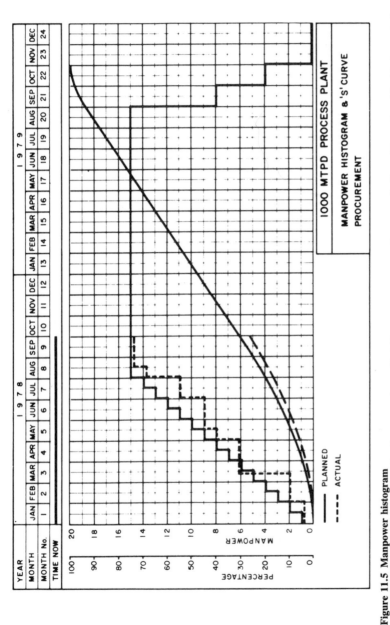

**Figure 11.5 Manpower histogram**

This graph illustrates the detailed development of one discipline – procurement – in terms of effort. (Reproduced by kind permission of Humphreys & Glasgow Limited, London.)

ance and reports to the project manager, who then proceeds to take such action as may be appropriate.

During the construction phase a similar procedure is followed, with the construction engineers and the planning engineer preparing their master task bar chart and manpower histogram from the overall master project programme. As contracts are let 'actual' (what actually happens) is measured against the plan. It is desirable that site meetings be held by the project manager at two-weekly intervals during the construction phase of the project to highlight variances and discuss possible action, review actions already taken and so monitor progress from the planning aspect.

### Control documentation

The project team's most important function is to communicate and so ensure effective, continuous and accurate sensing of the feedback control loop. The project manager's progress reports would be produced at regular intervals, usually monthly, for both the owner and his own company's management. One of these documents has already been illustrated (Figure 11.5). In order to demonstrate the type of detail available a material progress schedule is given as Figure 11.6.

Regular meetings between the project manager and his own senior management to review the project are of paramount importance. At these meetings the plan, the costs and the resources should be examined in detail. This ensures that potential problems are brought to the attention of management at an early stage and that priority on the allocation of effort can be planned in all its facets, to make proper use of company resources.

### Design

Design of the overall plant system of the project and the individual items of equipment would be carried out by process design engineers. They would be responsible for overall heat, mass and pressure balances, major control and safety requirements, the process specification of equipment, all the necessary calculations covering the startup and part load conditions in the plant, technical coordination of supplied equipment within the overall plant design, and the preparation of operating manuals. The development of plant flowsheets, piping and engineering instrumentation diagrams (usually known as the P & I), instrument and line schedules and the

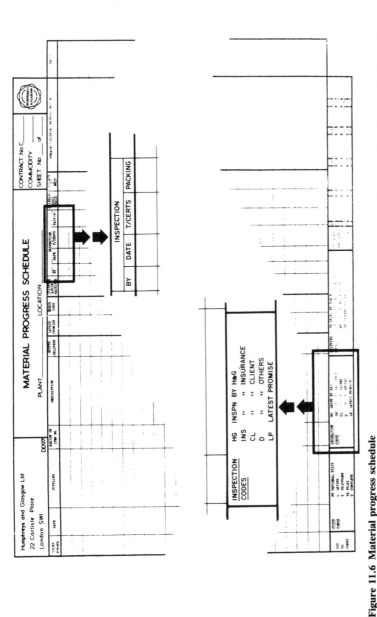

**Figure 11.6 Material progress schedule**

This form gives the status of all orders issued, and hence of all equipment and materials coming to the site. We have highlighted one aspect, inspection, to illustrate the degree of detail in which such reports are made. (Reproduced by kind permission of Humphreys & Glasgow Limited, London.)

preliminary functional layout of the plant are generally the responsibility of the specialist engineers. This ensures standardisation and continuity of the details involved in the key conceptual engineering of flowsheets and layouts. Other matters related to technical coordination of the plant, such as the assessment of hazardous areas and the calculation of plant and community noise levels may also be part of the function of these engineers.

Further services that may be made available within the managing contractor or contractor's organisation include advice on or supervision of activities during pre-commissioning and startup. This may range from the provision of single specialists to complete teams, and include operator training, troubleshooting and plant optimisation. Cooperation in the preparation of operating manuals and the review of operating problems and their remedy are also key activities. Such commissioning activities are carried out by process operating engineers (usually qualified chemical engineers) and process operating supervisors, fully experienced in the operation of process plants. Instrument, mechanical and other design and maintenance specialists may also be drawn from the contractor, permitting the formation of commissioning teams with the correct balance of theoretical and practical experience.

The design engineering activities of a contracting organisation form the major input to any project and include the following:

1 Civil/structural/building
2 Piping
3 Heat transfer
4 Vessel
5 Electrical
6 Instrument
7 Mechanical
8 Metallurgy
9 Computing

Each of the above disciplines would be responsible in its turn for the engineering design, together with the requisitioning of the equipment and materials required for the project, with the preparation of the necessary technical specifications and standards. They would also provide technical appraisal of the vendor's offers against the specified requirements, and liaise with each other to ensure that all interface activities are covered. As previously mentioned, members of the above design disciplines would be part of the project team, the numbers depending upon the size and complexity of the project.

## Procurement

Procurement activities these days comprise worldwide purchase, shop inspection, expediting and shipping to the construction site of all material and equipment. To facilitate these several activities the procurement function is generally divided into four sub-functions:

1 Purchasing
2 Expediting
3 Inspection
4 Shipping

Figure 11.7 shows the procurement function in some detail and thus illustrates the interrelationships and interactions within the overall corporate enterprise.

The purchasing function is responsible for all the purchasing activities, and should research and identify the best sources of supply all over the world. Purchase orders would be placed after careful technical and commercial evaluation of quotations, with firms of good repute, possessing the necessary manufacturing facilities and capacity to deliver goods conforming in all respects to the specifications, drawings and engineering standards, and to the agreed delivery schedules. Guarantees should be obtained from each manufacturer against defective material and workmanship. This must be one of the standard conditions of order.

Turning to expediting, resident expeditors would be located in all key industrial areas of the United Kingdom and also in certain locations overseas to ensure that the terms of orders are complied with. Regular liaison between the head office and such outside staff must be maintained and continued expediting carried out in the supplier's works and, if necessary in his sub-supplier's works to ensure that progress is on schedule and that the equipment complies with the necessary specifications. Regular expediting and materials status reports would be submitted as necessary through the project manager and his team.

Inspection engineers would be similarly located throughout the United Kingdom and overseas, thus ensuring worldwide expertise in the various manufacturing practices. The inspectors would carry out the normal stage inspection functions during manufacture with respect to equipment and materials being supplied, and of all the materials before final delivery, to ensure that the specifications had been met and the equipment correctly marked and packed. Regular, comprehensive inspection reports, together with all the relevant data on materials, welding, testing, and so on, would be issued to the project team.

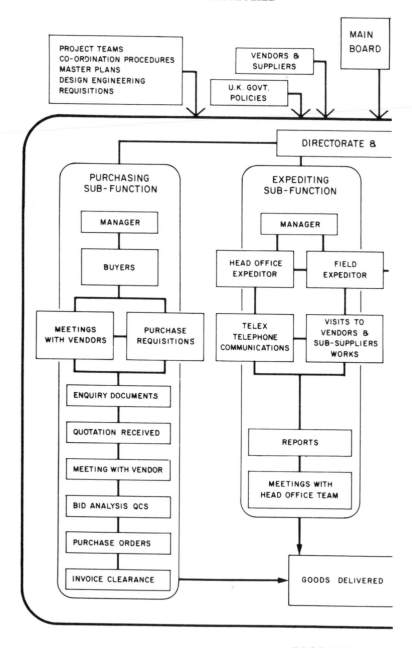

**PROCUREMENT**

**Figure 11.7 The procurement function**
A detail of the various activities involved in procurement. (Reproduced by kind permission of Humphreys and Glasgow Limited, London.)

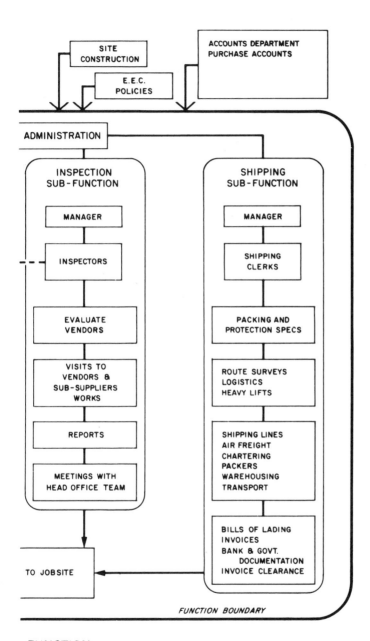

FUNCTION

The final exercise is to get the materials onto the construction site. This is the responsibility of shipping. This sub-function would be responsible for organising the international movement of equipment and materials. When forwarding agents have been nominated or retained by the owner, close liaison would be maintained in order to facilitate the most economical and expeditious method of movement and selection of routes. Bills of lading, freight accounts, commercial invoices and other such documentation would all be part of the responsibility of shipping.

### Construction

The responsibilities of the construction specialist on a project cover the planning and execution of site construction work and the activities with which he is concerned usually fall within the following categories:

1  Site planning
2  Site cost control
3  Industrial relations
4  Welding
5  Subcontracts
6  Field staff

Let us deal with each of these in turn. With respect to the site planning, this involves manpower resourcing, progress reporting and the preparation and issue of job cards. Close liaison is maintained with the project team.

With respect to site cost control, all site costs, including the delivery of materials to site, are monitored by the site cost engineer. With respect to construction on site, he prepares statements of all the commitments and forecasts on all facets of construction cost for incorporation in the overall project cost reports.

Industrial relations can be a problem. It is essential that both the contractor's and the owner's policies with regard to industrial relations are carefully administered and properly maintained. To achieve this, regular meetings must be held with trade union organisations at both local and national level and close liaison maintained with the owner. It is essential that the monitoring of the relevant legislation and that concerned with matters relating to the maintenance by the contractor and the owner on site of the proper standards of safety, health and welfare be fully maintained.

Welding is always a very significant factor in the total effort on site. The preparation of welding procedures and then ensuring the site welding is carried out in accordance with technical requirements, specifications and drawings calls for meticulous supervision. This, together with the non-destructive testing activities and assistance by design on the practicalities of the various fabrications are of paramount importance.

Turning to the letting of subcontracts, it is usual for the construction engineer on the project team to assume responsibility for the preparation of the enquiry documents, agreeing with the project manager on the selection of successful subcontractors. It must never be forgotten that each and every subcontractor must comply with any site agreement in force or established as part of the industrial relations programme referred to above.

Last of all, let us look at the field staff. This is the team put on site by the contractor, to supervise the construction phase of the project. The construction engineer will have transferred from head office at the start of site construction and heads a site construction team consisting of trade supervisors, field engineers, site cost engineers and quantity surveyors who control and administer all the activities carried out on site by direct hired labour or by subcontractors. The head office based construction personnel support and back up the construction engineer. Figure 11.8 illustrates a typical construction site organisation. The numbers and responsibilities of both supervisors and superintendents depend on the size and complexity of the project.

### Conclusions

It is hoped that this outline of the requirements of proper project management will give some idea, particularly to those who have never, as yet, been involved in a major project, of the breadth and depth of the various tasks and disciplines that are inevitably involved. It has been established that the prime objective of proper project management is to complete its project within the original budget. It is to be hoped that this will be an economic cost, within the optimum time and incorporating the latest technical, quality and safety standards. To achieve this objective it is necessary for many disciplines and specialists, bound together in a large organisation, to contribute their special skills and expertise in the most effective way.

In order to coordinate and marshall these skills project management has its own duties and responsibilities, which include:

1  Project definition
2  Coordination procedures

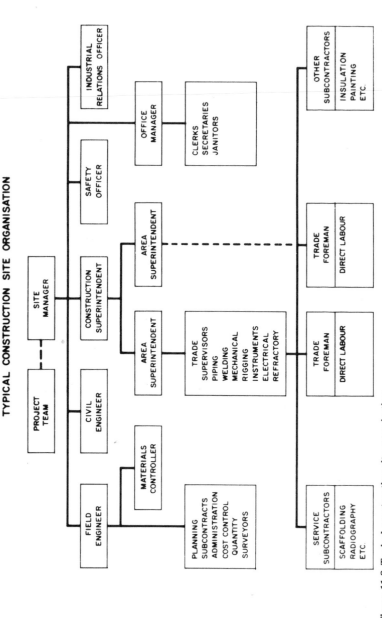

**Figure 11.8 Typical construction site organisation**
The numbers involved and the range of responsibilities will vary according to the size and complexity of the project.

3 Instruction and communication documentation
4 Delegation and liaison
5 Monitoring – internally and externally
6 Reporting
7 Controlling

There is no doubt that team effort is of paramount importance for the success of the project, with first class communication at all levels of responsibility. 'Who else needs to know?' must be the first question raised by the receiver of any information relative to the project. Concern and awareness by senior management of the project's progress and problem areas must be much in evidence. A caring attitude is essential if motivation of the various characters and personalities in a project team is to be maintained. At the same time the project manager must be given sufficient responsibility and scope so that he is in effect the 'managing director' of his own 'company', albeit for the life of the project only.

This chapter has highlighted the various responsibilities that are essential for a successful performance and outcome of the total project and at the end of the day that will be all that matters. Above all, it must be remembered that no matter how skilled and experienced the project manager and his team may be, they are still subject to the contraints we outlined in Chapter 3. Their most immediate constraint is their reliance on the numerous people giving them an efficient back-up service at all levels of responsibility within both the owner's and the contractor's organisation. Therefore, it must never be forgotten that no matter how efficient the monitoring, communication systems and reporting procedures may be, project management means above all that you are in the 'people business', and people *must* be seen to matter.

## Reference

1 Clarke, F. D. and A. E. Lorenzoni, *Applied Cost Engineering*, Marcel Dekker, 1979, 297 pp.

# 12　Successful case histories

This chapter seeks to reach and inform the uninitiated – those who become involved in capital investment in a major process plant after several years of minor expansion schemes or revamps. It discusses a few of the many problems presented to the project team in running and controlling a major project. Very rarely does a project run entirely smoothly – probably never – and the problems we present from experience are typical of what is to be expected in any system whose development depends upon the cooperation and mutual understanding of a great variety of people with different and sometimes opposing interests. Securing continuing, efficient co-operation, seen to be so necessary from what we have said previously, is a difficult problem. It becomes the day to day task of the project manager and his team to solve these problems for success to be achieved. It is hoped that the experiences presented here, culled from the construction of two very different overseas projects, will amply demonstrate the varied problems, procedures and documentation that a project team have to face, overcome and live through before success can be achieved. Hopefully, even the seasoned and experienced contractor may find something new here, or at least another angle from which to view an all too familiar situation.

## Overseas projects and contract conditions

We believe it will be useful to explain briefly some of the more important contractual conditions, especially bonding, imposed by overseas buyers these days on contractors, because they play an important role. They have considerable influence on the way the project manager and his team handle a project. Severe and sometimes onerous conditions can subject the project team to constraints and frustrations that are almost 'beyond the call of duty'.

Any contractor contemplating the undertaking of an overseas project must be fully aware of the contract conditions that are being imposed by the owner (buyer), especially in relation to performance and bonding. There has been a tendency lately in this area to move in the direction of adopting internationally acceptable forms of contract, such as are recommended by the Fédération International des Ingénieurs-Conseils (FIDIC). It is necessary, therefore, for the contractor to have staff available who are familiar with the requirements, and so capable of drafting suitable conditions of contract, offering the proper protection. Having got the contract, it is essential to keep a close control over the entire operation, since excuses for failure to comply with the conditions are not normally accepted. This means that a failure in performance of quite a minor character can be very expensive, since the bond will be called in.

The basic types of bond/guarantee required from contractors fall into four categories, relating to successive stages in the development of a project. There are definite reasons why each of the guarantees is required. The first is a bid bond/guarantee, given when the contractor submits his bid. This guarantee is designed to ensure that those who bid for a project are serious in their interest. Most such guarantees are for 1–5 per cent of the bid value. Second is the performance guarantee, given by the contractor at the start of the project. This is the main guarantee and its purpose is to ensure that the contractor completes the project in the manner required of him. Should his performance fail for any reason, then the guarantee sum can be called. The value of this is normally between 5 and 10 per cent of the contract value, sufficient to cover any potential loss by the owner because he has to start again. A typical performance bond is shown in Figure 12.1.

Third is the advance payment guarantee. Advance payments made to the contractor enable him to speed up work on the project and in many cases advance payments are made providing there is an adequate guarantee ensuring repayment of an advance in the event of default. Finally, there is the retention money guarantee, which operates during the maintenance period, after the project is physically complete. This enables the contractor to receive his money, rather than have certain payments held back until the maintenance period is over. Most overseas contracts have a period of one year during which these payments remain outstanding, to protect the owner against latent defects, not evident on completion.

---

### PERFORMANCE BOND

### To: GALA PRODUCTS LIMITED

We, Samuel Johnson Bankers Limited, have been informed that a Contract for the design, engineering supply and erection of an oil refinery to be built in Gala, was signed on the 1st July, 1970 between you and British Builders Limited, hereinafter called "The Contract". For the purposes of this Letter of Guarantee the Contract Price under the Contract is deemed to be £16,000,000.

In accordance with the terms of the Contract, British Builders Limited undertakes obligations concerning due fulfilment of the Contract to the satisfaction of Gala Products Limited.

With respect fo the fulfilment of the above obligations of British Builders Limited we, Samuel Johnson Bankers Limited, hereby irrevocably undertake, unconditionally and without reservation, notwithstanding any objections and/or claims by British Builders Limited and/or third parties and expressly refusing the benefit of all discussions and disputes, to pay you, Gala Products Limited on your first demand a sum up to £800,000 maximum, representing 5% of the total Contract Price as aforesaid.

For the payment of the sums in accordance with this Letter of Guarantee you shall present to us a written demand explaining in detail which obligation has not been fulfilled by British Builders Limited.
This Letter of Guarantee will come into force upon the date hereof and shall remain in force until 12 months after acceptance of the oil refinery, the subject of the Contract.

On expiry this Letter of Guarantee will become null and void and should be returned to us.

Dated this      day of      19XX      Samuel Johnson Bankers Limited.

. . . . . . . . . . . . . . . . . . . .

---

**Figure 12.1 Typical performance bond**
This illustrates the stringency of the obligations that can be placed upon a contractor by the owner. The names, added to make the document readable, are of course fictitious.

No contractor, whatever his size, could put up the cash for these guarantees. It would be far too big a drain on his cash resources. So he uses the services of an international bank, who will make the guarantee for him in a form acceptable to the owner. Thus the document illustrated in Figure 12.1 is actually issued by the bank. Then should the guarantee be called, the bank will pay the owner and reclaim from the contractor. The growth in such guarantee business has been phenomenal and bankers have had to develop a controlled risk strategy in relation to the guarantees in their portfolio. The bank charge for such facilities is usually some 1–2 per cent per year on the value of the bond given, so that on a large contract this can be a very costly business.

**Financing**

It is standard practice for buyers of turnkey capital projects to demand long-term finance and this is generally arranged within the framework of governmental export credit programmes. As the size of projects has increased individual companies have been less and less able to fund projects on their own. This has led to joint ventures and multi-country financing and it is not unusual to see projects financed simultaneously from three or four sources, with the financial package being seen by clients as an integral part of the offer they are being made. To illustrate the complexities we can take as an example a project that received wide publicity, since UK companies were in competition with the Japanese, the Bosporus Bridge. It appears that the credit deal proposed by the Japanese, outlined in Figure 12.2, was decisive in securing the contract for them: so much so that their approach was described as 'predatory finance'.

Of course, on other occasions it has been the British who have 'won out'. For instance, in connection with a tender to the USSR for two methanol plants, it seemed that Lurgi of West Germany would get the order, with Davy McKee (then Davy Power-Gas) as the runner-up. The British tender was some £20 million above that put in by Lurgi and award to them was imminent. But the ready availability of British credit, together with an improvement of some 0.75 per cent (yes, that's all) in their tender by switching from pounds sterling to US dollars just tipped the scales, and the British company was awarded the contract. This required in-depth liaison between the British consortium, their financial advisers (Morgan Grenfell) and the various government agencies.

But why should project finance now dominate in this way? It

---

## THE BOSPORUS BRIDGE CREDIT DEAL

*Credit secured by the winner to finance the contract*

| US$205 Million | – | Japanese credit confirmed by Government of Japan. Interest 5% over 25 years, 7 year grace period. |
| US$71 Million | – | Japanese Commercial Credit, Japanese Exim Bank. Interest 9.4% over 12 years, 4 year grace period. |
| US$140 Million | – | Italian Export Credit from Italian Export Financing Institution S.A.C.E. Interest 7.75% over 13 years, 3 year grace period. |
| US$30 Million | – | Italian Government confirmed Credit Guarantee. Interest not known, but very low, spread over 15 years with a 3 year grace period. |
| US$160 Million | – | Euroloan. Interest 7.25% over 7 years, 2 year grace period. |

---

**Figure 12.2 The Bosporus Bridge credit deal**
The credit terms secured by the Turkish authorities following intensive negotiation in the face of severe competition.

comes about because of the very high cost of money these days. Since the fifties and early sixties interest rates have more than doubled, whilst the rate of return on the investment was much higher then than it usually is these days. The result: in today's marketplace, especially in the process plant field, the best technology alone will not necessarily secure a contract. It has to be combined with the best financial package if it is to succeed. A new dimension has been added: a factor of which the cost engineer has to be cognisant. It is another cost factor which has to be monitored.

As a result of all this, the contractor, and often the cost control engineer in the contractor's organisation, will often find himself deeply involved in the financing of a project when he comes to make an offer. His client will expect financing arrangements that will enable him to:

- enjoy the benefits of a large capital asset, without having to finance the entire project
- undertake a project that might otherwise have not been affordable
- minimise his equity investment in the project by inviting other investors to take part
- shift some of the risk from himself to others

The contractor, for his part, has to:

- minimise the risk both to himself and his client
- obtain precise terms of payment
- determine currency used, and where and how paid
- establish good and clear conditions of contract
- obtain the appropriate insurance
- determine the risk period involved
- arrange any bonding requirements
- make financial arrangements with major subcontractors

To achieve all this, the contractor will have to make a detailed and accurate evaluation of project costs, establish probable sources for the equipment and materials, evaluate local suppliers and subcontractors, evaluate the sources of finance, have discussions with banks and credit agencies to get them committed and involved, and assess the foreign currencies involved, with the exchange risks. In addition, the arrangements made will have to have a degree of flexibility, since conditions can change over the two to three years or more the project will take to complete. The contractor is now involved in a complex and risky business and he *must* get his sums right.

Naturally enough, the owner will be seeking the best terms that he can get. There is thus the continuing danger of a 'credit terms race' between the different countries seeking business which would be damaging to all. Over the years the various countries in the Berne Union, the OECD and the EEC have sought to set guidelines, such as those set out in Figure 12.3. It will be seen that the buying countries are divided into three broad categories, related to per capita income. Despite this, terms are often put forward which cannot be matched, the competition for the Bosporus Bridge project being an outstanding example. If the terms obtained on that project, as set out in Figure 12.2, are compared with the proposals detailed in Figure 12.3, it will be seen that they are far better: rates of interest lower, length of credit period greater and substantial grace periods. This emphasises once again the importance of the financial package with international projects.

---

**CONSENSUS GUIDELINES**

MINIMUM INTEREST RATES:

| | Type of country | | |
| --- | --- | --- | --- |
| | Rich % | Intermediate % | Poor % |
| 2–5 years credit: | 10.95 | 9.65 | 8.80 |
| Over 5 years: | 11.20 | 10.15 | 8.80 |

MAXIMUM CREDIT PERIODS:

| | Years | Years | Years |
| --- | --- | --- | --- |
| | 5.0* | 8.5 | 10.0 |

NOTES:
*Exceptionally 8.5 years.
The minimum payment by delivery or commissioning is 15%.

---

**Figure 12.3 Guidelines for credit terms**
These are the terms considered equitable and generally on offer, but more advantageous terms can often be secured.

We have gone into this matter of project financing in some detail in order to give those who have never as yet been involved in a major project overseas the breadth and depth of the various tasks that will have to be undertaken, and the several disciplines that are inevitably involved. Whilst one learns by experience, this is undoubtedly a situation where 'first timers' should seek detailed advice and guidance from the experts, above all the banks and in the UK the Export Credit Guarantee Department (ECGD), the government department that will both insure the contractor against the risk of not being paid and guarantee 100 per cent repayment to the banks.

The project team will find that their workload and their responsibilities grow considerably in such cases, and it may well be necessary to have a financial expert in their team to ensure that the agreed financial protocol is duly followed, although this task often devolves on the cost control engineer. In any event, internal project procedures will have to be set up to facilitate the necessary actions, ensuring that the documentation is processed in the right way and at the right time. Let us now see how it all works out in action.

### A turnkey project – Case 1

Perhaps the phrase turnkey requires a little explanation. It describes an arrangement whereby a contractor is responsible for constructing a facility in its entirety, handing over the finished plant ready for work. All the owner then has to do is to 'turn the key'. Such is life that it is the failures that get all the publicity when it comes to plant construction: successes are never heard of. In Chapter 5 we took a look at some very public failures: failures in the sense that they were not built on time or to budget, even though the actual plant or product was a great success from an operational point of view. Let us now look at two successes: two projects that were indeed completed to time, and within budget.

Our first case concerns the construction of a small refinery on a turnkey basis. The contract price was sone £16 million sterling. The UK contractor was responsible for the plant process, plant design, procurement of materials and equipment, civil works, construction and finally commissioning. A banking house provided the finance for the prospective owner.

To give some idea of the financial complexities with which the project team, and the cost engineer in particular, were faced, we give outline details of the financial arrangements below.

| | | | |
|---|---|---|---|
| (a) | UK element | | £14 million |
| (b) | Local element: | | £2 million |
| | Total | | £16 million |
| (c) | Terms of payment to the contractor: | | |
| | | From loan | Direct from owner |
| | UK element | 80% | 20% |
| | Local element | 80% | 20% |
| (d) | Terms of repayment of the Loan: | | |
| | UK element: | | By twelve equal and consecutive half-yearly instalments |
| | Local element | | By ten equal and consecutive half-yearly instalments. |

In addition, part of the contract price was fixed: that is, not subject to any adjustment whatever. The remainder was adjustable, but only through the mechanism of an agreed contract price adjustment formula.

**Meeting the unexpected**

The original estimate breakdown for the refinery is given in Figure 12.4, whilst Figure 12.5 gives details of the construction element within the overall total. Notice that there is no provision for

| Cost Category | Cost in £'000s | |
|---|---:|---:|
| Furnace | 300 | |
| Heat Exchangers | 330 | |
| Compressors | 210 | |
| Pumps | 280 | |
| Other Machinery | 20 | |
| Tanks | 1,500 | |
| Vessels | 500 | |
| Diesel Generators | 200 | |
| Water Treatment Package | 30 | |
| *Total Equipment* | | 3,370 |
| Switchgear | 230 | |
| Motors | 120 | |
| Power Wiring | 110 | |
| Lighting | 90 | |
| Instrument Wiring | 11 | |
| Instruments | 300 | |
| Piping & Valves | 1,000 | |
| Steel Structures | 180 | |
| Catalyst & Chemicals | 210 | |
| Painting | 66 | |
| Insulation | 123 | |
| Fire Fighting | 210 | |
| *Total Bulk Items* | | 2,650 |
| *Total Equipment & Bulks* | | 6,020 |
| Spare Parts | 140 | |
| Site Survey | 15 | |
| Shipping Costs | 900 | |
| Vendors Specialists | 40 | |
| *Total Other Costs* | | 1,095 |
| *Commissioning Costs* | | 200 |
| *Field Construction* (Including Civil Works, Site Camp and Total Site erection of Equipment and Materials) | | 5,000 |
| *Home Office Costs* | | 3,685 |
| *Total Original Estimate* | | £16,000 |

**Figure 12.4 The budget estimate – Case 1**
This is a breakdown of the estimate for the refinery referred to in the text. Fuller detail of the item Field Construction is given in Figure 12.5.

| Category of Work | Cost in £'000s |
|---|---|
| Civil Works & Buildings | 900 |
| Structural Steelwork | 25 |
| Tankage | 200 |
| Erection of Equipment | 100 |
| Piping & Valves | 425 |
| Instrumentation | 110 |
| Electrical | 105 |
| Insulation | 45 |
| Fireproofing | 35 |
| Painting | 40 |
| Scaffolding | 55 |
| Small Tools | 85 |
| Consumables | 130 |
| Fuel | 65 |
| Material Transportation | 150 |
| Material Handling | 60 |
| Site Establishment | 200 |
| Transport of Personnel | 80 |
| Accommodation for Site Staff | 310 |
| Messing — Camp and Hotels | 520 |
| Site Staff — Expatriates & Local | 530 |
| Testing of Welders | 10 |
| Training of Local Welders | 50 |
| Attendance on Commissioning | 30 |
| Medical Facilities (Doctor incl. Staff) | 10 |
| Radiography | 55 |
| Mechanical Plant (Cranes, crawlers, diesel welding sets, tractors, compressors, etc.) | 600 |
| Heat Treatment | 20 |
| Refractories | 15 |
| Misc. Items — Thefts/losses/damages | 40 |
| | 5,000 |

**Figure 12.5 Breakdown of the construction estimate (Case 1)**
The number of separate and distinct items listed illustrates the scope of construction, particularly for an overseas 'green site' project, where no volume of technical skill is available locally.

contingency. This is a competitive situation and the contractor has to put forward his best possible price. The detail in Figure 12.5 gives some indication of the many site construction aspects that have to be considered and evaluated when preparing an estimate for an overseas project on a 'green site'. The detail also highlights the many facets of control that will be required in order to maintain adequate profitability on just one function within the overall complex.

One of the first tasks the design team leaders had to carry out as the project gained momentum and data sheets and flowsheets were being developed was to examine the first preliminary civil engineering designs and the related bills of quantity. The civil engineering aspect is always important, but in this case it was essential to quantify the design at an early stage since arrangements had been made that necessitated the use of local sand and cement. Special permission would have to be obtained were imports found to be necessary. As the project developed it was indeed found that the locally produced cement was somewhat inadequate for foundations where high quality and strength were required, such as the support columns for air coolers and compressors. So, not only had permission to be obtained for the import of some quality cement, but the strength of the concrete being poured had to be constantly checked and closely controlled. Test cube crushing was a regular occurrence. At times, when it was found that the crushing strength at seven days was too low, weak sections of concrete had to be broken out and replaced. Clearly all this put additional strain on the site staff, and led to repercussions in the home office because of the effect on time and cost.

It was during this time that another problem arose which is very often overlooked: the need for effective communication between the site and the home office. It became a bone of contention that the site were not receiving adequate answers to their questions. The distance involved, together with a desire for brevity in telexes and cables, led to misunderstandings and misinterpretation. Although telex and cable costs can mount, such costs are a cheap alternative to lost engineering time and the frustrations caused by inadequate and ineffective communication. It was therefore decided that all communication via cable and telex must be sent in full detail, leaving nothing to chance, or open to misinterpretation.

As work on the project progressed, mechanical construction requirements loomed up. All the constructional plant and buildings were being imported from Europe, and this called for extra effort on the part of the home office to ensure that the key items were continuously expedited. Costly decisions, such as the purchase of larger cranes than really necessary, were made in order to maintain delivery times. The availability and possible use of secondhand construction plant was also investigated in depth. Tankage had been estimated and included in the bid on the basis of erection by local labour, but after investigation by the project team it was decided that it would be better to subcontract the complete tankage package, including erection, to a specialist firm. This saved both time and money.

### Telling the tale

As the various problems were met and overcome they were noted in the monthly report prepared by the project manager, together with statements on progress in engineering, procurement and construction. Another important feature of such a report, and a particular responsibility of the cost engineer, is the financial status of the project, with reasons for the variances from the original estimate. This particular aspect of the report was found to be most useful when framing and formulating forward strategy and reaching policy decisions. A typical report on this particular project is presented as Appendix E. The most important features of the report have been retained and its length is such that we thought it better to relegate it to the end of the book. We hope our readers will nevertheless take the trouble to read it through, since thereby one can get a 'feel' for the way such projects progress. At this stage of the project the related monthly cost report was something like Figure 12.6 and work on the project had reached the stage illustrated by the photograph of part of a construction site given as Figure 12.7. This photograph, however, and the others we give later, are typical only to illustrate progress and have no direct relation to the narrative and the figures we have also discussed.

As mentioned above, it was found essential for the cost engineer to continually monitor the possibility of items overrunning the original cost provisions when making his estimates of final expected total cost. These possible extra costs were presented as an Appendix to the monthly cost report to management. Typical items and the relevant cost figures are given in Figure 12.8.

### The problems still come

Some of the other problems that beset the project team and had to be overcome one by one are listed below. Each one influenced both costs and programme.

MONTHLY COST REPORT – SUMMARY

ALL COSTS IN £'000s

| | Original Estimate | Approved Changes | Revised Estimate | Commitment and Expenditure | Forecast to Complete | Forecast Final Expenditure | Variance This Report | Variance Last Report |
|---|---|---|---|---|---|---|---|---|
| Equipment | 3,370 | 50 | 3,420 | 1,800 | 1,800 | 3,600 | + 180 | + 220 |
| Bulk Items | 2,650 | 20 | 2,670 | 1,200 | 1,350 | 2,550 | – 120 | – 130 |
| Sub-Total | 6,020 | 70 | 6,090 | 3,000 | 3,150 | 6,150 | + 60 | + 90 |
| Other Costs | 1,095 | 10 | 1,105 | 550 | 650 | 1,200 | + 95 | + 100 |
| Commissioning | 200 | – | 200 | 20 | 150 | 170 | – 30 | – 30 |
| Field Construction | 5,000 | 20 | 5,020 | 2,000 | 3,200 | 5,200 | + 180 | + 170 |
| Home Office | 3,685 | 10 | 3,695 | 2,500 | 1,200 | 3,700 | + 5 | + 5 |
| TOTAL | 16,000 | 110 | 16,110 | 8,070 | 8,350 | 16,420 | + 310 | + 335 |
| Forecast of Residual value of Construction Plant and Equipment after taking Shipping and other costs into Account | – | – | – | – | – 250 | – 250 | – 250 | – 250 |
| | | | | | 8,100 | 16,170 | + 60 | + 85 |

**Figure 12.6 Monthly cost report – Case 1**
This summary report shows the progress being made against the total project cost as first estimated.

**Figure 12.7 Placing concrete foundations**
Pouring foundations for equipment on a remote site (Photograph reproduced by kind permission of Humphreys & Glasgow Limited, London.)

1 Irregular power supply causing construction delays, especially in the welding of fabricated pipework, tanks and vessels. It became necessary to provide extra diesel welding sets and a large diesel generator for electric power on the site. Home office had to procure and airfreight the necessary equipment urgently.

2 The local fresh water supply eventually proved inadequate and a special large water storage tank had to be installed and filled each night. Rationing was necessary during periods of high demand.

3 Halfway through the construction period skilled labour became unavailable. So extra local nationals had to be recruited and trained. They were indeed 'raw recruits' so great pressure was put on the instructors.

POSSIBLE EXTRA CONTINGENCY ITEMS

| | £ |
|---|---|
| 1. SHIPPING<br>Possible additional shipping costs due to the<br>requirement of special charter — lack of lines<br>visiting the local port: | 50,000 |
| 2. SITE STAFFING<br>Additional turnover of site staff and also<br>possible further increase in overseas salaries<br>and allowances. | 50,000 |
| 3. MATERIALS<br>Loss on surplus piping materials. | 100,000 |
| 4. LOCAL LABOUR<br>Additional local labour required, travel<br>problems and costs not foreseen. | 75,000 |
| 5. PROGRAMME<br>Possible further extension by two months<br>or to be offset by uneconomical working. | 250,000 |
| TOTAL: | £525,000 |

Cover this month = £500,000

Last month's estimate = £450,000

PROBABILITY 90%.

**Figure 12.8 Contingency items**
This statement, prepared by the cost engineer, is part of the project manager's report to his management, since theirs is the risk. The owner pays no extra unless any item can be contractually demonstrated to be his responsibility.

4  Transport from the nearest town deteriorated and it became essential to request the government to instruct the railway officials to stop trains adjacent to the site – there was no local station! This was the only way local labour could reach the site at that time.

5  Turnover of site staff, especially expatriates, became excessive in the later period of construction. This had a major impact on both morale and costs. A high turnover of key personnel on any project is bad, and on an overseas project it can lead to serious delays.

6  Approaches from local contractors made it apparent that they

were anxious to obtain the latest in European construction plant and equipment at advantageous prices. The site cost engineer put residual values on this equipment, and the project manager was able to dispose of it locally. This offset overruns in other areas.

All these and many more and varied problems had impact on both site and home office manhours, which means costs, in addition to the direct impact on material and construction costs. Meanwhile, the plant was steadily growing: a further stage in construction progress is illustrated in Figure 12.9.

As will be seen, not all the incidents mentioned worked to the disadvantage of the project, but constant monitoring was essential, together with the allocation of responsibility and consequent costs to the correct source. It must always be remembered that all these extras, however minor, have to paid for by someone – owner, contractor or vendor, or perhaps a combination of all three. It is therefore most important in any cost control system to be able to identify and allocate responsibility both rapidly and accurately. However, good management is said to include a degree of anticipation. Certainly, some of the problems met were anticipated, and did occur, and costs were minimised thereby, but others took the project team completely by surprise. That led to unnecessary overruns and considerable extra effort had to be made in other areas to keep costs within budget. Nevertheless, the plant was completed on time. Figure 12.10 illustrates such a completed plant, in all its complexity.

## Meeting inflation – Case 2

Our second case history relates to the expansion of a fertiliser complex, where the contract was placed in 1974 for a sum of the order of £15 million sterling. So the amount of money involved was about the same as for Case 1, but that is where the similarity begins – and ends!

Since the contract was signed in 1974, the contract had to be executed during a period of unprecedented cost escalation in the United Kingdom. It was not unusual at that time to see process plant costs rising at a rate of 2.5 per cent per month: that is, doubling in cost within two years. The UK Retail Price Index hit an all time high, in rate of increase, of 26.9 per cent per annum, in August 1975. This factor, the abnormal increase in costs, put more than normal pressure upon the project manager and his team. In an

**Figure 12.9 Lifting equipment**
Getting ready for a heavy lift. (Photograph reproduced by kind permission of Humphreys & Glasgow Limited, London.)

**Figure 12.10 The completed installation**

Figures 12.7 and 12.9 showed construction work in progress. Now we have a general view of a completed plant. Warehouse buildings are in the foreground, distillation columns tower against the skyline in the background. (Photograph reproduced by kind permission of Humphreys & Glasgow Limited, London.)

endeavour to combat the impact of impending inflation – there was a degree of anticipation – the contract had been negotiated on the basis that part of the price would be fixed (not subject to escalation), part firm (with a price adjustment formula) and part reimbursable (the owner paying the actual costs). This complexity added to the difficulties of the project team because in effect they were running three different projects, embodying a degree of conflict of interest, all at the same time. Undoubtedly these conflicts of interest and the other interactions within the project were far above the 'norm' for a contract of this sort. Further, there was a sting in the tail: a penalty clause came into force if the contractor failed to meet the delivery date in its entirety.

An additional problem, and one that steadily worsened, was that of exchange rates. Provision had been made in the contract for material purchases to be made in Germany, France and Italy up to specified maximum levels, and now we had to face rapid fluctuation in exchange rates as well as soaring inflation in the UK. The problem was further accentuated by the fact that a high proportion, much higher than usual, of the total cost was in equipment purchased from these European sources. The size of the problem is perhaps best seen by studying Figure 12.11, and comparing this breakdown with that given for Case 1 (Figure 12.4).

It will be appreciated that such contractual conditions, with the accompanying restraints, puts the project team as a whole 'on its mettle', and makes great demands on their reserves of tact and patience. Certainly dynamic project management was required at all times. This was one project, above all, that called for 'TLC' – *tender, loving care!*

This project got it! Right at the outset the usual contract conditions and the inbuilt conflicts of interest were explained in such a manner that no-one on the project was in any doubt at all which portion was fixed, which firm and which reimbursable, and the impact of this on relations with the owner, suppliers and the contractor's own staff. This simple, but important step contributed greatly to full cooperation and understanding by all concerned, at every level in the organisation.

As the project developed, the anticipated difficulties in defining lines of demarcation between the three cost elements referred to above became more and more pronounced. It was not too difficult to establish the necessary division with equipment, but it was a very different story with the bulk purchases. Numerous detailed discussions and negotiations with the owner had to take place in order to clarify the position with his agreement. In turn, suppliers had to be instructed to separate costs they normally treated as one,

| ESTIMATE SUMMARY | | |
| --- | --- | --- |
| ALL COSTS IN £'000s | | |
| Description | £'000s | £'000s |
| Heaters | 500 | |
| Furnace | 2,300 | |
| Heat Exchangers | 1,800 | |
| Machinery, Compressors | 1,600 | |
| Pumps | 350 | |
| Turbines, Fans | 1,500 | |
| Tanks | 25 | |
| Vessels | 1,650 | |
| Stacks | 20 | |
| Sub-Total Equipment | | 9,745 |
| Electrical | 120 | |
| Instruments | 500 | |
| Piping & valves | 1,100 | |
| Structural Steel etc. | 400 | |
| Insulation & Paint | 135 | |
| Sub-Total Bulks | | 2,255 |
| Total Materials | | 12,000 |
| Home Office Costs | | 3,000 |
| TOTAL: | | 15,000 |

**Figure 12.11 Estimate summary – Case 2**
It will be seen that this estimate is very different to that for Case 1 (Figure 12.4).
Equipment is now more than 60% of the total estimated cost, instead of some 20%.

so that the contractual arrangements could be complied with. Once again, a multitude of problems for both project team and procurement staff.

It became apparent that as costs were rising so rapidly, time was of the essence. Early process and engineering definition was of paramount importance. This was achieved in certain areas and as a result not only were economies secured in design, but also currency movements on the Continent were used to advantage with respect to purchases there. This was really *cost control in action*! Another area where cost control was seen to be really effective was in the design and procurement of the major machinery. Costs had originally been estimated on the basis of preliminary discussions with the appropriate vendors. Immediately the contract was signed, firm negotiations with those vendors were set in motion and pursued with vigour until the final design work was complete. This allowed fixed price contracts to be placed well ahead of the time such contracts are normally placed, with consequent savings in forward escalation.

## We are fighting a battle

As in all projects not everything ran smoothly, or was a success story. There *were* delays, things went wrong, some of the original conceptual engineering proved to be weak in certain areas and changes had to be made. As we have said already, cost escalation in the process plant industry was excessive in the UK during 1975 and suppliers were loath to give firm prices for more than three months ahead, let alone fixed prices. Constant monitoring of price movements was absolutely essential, and the checking of suppliers' claims, based on price adjustment formulae, with the subsequent negotiations, grew into yet another time consuming and costly activity. This processing of escalation claims applied, of course, to both the UK and the European suppliers and everyone became vividly aware of the great differences in rates of escalation, and the attitudes in relation to this adopted in the various countries involved in supplying plant and equipment.

The situation that developed in relation to the major cost item, materials, is well illustrated by an abstract from a typical cost control report made at this time. You will find it as Figure 12.12. This report brings out most clearly the cost variances that had to be faced at that time. The variance *was* being reduced: that is something else that comes out of the report. This was achieved, largely, by successful negotiation of claims for changes in the contract price, based on the relevant clause in the agreement. All in all, this was also a very enlightening and educative period for the owner, since he had to be confronted with the consequences of this drastic inflation. The problems and claims had to be brought to him for his approval.

Yet once again we stress the importance of the continuing prediction and control of the cash flow on the project. With this particular project it was absolutely essential to maintain day to day knowledge of price movements and their effect upon project cost. This enabled the effect of exchange rate fluctuations, the increasing impact of the high rate of escalation in the UK, and the general

## COST REPORT SUMMARY – MATERIALS ONLY
### ALL COSTS IN £'000s

| | Original Estimate | Approved Changes | Revised Estimate | Commitment & Expenditure | Forecast to Complete | Forecast Final Expenditure | Variance this Report | Variance last Report |
|---|---|---|---|---|---|---|---|---|
| Heaters | 500 | 20 | 520 | 550 | 30 | 580 | + 60 | + 60 |
| Furnace | 2,300 | 100 | 2,400 | 2,300 | 100 | 2,400 | – | + 50 |
| Heat Exchangers | 1,800 | 50 | 1,850 | 1,800 | 70 | 1,870 | + 20 | + 20 |
| Machinery | 1,600 | 55 | 1,655 | 1,700 | 20 | 1,720 | + 65 | + 85 |
| Pumps | 350 | 10 | 360 | 380 | 10 | 390 | + 30 | + 30 |
| Turbines, Fans | 1,500 | 40 | 1,540 | 1,600 | 20 | 1,620 | + 80 | + 80 |
| Tanks | 25 | – | 25 | 35 | – | 35 | + 10 | + 10 |
| Vessels | 1,650 | 90 | 1,740 | 1,850 | – | 1,850 | + 110 | + 150 |
| Stacks | 20 | – | 20 | 25 | – | 25 | + 5 | + 5 |
| SUB–TOTAL | 9,745 | 365 | 10,110 | 10,240 | 250 | 10,490 | + 380 | + 490 |
| Electrical | 120 | 10 | 130 | 150 | 10 | 160 | + 30 | + 50 |
| Instruments | 500 | 15 | 515 | 510 | 20 | 530 | + 15 | + 15 |
| Piping & Valves | 1,100 | 85 | 1,185 | 1,350 | 50 | 1,400 | + 215 | + 250 |
| Structural Steel | 400 | 20 | 420 | 450 | 30 | 480 | + 60 | + 60 |
| Insulation & Paint | 135 | 15 | 150 | 180 | 20 | 200 | + 50 | + 50 |
| TOTAL MATERIALS | 12,000 | 510 | 12,510 | 12,880 | 380 | 13,260 | + 750 | + 915 |

**Figure 12.12 Cost control report – Case 2**
We are approaching completion and face a loss, unless the various claims being made to the owner can be substantiated.

overall hardening of the market, to be evaluated, and its ultimate effect on project cost forecast with a high degree of reliability. Certainly this made quick decisions not only possible but effective. The project manager could have confidence in the knowledge that the information he was basing his decisions upon was as up-to-date and as accurate as was possible.


## Conclusion

Our presentation of these two very different case histories has tended to emphasise the difficulties that were encountered and we make no apology for this. It is the difficulties that make this work – project management – so interesting and so full of challenge. Perhaps the most outstanding quality of any good engineer – project manager in our particular case – is his ability to get himself in *and* out of trouble *at no extra cost to his employers*. We hope that we have demonstrated that it is indeed possible to complete projects on time, and within the estimated cost, despite the impact of the unknown and the unexpected. But there has to be a degree of anticipation. With our first case, in illustration of this, it was appreciated that the civil works would be a sensitive area and special attention was paid to this from the start. This allowed the problems that arose to be resolved in good time, so that the project did not suffer. Anticipation prevented delay. Our second case demonstrates that properly worded contracts are another key to success. Although the drastic upsurge in costs was entirely unexpected, properly drawn escalation clauses protected the contractor to a material extent. Anticipation prevented the problem getting out of hand. Of course, in that instance the owner had to pay, but his circumstances are very different to those of the contractor. Whilst the owner has to face the cost of inflation on his capital investment, at the same time all his other costs, *and* his selling prices, are keeping more or less in step, so ostensibly he is no worse off.

# 13    Projects come in all sizes

There is really no limit, either lower or upper, to the size of process plant projects. A plant can be built for as little as £50,000, whilst at the same time a US$16 billion hydroelectric power plant is built in Canada. However, the normal project will range in size, when expressed in monetary terms, between £1 million and £200 million, and it is across this range that the cost control techniques discussed in this book are particularly applicable. However, the size of a project does very little to change the approach to project cost control: a point that we, with purpose, have emphasised time and again in this book. That installation in Canada, known as the 'James Bay Complex', has been built over the years 1972 to 1985 and was built to plan and within budget. The project management techniques employed on the project have been well publicised. As a result we know that the pre-award phase was considered to be of prime importance in terms of project cost control and scheduling, but that in spite of its magnitude and complexity those involved in the project *knew where they were going*! This has been ascribed to the excellent leadership of a competent project team using straightforward control systems.

## Size is a relative term

Yesterday's large project is today's medium project, and is quite likely to be tomorrow's small project. The time scale seems to be roughly: one day equals ten years. The Humber Refinery contract, to which we referred in some detail in Chapter 5, valued at £25 million, was called a very large project: the year, 1968. A project of this size today, in money terms, would never merit that description. Thanks to inflation the cost of process plants increases with time, and the cost increase can well be two or fourfold in ten years, depending upon the country we are looking at. The inflation rate over the years is, of course, different from country to country, being dictated by the economic conditions of each country, the money supply, and numerous other factors. This factor of from two to four over ten years may be considered to be quite normal. There are, however, countries with what is called hyper-inflation. We see some examples of this in Latin America, and there the inflation factor over ten years will range from four to ten.

INFLATION INDEX

| Year | Australia | Canada | France | West Germany | Spain | Israel | India | UK | USA |
|------|-----------|--------|--------|--------------|-------|--------|-------|-----|-----|
| 1975 | 106 | 103 | 104 | 100 | 105 | 106 | 100 | 109 | 99 |
| 1976 | 121 | 105 | 119 | 109 | 130 | 141 | 97 | 129 | 105 |
| 1977 | 131 | 128 | 132 | 111 | 158 | 204 | 104 | 139 | 114 |
| 1978 | 144 | 138 | 150 | 117 | 190 | 342 | 103 | 160 | 126 |
| 1979 | 156 | 156 | 166 | 122 | 230 | 634 | 118 | 177 | 138 |
| 1980 | 175 | 176 | 185 | 130 | 277 | 1470 | 143 | 202 | 151 |
| 1981 | 190 | 191 | 211 | 136 | 340 | 3469 | 156 | 216 | 167 |
| 1982 | 212 | 207 | 251 | 147 | 389 | 7887 | 155 | 232 | 177 |
| 1983 | 233 | 214 | 265 | 145 | 448 | – | 166 | 245 | 184 |
| 1984 | 258 | 279 | 302 | 158 | 535 | – | 188 | 255 | 188 |

**Figure 13.1 Process plant inflation index**
These indices for a range of countries illustrate the way in which inflation varies. Israel has been included as an illustration of hyper-inflation. The figures there for 1983/84 are available, but they are meaningless (20,000, then 100,000). All the indices are based on 1975 (first quarter) equals 100 and the yearly average is given. It should be remembered that, although the index for each country begins with a value of 100, the costs in the several countries were not then the same in absolute terms, so further adjustment is necessary: in particular, fluctuations in the rates of exchange have also to be taken into account. (With acknowledgements to *Process Economics International*.)

As an illustration of the way in which inflation affects process plants in particular, Figure 13.1 gives the PEI (Process Economics International) plant cost index for eight selected countries for the past ten years, on the basis 1975 = 100. It will be seen that by 1984 the index is a low of 158 for West Germany, against a high of 535 for Spain. Thus a process plant costing £100 million in 1975 would today cost approximately £170 million in West Germany or the USA, but £500 million in Spain. All this is in round numbers, but that is about as accurate as these indices are anyway. So we see that size, when measured in money, is tempered by time.

## Small is beautiful

Inflation is one of two major factors causing the monetary investment in process plants to grow, as compared with yesteryear. The other major factor is that of plant capacity. The capacity of the individual process plant units has also been increasing steadily over the years. This is because of a desire to reap the benefits of what is called 'economy of scale'. This means that the larger the plant, the cheaper the capital investment per unit of production.

There is an empirical law, of great value to estimators, which says that:

$$\text{Cost} \propto (\text{Capacity})^n$$

where 'n' is the 'economy of scale' factor. This factor can vary from 0.4 to 1.4, but lies more usually in the region between 0.5 and 1.0. A factor of 1.0 means, in effect, that there is no economy of scale. This happens when the process unit cannot be increased in size, but has to be duplicated, as for example happens with caustic soda/chlorine plants. However, cost analysis over the years has led to the conclusion that for process plants in general this factor lies between 0.6 and 0.7 and the relationship has become known as 'the six-tenths rule'. This rule means that doubling the capacity of a process plant results in the capital investment increasing by only 50 per cent, instead of doubling as well. This *is* the economy of scale and, as you will see, it is quite substantial. We must issue the warning that this exponent 'n' is not necessarily a continuous function, because the size of individual items of equipment incorporated in such plants often goes up in 'steps', because of the limitations of design, standardisation and other considerations. This occurs particularly in the case of proprietary equipment.

Theoretically there is no upper limit on the way the size of a plant can be increased to gain this benefit of economy of scale. As a result many, if not most process plants have been getting steadily bigger and bigger. Whilst the reduction in investment cost per unit of production creates this pressure to increase size, technological considerations often play a decisive role. For example, in the case of ammonia plants, the introduction of the centrifugal compressor had a revolutionary effect on the possible size of such plants. The end result of this was that despite inflation the selling price of ammonia has been maintained at the about the same level for several decades now. The cost of operation has climbed, but not the cost of the end product.

We have said that theoretically there is no upper limit on the size of a process plant, but in practice, of course, there is. We have already mentioned one: the inability to build certain items of equipment still larger. There the problem was solved by the development of an entirely different type of equipment to do the same thing, but there are other, and more intractable problems. There is, for instance, the fact that even centrifugal compressors have size limitations, that items above a certain size cannot be transported. If they come in pieces, then complicated operations, such as stress relieving, may have to be performed at site, rather than in the factory. There is the further constraint, particularly in developing countries, of purchasing ability, occasioned by the limited market and scarce capital resources. However, at any moment in time there is an optimum size for any particular plant, and this aspect has been thoroughly analysed (1). It has been found that the cost-capacity curve is rather flat in the region of the optimum capacity, indicating that the influence on production cost of choice in capacity is rather small in this area. For instance, a 20 per cent move away from the optimum size brings a change of but 1–3 per cent in the capital investment, and the effect of this on production cost will be marginal. The extra capital cost, perhaps some 5–10 per cent, per unit of production, incurred by installing a plant half the optimum size may well be considered as an insurance premium: a protection against loss if the market demand does not increase at the rate originally forecast – and it very often does not! It can also be considered as an insurance against obsolescence. Certainly such a premium is small enough to be fairly readily justified. There is no virtue in size as such. Indeed, as we follow this story through, you may well come to agree with us that small is indeed beautiful.

Let us look at another aspect, because the capital cost of a plant is only half the story. The other half, and perhaps the 'better half', is the cost of raw materials and the cost of operation. The relative magnitude of these two halves, in their influence on product cost, varies quite considerably. However, on the basis of a certain assumed weighting, the influence of the three factors we have mentioned, capital cost, raw materials and operating cost, can be calculated as demonstrated in Figure 13.2. Thus, if the weighting we have adopted – 70:15:15 – is anywhere near realistic, the low exponent means that large changes in capital investment have a minimal effect on product cost. This is a theoretical approach, but it can be demonstrated as a practical reality by considering the price of urea in various different contexts. Look, for instance, at the data given in Figure 13.3. Here we have a ten-fold increase in capacity of the manufacturing plant, but the final product cost to the end user,

| COST COMPONENT | EXPONENT | WEIGHTING |
|---|---|---|
| Raw materials | $n = 0$ | 70% |
| Capital charge | $n = 0.6$ | 15% |
| Labour & utilities | $n = 0.25$ | 15% |

Hence:

Average exponent $= 0.13$

Then: If plant capacity x 10

Reduction in production cost $= (10)^{0.13} = 1.34$

That is: Production cost is still 75% of the previous production cost, despite a capacity increase of ten times.

**Figure 13.2 Production cost versus capacity**
This calculation shows the relatively small reduction in production cost achieved by a vast increase in capacity.

the farmer, remains substantially the same. The concentration of production in one location adds substantially, for instance, to distribution cost, and so the benefit of a low production cost is dissipated.

Now we have two factors, both working in the same direction. A typical production cost *versus* production volume graph has been published and we reproduce its shape in Figure 13.4 because it is the shape that is significant (2). Notice the broad, flat region around the optimum, showing how insensitive product cost is to change in this area. This confirms our earlier conclusion that, keeping in mind the uncertainties of market demand and the certainty of technical obsolescence, a smaller plant has many advantages, even though it is more expensive in terms of the capital investment per unit of production.

In the developing countries in particular there are additional considerations such as the influence of distribution and transport costs on a bulky and cheap product such as urea. Such an infrastructure may well be non-existent and as a result the cost could be quite substantial. A study by an Italian plant supplier led to the suggestion that developing countries could well do much better by setting up a number of small plants for such a product (100 to 200 tons per day) rather than one large plant, with a capacity of say 1,000 to 2,000 tons per day, as is the practice in the West. Look at Figure 13.3 once again, because this data reflects precisely such a difference in approach. The two sizes considered there are 150 and 1,500 tons per day, a difference in scale of ten times.

| PRODUCTION COST – UREA | | | | |
|---|---|---|---|---|
| | DEVELOPED COUNTRY | | DEVELOPING COUNTRY | |
| | $/ton | $/ton | $/ton | $/ton |
| Depreciation: | 42 | 32 | 50 | 48 |
| Fixed costs (1): | 92 | 69 | 96 | 85 |
| Variable costs (2): | 58 | 58 | 24 | 24 |
| Production cost: | 150 | 127 | 120 | 109 |
| Distribution cost: | 8 | 30 | 15 | 40 |
| TOTAL COST (3): | 158 | 157 | 135 | 149 |
| Plant capacity:* | 150 | 1500 | 150 | 1500 |

(1)  This includes depreciation interest, labour, maintenance overheads and insurance.
(2)  This is the cost of natural gas, chemicals and bags, in particular.
(3)  This is the final cost to the farmer.

*Expressed as tonnes per day of urea.

Source: ECN – 1978.

**Figure 13.3 Production cost of urea**
This table illustrates that a ten-fold increase in capacity may well have but a marginal influence in reducing the cost to the ultimate user.

Production costs are based on natural gas as a raw material. The figures do not refer to any specific country, but they would be typical of one of the oil producing countries, with large volumes of cheap natural gas readily available. The price of the gas is therefore assumed to be one-third of that prevailing in a developed country. The production cost from the larger plant is only 15 per cent lower than that for the small plant in the developed country, and the difference is even less for the developing country, some ten per cent. When the costs of distribution are taken into account, making certain assumptions with respect to logistics, this initial cost advantage practically disappears in the case of the developed country. For the developing country the situation is reversed: cost to the farmer is some ten per cent *cheaper* if small plants are built. Small is indeed beautiful.

We have dwelt on the problem of small scale process plants here at some length for two reasons. Firstly, the bulk of future expansion

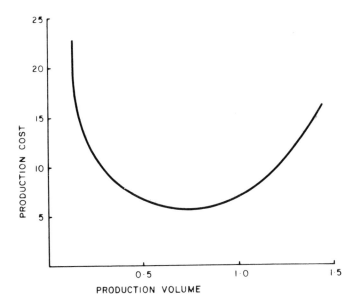

**Figure 13.4 Production cost versus production volume**
This curve, typical only, illustrates the relationship between production cost and
production volume.

in fertiliser capacity will in all likelihood take place in the
developing countries, who therefore have to learn not to ape the
West, but to think first. Secondly, cost consciousness and therefore
the importance of cost control has yet to be appreciated in these
countries. This is a point well illustrated by the examples from the
fertiliser industry in India that we gave in Chapter 5. We have
already said that cost control is no different, and no less important,
on a small project, as compared with a large project. But there *is* a
benefit. Mistakes will be smaller in their effect, so the small plant
provides a better and cheaper training ground: yet another
advantage in countries where they have a long way to go with
respect to project cost control.


## Some typical projects

What *is* a typical process plant? There is none. We pointed out right
at the beginning, in Chapter 1, that in general process plants are
tailor made and almost invariably one off. No two projects are

identical. If they were for precisely the same duty, for the same company, they would be built on two different sites, and that would immediately give rise to differences in design.

Perhaps the diversity of plant and project with which the project manager and his team may have to cope, and the project cost engineer watch over, is best illustrated by taking a few rather extreme examples. As we have already seen such plants can be built onshore or offshore, and back in Chapter 1 we gave a notable example of an offshore project – the Brae 'A' platform in the North Sea. But similar projects to that are being constructed all over the world: the North Sea is singled out here because the conditions there are rather severe. But we can also meet severe conditions of another sort if we built in the Arctic or at the Equator. We also come to learn, as we travel the world looking at projects, that without effective transport no project can succeed. Transport is needed to get both men and materials to the project site. Transport is needed to get men and materials around the site. Projects built in the open sea demand a helicopter service to ferry the people working on the project to and fro. A project built on the Falkland Islands resulted in a ferry service from Cape Town to the Islands once a fortnight for the same purpose whilst the project was under construction. When one looks at the problem of bringing materials to a remote site, the situation is further complicated by the desire to reduce the number of people working at site to a minimum. This has resulted in larger and ever larger prefabricated constructions, usually called modules, that sometimes have to be transported half across the world. But it is no use building bigger and ever bigger modules unless the means of getting them to site are also there. So the project team has to look beyond the flowsheets to take account of the logistics: the route to the site and the available transport facilities.

The Dutch, a seafaring nation, were pre-eminent for a great many years on the high seas with their seagoing tugs, but the importance of maritime towing has now declined, insofar as the *towing* of large objects is concerned. Instead there are a variety of specialised purpose-built vessels: dock vessels, self-propelled pontoons and heavy-lift module carriers. To illustrate the present sophistication in this area, the latest heavy-lift vessel operated by the Dutch company Mammoet Transport is capable of transporting a 2,000-tonne module across the world. Details of its size and capacity are presented in Figure 13.5. You will see that it has container capacity and this is a novel feature that would contribute much to its operating economy. One of the problems of transporting anything from one place to another is the 'return load' and here

### M.V. 'HAPPY BUCCANEER'

| | |
|---|---|
| Length o.a. | 145.86m |
| Length p.p. | 135.80m |
| Breadth | 28.30m |
| Depth | 14.80m |
| Draught open | 7.02m : Deadweight 9,493 tons |
| Draught closed | 8.22m : Deadweight 13,740 tons |
| Gross tonnage | 16,341 tons |
| Net tonnage | 4,902 tons |
| Service speed | 14.6 knots (Trial speed 16.6 knots) |
| Engines | 2 × 5, 220HP (Hitachi Zosen Sulzer 6ZAL40) |
| Bow-thruster | 1,200HP |
| Lifting capacity | 1,100 tons (2 × 550 tons) |
| Aux. hoist | 2 × 25 tons (Trolley type) |
| Ro/Ro capacity | 2,500 tons (Ramp length 7.5m, width 20m) |
| Lower hold | 68.88m (L) × 20.6m (W) × 5.4m (H) |
| Tweendeck | 112.56m (L) × 20.6m (W) × 5.4m (H) |
| Deck | 112.0m (L) × 24.0m (W) |
| Bale capacity | 19,908 cbm |
| Container capacity | 1050 TEUS or 508 FEUS + 34 TEUS |

**Figure 13.5 Specification – *The Happy Buccaneer***
The above table details the principal particulars of this twin screw heavy-lift Ro/Ro vessel. (Data provided by Mammoet Shipping BV, Amsterdam.)

there is a neat solution to that difficulty. Let us see how this transport is used.

Typical of the way in which modern transport facilities unite with modular design to make yet another successful project is the provision of a seawater treatment plant that represented a series of 'firsts' in relation to Arctic oil production. The plant was a single huge barge-mounted facility that arrived at Alaska's North Slope during the brief summer sea-lift – the only time when Prudhoe Bay is free of ice. This is the 'weather window', the impact of which we discussed in some detail in Chapter 5 (the section on Productivity). We tell you the details so that you can see the wide range of considerations that the project manager and his team had to take into account.

This plant was the largest piece of equipment ever transported to the Prudhoe Bay oilfield. It is also the largest seawater plant in the United States and the first offshore plant to operate in the Arctic – the barge was berthed in Beaufort Sea and the plant then piped up. The 26,000 ton, 610-foot long plant will treat two million barrels of seawater a day, which will then be pumped into the oil reservoir to 'waterflood' the formation and maintain its pressure. The plant was assembled at the huge Opko, Korea, shipyard of Daewoo Shipbuilding & Heavy Machinery Limited. The location of the shipyard was determined in part by the fact that, at 150 feet wide, the barge was too wide to go through the Panama canal.

This plant is however but one of many examples of the modular approach to plant design and construction and the keys to success with this type of project implementation are said to be:

Think modular from the start
Select the module fabricators early
Enquiries to module fabricators should include dimensions, weight and applicable codes.
Make no compromise in plant design from a process viewpoint
Assess the 'trade-off' between module dimensions and weight

There is no doubt that the plants of the future will tend more and more to be a series of modules and project engineers will have to be well aware of the impact of this approach on process plant design.

### A dairy on the permafrost

Major modules are not always the answer. It all depends on location. Finn-Stroi Limited of Helsinki secured the contract for the design and construction of the Norilsk Dairy Project. Norilsk is located in the USSR in Siberia, north of the Arctic Circle, in a region of permafrost, some 3000 km east of Moscow. The weather conditions are severe, with winter nine months long and temperatures down to $-50°$. The discovery of large nickel and copper deposits in 1922 led to the founding of the Norilsk mining complex and Norilsk is currently a town of some 250,000 inhabitants. Finn-Stroi had the job of building a dairy to serve the entire city: a project worth some US$35 million. Because of Norilsk's location fresh milk is not available in sufficient quantity, so that the milk products from the dairy are based on milk powder reconstitution. The reconstitution department produces some 25,000 litres per hour of milk, and the factory produces not only milk but a range of milk products, such as kefir, ryashenka, sour cream, quark, mayonnaise and ice cream. The project was completed in thirty-four months, including startup trials and the training of the operators.

Having pictured the project, what is of interest is the way in which the plant was built. Careful planning, once again, was at the heart of successful project completion. Because of the location prefabrication in Finland was used to the maximum extent possible, but size had to be carefully watched because of the means of transport that had to be used. The prefabrications had to be shipped from Helsinki via Murmansk across the Arctic Ocean to the port of Dudinka, and then by train to Norilsk and everything needed had to be contained in three shipments at the appropriate time of year. A sizeable problem in logistics, but the challenge was met and the project has been a success.


## The Ok Tedi project

Mention of this project allows us to present you with a great contrast to the previous two projects, both of which were built on the Arctic Circle and used the modular approach to minimise work on site. There is no doubt that the Ok Tedi project ranks as one of the most ambitious projects ever undertaken in the mining industry and the greatest challenge was getting to the site. Mount Fubilan, in the heart of Papua New Guinea, has steep slopes. Absolutely everything required had to be shipped to the site from suppliers spanning the world.

Ok Tedi Mining Limited is owned by a consortium of mining interests and a joint venture was formed by Bechtel Civil and Minerals Inc. and Morrison-Knudsen International to provide the design engineering, procurement and construction services required to implement the project. The materials and supplies entered Papua New Guinea at Port Moresby. At that port the materials were transferred to barges and shipped some 500 km across the gulf to the mouth of Fly River, a further 800 km up that river to the town of Kiunga and finally another 160 km up a steep mountain road to the construction site. With the previous two projects reviewed, prefabrication was maximised: here the reverse was the case. The grinding mill was probably the most important item of equipment, the heart of the process. That came from Canada. But because of its size and weight, over 200 tonnes and some 10 metres in diameter, it had to be shipped in pieces and hauled in special multi-wheel trailers.

Just to let you see the spirit in which the project was carried out, we finish this series of examples with a quotation from the contractor's project manager (3):

> This was a project that you like to tell people you worked on. It was a mega-project, a one-of-its-kind challenge, something that provided much more than a new mining complex. There's a tremendous amount of satisfaction when you complete something that seems so difficult. It's just a hell-of-a good feeling for all of us to see this job come together knowing what was accomplished to get it there.

Yes, the projects we have chosen to illustrate the sort of thing the project team may well have to cope with at some time or another are special, but it is a true saying that 'the exception proves the rule'. Most projects will not make the same extreme demands on the project manager and his team, but all projects should be approached with the same resolution and determination.

## Billion dollar projects

We have already commented earlier in this chapter on the fact that (a) inflation and (b) economy of scale result in process plants being built and planned that require ever greater investment from year to year. This process has accelerated to the extent that a number of projects have now reached or crossed the 'billion dollar' (US $1,000,000,000) frontier. Whilst it is true that such projects can have problems all their own, much can be accomplished in terms of mitigating the impact of size by breaking down the whole into recognisable, assessable and manageable units, or 'projects'. The Sasol Two and Sasol Three Synfuel plants now built and in successful operation near Johannesburg in the Republic of South Africa cost in total some US$7 billion. But the total plant area of some 15 square kilometres (15,000 hectares) was divided into some 120 areas, each area being treated as a project, with its own estimate and critical path network (4). From then on the project teams were using standard procedures with which they were completely familiar, applied to a project size with which they were also familiar. We call this 'project decentralisation'.

It is so easy, with such vast numbers of people involved, for the right hand not to know what the left hand is doing. Decentralisation passes detailed control down to a level where a good overview of the work in the 'unit', 'area' or 'section' (all these words are used) is possible and practicable. The work to be done is scaled down to human proportions. Those involved in the project then have short-term goals, can see the completion of an assignment and get recognition for a job well done.

If this type of project subdivision is not carried out, the inertia within the organisation will be such that movement forward becomes almost impossible. The same is very true of management in general and the words of Alfred P. Sloan, Jr, the former head of General Motors are very relevant (5):

> In practically all of our activities we seem to suffer from the inertia resulting from great size ... Sometimes I must be forced to the conclusion that General

Motors is so large, its inertia so great, that it is impossible for us to be real leaders.

The lesson for the project manager is that with major projects he *must* delegate and decentralise. Nevertheless he and his key team members must have an overview of the entire project or projects, otherwise the 'right hand' may never know what the 'left hand' is doing.

The cost control engineer will no longer be one man, or even an office with a small team, but a number of separate offices, each with a group of units to watch over.

We have said more than once – it is a habit with us to repeat ourselves to drive a lesson home – we have said, then, that cost control is no different in principle with large projects, as compared with small. The philosophy, the basic practices and procedures, the techniques, will be identical in either case. Very large projects have bigger stakes, are more complex, involve the monitoring of a much larger number of contractors and subcontractors, and the total labour force may well run into six figures. Such size can, and will, create problems of its own. Cost control, in such cases, will have to be decentralised and yet there must still be *one* central authority who can 'feel the pulse' of the entire group of projects, in order to see that the very large number of pieces of this giant 'jigsaw' each fall into their proper place, slowly building up the total picture – the billion dollar project. To the extent that this does *not* happen, money will be wasted and time will be lost.

## Developing countries have additional problems

Project execution to time and within budget is a difficult task anywhere and at any time, no matter what the size of the project. We have not attempted here, nor will we ever attempt, to pretend that it is easy. Keeping it simple is not making it easy: that but makes it *effective*. In earlier chapters we have likened the task of project management, quite appropriately we feel, to:

1   Climbing a mountain peak
2   Fighting a battle

and we have likened the role of project manager to that of:

1   Captain of a ship or airplane
2   Conductor of an orchestra

These simple parallels should be graphic enough to give an

indication of the type and magnitude of the problems that are going to be encountered in project execution. There is absolutely no substitute for:

1 Meticulous planning
2 Starting cost control right at the beginning – before design begins
3 Watching the trends and early warning signals
4 Acting promptly to keep the project on an 'even keel'

To sum it all up: not an easy task anywhere, at any time. The last of the actions mentioned above is made much more difficult in the developing countries due to factors such as:

1 Lack of infrastructure
2 Strict government regulations
3 Irrational decisions (or so they appear to the onlooker)

As a result, project management is least effective in developing countries, and cost control goes out of the window. In Chapter 5 this point was made very clearly when we surveyed the various fertiliser projects constructed in India over the years: look again at Figure 5.2. Some of the other developing countries, particularly in the Middle East and the Far East have had to face all the problems that are to be faced in India, *plus* many more, typical of which are:

1 Lack of a skilled labour pool
2 Lack of middle level managers

These factors can only make the problem of proper project management and cost control even more difficult. Such factors also contribute significantly to construction costs, even assuming effective cost control. This is one of the reasons why construction costs in such countries can double, or even treble, as compared with what happens elsewhere in the world. This will also account for the glaring differences in capital investment for seemingly identical projects, when one studies the published information. It is not necessarily wrong: only that the circumstances are so very different.

Once the plant is built, the problems are not over. The plant has to be operated and maintained, and these same factors will affect those costs as well. However, that aspect of the matter is beyond the scope of this present book. The fact remains, however, that in planning and setting up major projects in countries lacking the facilities noted above, the owner-consultant-contractor team must view the situation as a whole and realise what may be missing. Otherwise, we can well have white elephants – a rarity even in

India – dotted all over the place. This would, of course, be a sheer waste of both national and international resources.

### The basic principles do not change with size

We have already said in this chapter and in several earlier chapters, particularly in Part 1, that the basic principles of good project management and cost control remain the same, whatever the context. Size makes no difference. Location makes no difference. Language makes no difference.

In this present chapter we have sought to get a feel of what is implied in this area in projects of all sizes, right up to the billion dollar range, where the majority of our readers may well say: 'What has that to do with me?' But the small can still learn from the large – *and* the large from the small. Large projects call for more money, more men, and they have many more activities. By the same token, therefore, there are a great many more things that can go wrong. So management has to be more careful.

So let us repeat yet once more: no matter what the size of the project with which we are concerned, the basic principles of project management and cost control remain the same. Because a project is bigger, the systems do not have to be more complex. A small project deserves and should receive just as much careful and considered attention from the very beginning. A small tragedy is no less a tragedy, just because it is small. The principles have been discussed at length in Part 1, and their application in Parts 2 and 3 of this book. Throughout, we have tried to show you cost control in action, by bringing forward the results on actual projects.

### Let's listen – at least for now!

The havoc created by cost and time overruns on process plant projects has been amply demonstrated in Chapter 5, where we hoped that if you were forewarned, you would be forearmed. Did you listen? Or did you say: that will never happen to one of our projects. Did you realise that a ten per cent overrun on capital cost, with its concomitant time delay, can cause a 25 per cent drop in the rate of return on the project? Did you notice that one year's delay in completion of an ammonia plant, where the profit margin is small, will delay the break-even point by more than four years?

These are the *direct* losses. The indirect losses, though more difficult to assess, are undoubtedly much greater. Delays are not only very expensive for those who have to pay for them, but we all suffer from the loss and waste of scarce resources. If we could save ten per cent on ten plants, we could build another one for nothing! What is the moral of all this?

Is it not all too obvious, seeing how long everyone has been at it, that we did not listen *then* – when we built our last project. We know what happened. It was very painful. The project, when completed, had to live with the consequences. Many an owner has had to live with a lossmaker for years, labouring constantly in an endeavour to transform the situation, and make a profit. Think how much happier everyone would have been had it never happened: had it been a success from the word 'go'.

So, the next time we start, let us listen to the past, try and be a little wiser, try and learn from the mistakes we and others have made in the past, so that the same mistakes are not repeated time and again.

This is indeed vital. We take up this theme in greater detail in Chapter 14, where we ask the question: Will we ever learn? But most contractors, whose daily bread and butter this is, are already aware of the problem. At times even they are called in to 'rescue' a project and on this background one contractor had this to say:

> *The light at the end of your tunnel could be a freight train.*
> In the engineering and construction of process facilities it is easy to promise an early completion date ... but not easy to deliver. To use an analogy, you may get deep into the tunnel, only to find that the light at the other end is an oncoming freight train. Delays can seriously jeopardise a project's feasibility – but by then it will be much too late to do much, if anything, about it.
>
> As contractors, we know how disastrous an inaccurate initial estimate can be. A number of times in recent years we have been called in to rescue projects where costs and construction time have gotten out of hand. We know that unmet schedules can increase the total economic cost of a project by *25% or more per year* of the original capital cost. So we take into account potential management and financing difficulties, as well as engineering, procurement, construction and operating problems, before we bid. Others may match our initial bid, but no-one can match our record of completing process facilities on time, in budget. And they run. For any job, large or small, our experience really pays.
>
> Next time you're considering a project, ask for a bid from us. It is the best way to avoid getting run over by overruns.

They think they know. Perhaps they do; experience is everything in this game of project management.

## References

1  Rose, L. M., *Engineering investment decisions*, Elsevier, 1976, 477 pp.

2  Wei, J., T. W. P. Russell and M. W. Swatzlander, *The Structure of the Chemical Processing Industries – Functions and Economics*, McGraw-Hill, New York, 1979, 397 pp.

3  Brochure: 'Ok-Tedi – ready for the production of gold', published by the Mining and Metals Division of Bechtel Civil and Minerals, Inc., California, USA.

4  Stallworthy, E. A. and O. P. Kharbanda, *Total Project Management from Concept to Completion*, Gower, 1983, 329 pp.

5  Sloan, A. P., Jr., *My Years with General Motors*, Doubleday, 1972, 560 pp.

# 14 Will we ever learn?

We remember reading somewhere that 'cost control is the name of the game', followed by a series of statements illustrating the all pervading influence that cost control *should* have, from the conception of a project to the final demise of the plant and its scrapping. Cost control principles should influence:

1 *Feasibility studies* – they are made to determine the profitability of a project
2 *Equipment* – each item of equipment should be designed for optimum operation and possible purchase at an economic cost
3 *Design* – the entire plant should be designed with cost in mind
4 *Implementation* – suppliers and contractors are chosen on the basis of competitive tendering
5 *Operation* – the plant should be operated and maintained economically
6 *Disposal* – when the plant ceases to make a profit, the asset should be disposed of in the most economical way

We have been concerned in this book with the central phases in this sequence of events, covered broadly by the words 'design and implementation'. We have sought to demonstrate cost control *in action*. What is the action?

## The key actions

One basic outline of the cost control function goes thus:

1 Monitor and report cost at all stages of a project;
2 Evaluate and project cost trends;

3 Produce forecasts of final cost for the total project and specific elements within the project;
4 Provide cost data sufficiently ahead of events to permit decisions to be made in full knowledge of the effect on the cost of the project.

Simple and direct. Not our own words, precisely, but adapted from a statement made by a past President of the American Association of Cost Engineers in the USA. We began by demonstrating that cost control was really as old as time: it has been in existence as a separate discipline now for some thirty years. Yet we felt it necessary to set out an approach that would result in a series of activities as described above.

In our approach, we have continually emphasised the need for the projection of cost trends: the need to provide final cost forecasts: the need to forecast a completion date: the need to provide this information early: the need to watch this dynamic entity and see where it is going. Why is this reemphasis necessary? We say reemphasis, because it has all been said many, many times before. These are the difficult areas in cost control, and we tend to forget, ignore the unpleasant and the difficult as fast as we learn it. Cast your mind back over the holidays you have had from year to year. Which do you remember vividly after many years – the good or the bad? Yes, we forget very easily, and the more easily when the thing is unpleasant.

## The 'forgetting' curve

Like everything else these days, even forgetting has been formalised. We hear a lot about the 'learning curve'. Did you know that there was also a 'forgetting curve'? Somewhere, sometime – we have forgotten when and where! – we saw a very illuminating little graph over the title: 'A picture to think about'. This diagram, which we reproduce as Figure 14.1 was, we were told, developed for the promotion of continuing education and professional development. This being so, we feel sure that there can be no objection to our making the point once again: this is what the authors are anxious for everyone to do. This is a further attempt to promote the same idea: that not only the beginners but also the professionals have a lot to learn. The implications of the graph are quite clear, when we consider its lesson in the field of project cost control. It is still true, very true, that each new project is approached by owner and contractor alike, almost as if they had never built a plant before.

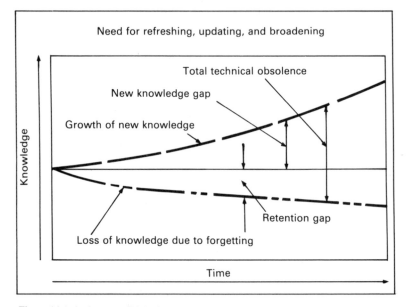

**Figure 14.1 A picture to think about**
To quote: 'a diagram for the promotion of continuing education and professional development. I leave you to ponder its meaning.' (Author unknown.)

Part of that is due, of course, to a law discovered by students of human behaviour. To quote:

> All human activity systems have this characteristic – the solution of one set of perceived problems creates another set.

So need we wonder, if we forget so easily, and continuously create problems, that now as we write, and next year, and in the years to come, they will still be 'implementing cost information systems to provide benefits' – the provision of information which is *more* timely, *more* readily accessible, *more* accurate than at present, making a *more* profitable utilisation of human skills.

Yes, whilst we have had much to say about management techniques and have emphasised the need for sound *simple* management – we also have to realise that both the managers and the managed are people – individuals with weaknesses, frailties, ambitions, longings and desires. A new book on making money that has become a cult with US investors contains nuggets of Swiss wisdom that are very relevant in this context (1). For instance, we have stressed the importance of sound planning, but always in what we might fairly call a 'short-term' context, even although many projects can take five years or more from concept to completion. The distilled wisdom here declares:

Long-range plans engender the dangerous belief that the future is under control.

This comment incorporates a very important principle which should never be lost sight of. The future is uncertain, no matter how refined the technique which you may be using for forecasting purposes. Another very human failing is a reluctance to recognise the inevitable. The comment here is:

When the ship starts to sink, don't pray. Jump.

The lesson there is that the cost control engineer should never be afraid to speak the whole truth, whatever the consequences. We read one paper dealing with what happens when a project overruns in terms of cost. The writer outlines the way in which he feels the problem should be tackled and has a section headed: 'abandon if necessary' (2). We are told that when a new project overruns its budget, managers should seek causes before remedies. One is warned against indiscriminate cost cutting and advised rather to recost the entire project. If, following such a review, the project is not viable, then it should be abandoned. The comment is made that the number of bad projects that reach the operational stage serve as proof that their supporters often balk at this decision. There are a number of reasons for what amounts to irrational behaviour when such a crisis occurs and it is a brave project manager indeed who dares to recommend abandonment once a project is well on the way. But it should be done when the situation demands it. Once again, we come up against very human traits: the desire to save a reputation, the fear that one's career will be wrecked. The solution lies in good management, yet once again. The good project manager will face up to the decisions he has to make and make them, however unpleasant the results may be. Almost invariably the good decision is the hard decision to take and there is no 'soft option'. Yet to let the project drift on is a sure recipe for disaster.

We need to maintain that same critical approach to the systems we employ, even the systems we have recommended in this book. They have stood the test of time, but there is always the possibility of improvement. We have mentioned the implications of 'forgetting', but Peter Drucker suggests that there are some things that are better forgotten (3). Indeed he proposes a policy of 'systematic abandonment'. Everything we do should get a regular 'live-or-die' scrutiny. This automatically demands innovation, since the gaps left by discontinued procedures would have to be filled. This analytical approach would encourage the habits of flexibility and continuous learning, with the result that change would be accepted as normal and providing opportunity. So we reiterate: you are never too old to learn and learning should be a continuing process – always!

The last point we wish to make in this context is that since 'learning' should be a continuous process, it should – nay, *must* – be going on throughout each and every project. The several parties to the contract – owner and contractor alike – should not only be learning, but sharing their newly acquired knowledge. We learn most from the mistakes that are made as a project goes forward and this means that those who observe those mistakes should be *constructive* in their criticism, not destructive. If this is true then those who make mistakes will not be so likely to conceal them whenever that is possible. We should not be embarrassed by the mistakes we make or the weaknesses that may be exposed. Far better to see them in full view, so that the reasons for failure may be established. Then we will do better next time. It is still true, as it has always been true, that 'the man who never made a mistake never made anything'. We know this is true – we have made a good many ourselves!

**Take the time**

Having looked at a number of 'real life' projects to learn from them, it has become apparent that whilst the project itself may be full of high technology, may demand a high level of technical skill in design, the *management* of that project and the cost control systems should remain straightforward, even simple. May we repeat yet once again our acronym as being very sound advice in this context: *KISS* – *K*eep *I*t *S*imple, *S*tupid! – although, if that sounds a little arrogant, perhaps we should have kept with the version we have brought to you more than once in this book: *K*eep *I*t *S*tupid *S*imple.

It does appear, however, that the planning and particularly the pre-planning, is one very important ingredient in success. The proper time must be taken in planning the project before it is set on the road and by this we mean not only the project itself, but also the project administration in all its detail. Competent subcontractors also contribute much to the success of a project and competence is very largely the result of experience. This may be summed up in two simple rules:

1 Take the time to make a sound assessment of project cost and duration *before* you start
2 Always ask yourself to what extent this project is a 'development' project, and then try to make the appropriate allowances for that fact.

We have also learnt that change costs dear and everyone with any experience of project work knows this very well indeed, yet changes will still come. With the best will in the world to 'freeze' the scope of a project and so inhibit change, it never works in practice. So the administrative procedures must take full account of the possibility and legislate for it.

## Let both past and present teach us

We have already said that it seems as if each new project is approached as if it was the first. Let us try and get away from this. Let us try and avoid starting each and every project with, as it were 'a blank piece of paper'. This applies to every discipline involved, but more especially to the conceptual process and engineering design. Each and every new project *must* have the lessons of the previous work that has been done both available to it, *and* built into it.

How are we going to achieve this? At the end of each project the project team should prepare a technical and commercial report of 'dos and don'ts' for study and action. Each project starts with what is euphemistically called a 'kick-off' meeting: let it end with a 'final whistle' report. What is more, this report should be compulsory reading for management, including in particular the project teams not involved in that particular project.

This applies to both the managing contractor and the owner. We know at least one owner where one of the rules with respect to new construction is the writing of what is called a 'construction report'. This has, says the contract, to be produced by the managing contractor within three months of the end of the project. What happens? Contractors are only human: the report tells us how clever they were, and then proceeds to gather dust on the shelves. No: both owner and contractor should write reports for their own edification, not the edification of others. The report should highlight the weaknesses that have been discovered, the lessons to be learnt. But we have yet to see such a report written and widely published amongst those whom it most concerns. The situation is not helped by the fact that those involved tend to disperse as the project draws to a close, taking their knowledge with them.

But, in any event, learning should be limited to examining what has happened at the end of the project, in order to apply the lessons next time round. Learning should also be going on whilst the project is in progress. To achieve this we should make more effective use of the monthly project progress meetings. See them, not as a 'blame placing' exercise, but as part of the 'learning process' for all concerned. We should also encourage everyone involved – owner, contractor, supplier – to be *constructive* in their criticism, so that *all* may learn. Let us be open with one another. Do not hide things because we might be embarrassed by the mistakes or weaknesses exposed. It is still true, even in this day and age, that 'the man who never made a mistake never made anything'.

We should also be able to learn from the others in the business. We should therefore use the intelligence reports that come to us about the way in which our competitors' projects are going. We should seek to hear about these things, not to 'crow', but so that we can use the knowledge to our own advantage, learning from one another even though we may be in competition.

Another trap that we can easily fall into is to become rigid and bigoted in our approach, especially in the fields of administration and project management. But we must learn to be flexible, and recognise that others can also have ideas as well as we. The managing contractor, for instance, should try and find out why certain owners, certain suppliers, prefer information presented in a certain way, even though it may be in conflict with his own methods and practice. This is a basic need – the subject of 'good communications' rearing its head once again.

Now a brief exhortation. Never try to be too clever. The simple approach almost invariably pays off in the end. By all means use the latest techniques and methodology, but remember at all times to control costs. Do not spend £100 unnecessarily when £10 will do the job just as well. Man seems to have a tremendous ability to complicate problems which cry out for simple solutions. Common sense is so often the key, but so rarely applied. We have been trying to make what is perhaps quite a dry subject palatable, because we want to drive home the lesson that it really can be interesting, simple to understand: the simple approach being completely effective. We have emphasised that today's decisions are tomorrow's costs and that the *only* way to control cost is – not to spend the money!

It is true that cost control can only be improved if those who are involved are provided with relevant information, that will enable them to take action to avoid costs. We control when we take action to avoid waste. We control when we take action to correct a deviation from the target or standard that we have set up. If we know what is going on, but are unable to act, then that is *not* control: nor is finding out what has happened after the event. To ensure that cost control is effective we must look carefully at what we mean by control, and then know how we propose to go about it. These are the simple, fundamental factors surrounding what we are trying to do.

One simple thing has been brought forward time and again: watch the trend. Let us look at that just once more.

## The trend curve

We have laid continual emphasis on the need for early warning, and the way in which trends must be studied and projected if we are indeed to receive early warning. Trend extrapolation, whilst highly desirable and giving clarity of perspective, particularly in times of considerable uncertainty, can nevertheless be a dangerous tool. It *can* mislead. To quote A. K. Cairncross:

> A trend is a trend is a trend. The question is: when will it bend? Will it climb higher and higher, or eventually expire, and come to an untimely end?

We quote these words because they may stick in your memory and help you appreciate, as you look forward – and it is the proper thing to do – that we are fallible. 'The best laid schemes o' mice an' men gang aft a-gley' (Burns) is a saying particularly appropriate to investment in new process plants and if we can but minimise the risk of a disastrous outcome, then the means that we use to that end can but be welcome, even if they are not 100 per cent effective, and infallible. So let us, despite the fact that the future is full of uncertainty, examine the trend, heed its warnings, even if at times it leads us in the wrong direction. Success in the end depends upon a large number of individual actions, many of them small, but which, if neglected, can imperil the whole. To quote:

> the provision of a bag of nuts and bolts at the right time and place – especially if they are of the right length and diameter – may well bring its due reward ...

And this is true. The work on the project, which leads to the finished result, is indeed built up from thousands of small, individual actions which make or mar. We have sought to be practical and down-to-earth. The management techniques that have been presented, derived from the best laid schemes o' the men of industry, can also be of great value to the mice.

## Is it success or failure?

Discussions on project cost control are often fruitless because all that is actually discussed are the various problems that were encountered on the project. But those problems, burdensome though they may have been at the time, rarely have anything to do with cost control. To take an example, a strike could occur in a basic industry such as steel manufacturing or transport, which would delay all the suppliers to a particular project, delaying completion and causing costs to escalate. Management would be concerned at the increase in cost but, nevertheless the project team could have done an excellent job so far as cost control was concerned.

On the other hand, an underrun is not necessarily a cause for pride. An underrun can give a great deal of satisfaction to both owner and contractor but the cost control could still have been extremely inefficient. Better control could have resulted in greater savings. It was just that the estimate was too high in the first place. A good estimate, but the plant was built on a 'buyer's market'.

It is very apparent, from all this, that the budget estimate, set up right at the beginning, when so little was known about it all, is nevertheless the arbiter of our destiny. For better or worse, it becomes the standard of comparison from the moment that it has been made and accepted. So we emphasise yet again the importance of the decisions made, the estimates prepared, the plans developed, in those early days. Let them be good. Take the time to make them good. It is time well spent.

## Conclusion

Let us make one last comparison. We have compared our efforts to climbing a mountain, piloting a plane, being captain of a ship, fighting a battle, conducting an orchestra. Let us conclude by saying that building a process plant is rather like *painting a picture*. The project manager, the design engineers, the procurement and construction personnel are the ones who actually paint the picture, or achieve the result. The cost control engineers and the accountants provide the frame which enables the picture to be clearly seen. So then, if the project manager and his team do not think and practise cost control, then costs will *not* be controlled, however elegant the frame: however sophisticated the cost control techniques: however many cost control engineers are employed.

The next point that we have to appreciate – and we have spent a lot of time making it – is that the picture has been drawn in outline, and its size set, at a very early stage in the project. Most of the time is spent in filling in the detail. What was that? 'Cost control occurs when the engineering decisions are made'.

Of course, the *real conclusion* is the completed plant, built within budget, and making a profit. This is the objective: this is the goal to which one and all should be striving. If that end result is in fact achieved, it should not be seen as a matter for pride, rather should it have been a humbling experience. So much could have gone wrong, but did not. Many things did go wrong, largely due to ignorance, but sometimes it was indeed just bad luck. The end result would never have been achieved but for the cooperation of a multitude of people doing humdrum, routine jobs. All played their part.

## References

1  Gunther, M., *The Zurich Axioms*, Souvenir Press Ltd, 1985.
2  David, D. M., 'New projects: beware of false economies', *Harvard Business Review*, March–April 1985, pp. 95–101.
3  Wilson, J. W., review of 'Innovation and entrepreneurship', by Peter F. Drucker, Harper & Row, 1985, in *Business Week*, 10 June 1985, pp. 7–8.

# APPENDICES

# Appendix A  A typical position description

**Department** : Project Team

**Position** : Manager, Project Cost Control

**Reports to** : Project Manager

**Responsibilities**: Establish, build up, maintain and improve a system for project cost control and the related estimating and reporting activities appropriate to the proposed project, in accordance with the principles set out in the 'Cost and Progress Control Manual' and the related 'Material Management Manual', together with the relevant sections of the project specification.

This will include, inter alia:

1  (a)  Institute and maintain the appropriate administrative procedures in order to enable the above responsibility to be properly discharged.
   (b)  Ensure the systematic development of site current estimates and cost control reports.

2  Receive commitments data from various sources, and data on the progress of work in the field from the various main and/or subcontractors for further progressing, including analysis and the preparation of the relevant reports.

3  Establish and maintain a system of monetary control on all bulk materials ordered, which can be related to the physical disposition of those materials.

4  Establish and maintain specific cost control activities in

relation to open contracts (for example, cost plus or schedule of rates contracts), giving advice on the validity of invoices received, and appraisal of the efficiency or otherwise of such contracts, using the appropriate norms.

5 Establish and maintain a system of cost control, involving the comparison of actual with forecast progress in terms of both money and erection manhours, in order to discern trends, and report on exceptions, for others to take action as may be appropriate.

6 Provide forecasts, based on site current estimates, of the cash flow for the various separate projects constituting the investment.

7 Provide a service in relation to spot checks on the site activities, to enable reports to be issued on the effectiveness of the utilisation of labour, on the validity of work in progress appraisals made by the main contractors for the payment of subcontractors.

8 Contribute to the negotiation of contracts and variations to contracts for site work, estimating and agreeing where appropriate the value of such contracts, prior to approval by the Project Manager.

9 Coordinate with other departments both within the Project Team and at Head Office, to ensure that the projects are executed efficiently.

10 Coordinate with the Engineering and Finance Departments of the Owner to ensure that project cost control procedures are harmonised, and that there is a proper exchange of experience and data.

# Appendix B    Code of accounts for process plant construction

## Design and engineering

01  *Design and engineering services by owner*
Process and engineering design work, where provided in whole or in part by the owner, directly related to the project.
02  *Design and engineering services provided by contractors*
Process and engineering design work, provided in whole or in part by a managing contractor or contractors, consultants and the like.
03  *Project supervisory services – owner*
General supervisory services provided by the owner in head office, or on site, with cost of support services, allocated in the form of overhead.
04  *Project supervisory services – contractor*
Site supervisory services provided by a managing contractor. The supervisory services provided by subcontractors are considered to be part of the direct cost of the works they are doing, and allocated with the appropriate cost code.

## Civil works

10  *Building and civil engineering works*
The costs, including materials, labour, supervision, preliminaries and similar expenses (including the contractor's overheads and profit) for the construction of building and civil engineering works, as described in detail under cost codes 11–19.

11 *Site preparation and development, including fencing*
The cost of developing the site, including levelling, removal and supply of soil, reclamation of land, dredging and fencing, with gates and the like.

12 *Roads and railways*
Roads (including trenching, cleaning, scrubbing, scraping and topping), dykes, railroads, bridges, parking areas.

13 *Piling*
Piling for foundations, tanks, retaining walls, channels, including sheet piling whether temporary or permanent, including the provision of all the necessary pile-driving equipment and the piles (but not pile-capping).

14 *Foundations and concrete substructures*
Foundations, pump blocks, footings, supports, sleepers, ground floors, pipe trenches, cable trenches, sumps, oil catchers (including skimming devices, but excluding pumps, drives and pipelines): paving, gutters, trench covers, curbs, angles, including excavation, backfill, gravel, sand, cement, timber, reinforcing rod and fabric, HD bolts embedded in the concrete.

15 *Buildings (above DPC level)*
Concrete, brick, masonry and steel framed buildings, houses, main offices, churches, clubs, schools, hospitals, clinics, gate houses, fire stations, canteens, control houses, switch houses, pump houses, including natural ventilating systems, windows, doors, gutters, down pipes, sanitary equipment and plumbing, and chimneys part of the building structure.

16 *Steel structures*
All steel structures other than those forming part of a building, or supplied as an integral part of an item of equipment, for the support of, or access to columns, vessels, and other plant and equipment, including pipebridges, supports, masts (but not lighting masts), platforms, railings, staircases, gratings, hoisting beams. (Note: travelling cranes, hoist blocks, and special rails are part of cost code 25.)

17 *Storm and water drainage*
Storm and water drainage systems for the discharge of rain water, domestic water and other waste, including soil drains, but excluding chemical effluents. Purely mechanical work such as steel pipelines, pumps, is excluded. Works include gutters, sumps, channels, trenches, weirs and culverts.

18 *Effluent drainage*
Chemical and other process effluent drainage systems, including separating, purification, clarification and filtering equip-

ment, including mechanical equipment related thereto, with gutters, sumps, channels and trenches.

19  *Arboricultural amenity works*
Architectural and aesthetic treatment of the site, with land-scaping, provision of trees, shrubberies, grass areas and the like, but excluding grass sown to bind surface soil or sand (which comes in cost code 11, Site preparation).

## Mechanical works

20  *Columns*
Strippers, absorbers, fractionators, scrubbers, evaporator columns, extraction columns, including all internals, such as linings, trays, fillings, and externals provided with column, such as manhole covers, davits and brackets.

21  *Unfired heat transfer equipment*
Reboilers, coolers, condensers, heat exchangers, chillers, scraper type exchangers (including drives), condensers and cooling boxes (including coils and supports), barometric condensers (including ejectors), evaporators, suction heaters, preheaters, and waste heat boilers, including all accessories such as gaskets, bolts, linings, test rings

22  *Tanks and vessels, MS*
Vessels operating at atmospheric pressure and those operating above or below atmospheric pressure, with all internals such as blades, partitions, heating or cooling coils or jackets, fabricated from mild steel materials (including nickel steels for low temperature applications).

23  *Tanks and vessels, alloy*
Vessels operating at atmospheric pressure and those operating above or below atmospheric pressure, with all internals, such as blades, partitions, heating or cooling coils and jackets, fabricated from alloy steels, non-ferrous metals and synthetic materials such as glass, fibre glass, rubber, keebush and the like.

24  *Tanks and vessels, lined*
Vessels operating at atmospheric pressure and those operating above or below atmospheric pressure, with all internals, such as blades, partitions, heating or cooling coils and jackets, fabricated primarily from mild steel, and lined; for instance with rubber, pentaphane, glass, teflon, special paints, or other metals.

25  *General plant and equipment*
Furnaces, heaters, ovens, kilns, incinerators, including related stacks, flues, ducting, tubes, air heaters, induced and forced draught fans (including drives), soot blowers, burners, vacuum filters, filter presses, centrifuges, cyclones, extruders, mills, kneaders, dryers, screens, crystallisers.
Mechanical handling equipment, including equipment for the transport of materials or personnel, including elevators, conveyors, hoisting and lifting equipment, stackers and lift trucks, trucks, tractors and trailers, locomotives, marine small craft, miscellaneous vehicles: packing plant. Lifts are included in cost code 40.

26  *Pumps, compressors, fans, blowers*
Reciprocating, centrifugal, rotary, screw and miscellaneous pumps, including bedplates, couplings, gearboxes, and reciprocating steam engine, turbine or electric motor drives to such pumps.
Reciprocating, centrifugal, screw and other compressors, vacuum pumps, induced and forced draught fans and blowers, including bedplates, couplings, gearboxes, and reciprocating steam, gas or oil engines, turbine or electric motor drives to such units.
Electric motors purchased separately and delivered to the manufacturer for mounting are, however, considered to be part of the electrical function, and allocated to cost code 46.

27  *Mixers, stirrers, agitators*
Mixing, stirring, agitating and scraper devices, including gearboxes and also including drive if integral with device. Electric motors purchased separately and delivered to the manufacturer for mounting, however, are allocated to cost code 46.

28  *Fixed inventory*
Portable machinery and tools for workshops and stores, consisting of small tools, pneumatic tools, welding equipment and the like, and fixed plant and machinery for mechanical, electrical, carpentry, instrument and other workshops: storage racks and bins: machine tools.
*Note*: This cost code also includes such equipment when requisitioned in the first place for construction purposes, and retained on the project, credit being given for all such equipment ultimately passed to general construction stores in a usable condition.

29  *Erection*
All site costs related to the erection of the plant and

equipment included in cost codes 20–28, including the provision of all necessary temporary facilities, construction plant and equipment, scaffolding, skilled and unskilled labour and supervision.

30  *Process pipe and fittings*
Screwed, welded, socketed, pipe in mild steel or alloy, or non-ferrous materials, including all linings, coatings, CI fittings and ductwork. Flanges, weld fittings, screw fittings, gaskets, bolts, nuts, expansion fittings: steam traps, strainers, filters, hoses, pipe support brackets and anchors.

31  *Process valves*
Gate, globe, check, butterfly valves and dampers in mild steel, stainless steel, copper, metal or other alloys, lined valves and valves fabricated from synthetic materials.

32  *Off site fabrication of pipe and fittings*
The fabrication by a manufacturer in his shops of pipework and fittings requisitioned under cost code 30, including the value of such pipe materials when purchased from the fabricator as part of his work.

38  *Site erection of pipework*
The fabrication and erection on site of the pipe, fittings, valves, and/or fabricated pipework enumerated in cost codes 30–37 (33–37 are spare).

39  *Site erection, general*
The site erection of plant, equipment, pipework on process units, as detailed under cost codes 20–37.
*Note*: This cost code to be used only when it is not possible to requisition the work separately, as detailed in cost codes 29 and 38.

## Electrical works

40  *Electrical equipment (general)*
Electrical equipment, materials and supplies. This cost code is only to be used when analysis of requisitions under cost codes 42–48 is not possible. Telecommunications equipment, radio, special electronic equipment, lifts, fire alarm systems. Telephone installations, when purchased and not part of PTT service.

41  *Spare*

42  *Transformers*
Transformers, batteries, rectifiers and protective apparatus (capacitors, reactors, resistors).

43  *Switchgear, starters and controllers*
HV (over 650 V) switchboards, busbar chambers, isolating
switches (air break or oil immersed), with related metering and
control devices. MV (250–650 V) switchboards, busbar
chambers, isolating switches (air break or oil immersed), with
related metering and control devices. Motor starters and
controllers, push button stations.

44  *Power wiring*
HT and LT wires, cables, distribution boxes, channels, rails
and racks, connectors, earthing systems, cable markers,
insulation materials (tapes, liquids, compounds), insulators,
poles, lightning conductors.

45  *Lighting systems*
Lamps, lamp fittings and accessories, lighting cable and
conduit, switchboards, switches, fuses, distribution and cable
boxes, socket outlets.

46  *Motors*
Motors, where purchased separately, are to be requisitioned
under this cost code. Where the motor is requisitioned with the
equipment it serves, and so purchased from the supplier of that
equipment, it carries the cost code of that equipment.

47  *Electrical services, LV*
LV (under 250 V) services to instruments and instrument
panels, mobile tools, emergency lighting, with cabling,
switches, distribution boxes, outlet sockets.

48  *Site erection of electrical equipment*
The site erection of electrical equipment, materials and
supplies requisitioned under cost codes 40–47.


**Instrumentation**

50  *Instrumentation (general)*
Instruments, including flow, level, pressure, temperature
instruments, analytical instruments, switches actuated by a
hydraulic, pneumatic or electric impulse, pneumatic or electric
relays, thermocouple assemblies, thermocouple extension
cable, instrument panels.

51  *Control valves (instrumentation)*
Instrumentation valves only (that is, not motor driven on–off
valves), operated pneumatically, electrically or hydraulically,
with or without integrally mounted controllers. Air reducing
valves, steam reducing valves, valve positioners, actuating
cylinders.

52  *Instrumentation installation materials*
Instrument installation materials, such as nameplates, instrument air piping (including copper tubing, fittings, but excluding air headers and main supply lines, which are in cost codes 56–59), air headers behind panels, air valves, conduit and conduit fittings for instrument cables, flexible metallic tubing, cable channels (solid or perforated), instrument pressure piping and fittings. Equipment for instrument air supply, such as instrument air compressors, with drives and coolers, air vessels and air dryers, are included in cost code 61.

53  *Site erection – instrumentation*
Installation on site of instrumentation materials, including items pre-assembled off site, as included in cost codes 50–53, including calibration and testing.

## General services

56  *Services pipe and fittings (supply only)*
Screwed, welded, socketed, MS, CI, alloy or plastic pipe, including all linings and coatings: pipe fittings: pipe support brackets, expansion fittings, steam traps, strainers, filters in pipelines.

57  *Services valves*
Gate, globe, check, plug, butterfly valves and dampers in mild steel, stainless steel, copper, metal and other alloys, lined valves and valves manufactured in synthetic materials.

58  *Off site fabrication of services pipework*
The fabrication by a manufacturer in his shops off site of pipework, utilising the pipe and fittings requisitioned under cost code 56, including the value of such materials when requisitioned from the fabricator.

59  *Site erection, services pipework*
The fabrication and erection on site of the pipe, fittings, valves, included in cost codes 56, 57 and 58.

60  *Service equipment*
Plant and equipment as required for compressed air services.

61  *Instrument air service*
Instrument air compressors, air dryers and related equipment for instrument air services.

62  *Vacuum service*
Vacuum pumps and related equipment for vacuum services.

63   *General services equipment*
Plant and equipment as required for general services, including oil storage tanks, pumps, heaters, loading and unloading facilities, storage for nitrogen and other gases, brine services.

64   *Fire protection service*
Sprinkler systems, hydrant and other similar piped systems for fire protection purposes, hose reels.
*Note*: Fire doors, whilst specified by services, will be requisitioned as part of the building, cost code 15. Miscellaneous 'loose' fire fighting equipment will be requisitioned under cost code 81.

65   *Water purification and treating*
Treaters, softeners, chlorinators, clarifiers, filters, screens, rotating screens (including drives) and ancillary equipment, with related instrumentation.

66   *Cooling towers*
Forced or induced draught cooling towers, including fans and drives, water basins, circulating pumps, control systems.

67   *Steam service*
Fired steam generators, including waste heat boilers, flue gas boilers, with all auxiliary equipment and accessories, such as superheaters, desuperheaters, air heaters, induced and forced draught fans (including drives), pumps (including drives), soot blowers, flue stacks (including those in brick, stone or cement), insulation, platforms, steel structures, instrumentation, internal pipework, ducting, fuel handling (but not storage), ash disposal plant.

68   *Electrical generating equipment*
AC and DC generators, including related drives and all control equipment, such as switchgear, and service equipment, such as metering, lubricating oil installations, related HP and LP piping, circulating pumps, with buildings.

69   *Air conditioning and heating service*
Air conditioning and heating installations, including plant for heating and domestic water services, ventilation fans (with drives), heaters and filters: air filters and washers, automatic louvre and shutter systems (but not natural ventilation systems): heating and chilled water piping systems, lagging, steel structures, ducting and instrumentation. Refrigation plant as required solely for HV and C duties.

70   *Refrigeration service*
Refrigeration plant units, with pumps and compressors, and including local pipework, valves and fittings (but not

distribution pipework): instrumentation, metering, storage equipment, anti-freeze systems, insulation and steel structures.

## Preservation

71 *External insulation*
External heat and cold insulation, including personnel protection, for columns, vessels, pipelines, pumps, tanks, heat transfer equipment (excluding oil furnaces and steam generating equipment, where it is considered part of the service supply), including all materials, and installations.

72 *Painting*
Paint, varnish, and the application thereof to plant, equipment, pipework.
*Note*: Painting to buildings included in cost code 15. Galvanising to steelwork included with steelwork supply, for instance in cost code 16.

## Miscellaneous

80 *Laboratory equipment*
Specialised equipment, glassware, experimental apparatus and supplies for use in laboratories.
*Note*: Benches and services included with building, cost code 15.

81 *Miscellaneous fire fighting and safety equipment*
Trucks, trailers, foamite, extinguishers, crash tenders, safety supplies (clothing, boots, goggles, masks, respirators): similar loose equipment for personnel protection. Initial supply only.

82 *Testing and initial startup*
Provision of engineers and supervisory staff for initial testing and startup of plant and equipment, with standby of necessary trades, such as mechanical, electrical and instrumentation, prior to commissioning.

83 *Catalyst and chemicals*
The initial supply of transformer and lubricating oils, fresh or used catalyst, acids, soda, when treated as 'capital'.

84 *Spare parts*
Capital (or insurance) spare parts, spare parts (for one year's operation), spare parts for startup and commissioning. This cost code does not include installed spares, or standby equipment.

85 *Miscellaneous supplies*
Medical equipment and supplies, first aid equipment, warehouse equipment, other items not specified elsewhere.

86 *Remedial site work*
Expenses involved in repairs or alterations to plant in course of construction, occasioned by the restitution of items subject to damage or replacement due to theft, fire, accident, wilful damage, sabotage and the like.

87 *Rectification work*
Expenses involved in repairs or alterations to plant on setting to work, to achieve guarantees or other commitments, or during any maintenance period which is part of the original supply contract. (These costs can arise after a project has been physically closed.)

88 *Travelling expenses*
All expenses incurred in the sending out of engineers, specialists, supervisors, such as board, lodging, travelling expenses, allowances and the like, when separately charged.

89 *CIF expenses*
Packing, transport costs, dock charges, dues on imported items, where charged as a separate expense.

90 *Packing and handling*
Packing, storage and handling costs, including warehousing, when items are assembled and handled off plot for shipment in bulk, or storage prior to further processing.

91 *Carriage*
Carriage and trans-shipment costs, when not incorporated in the cost of equipment. This applies particularly when coordinated deliveries to site are arranged, with 'group' or 'bulk' transport, chartering of ships, etc.

92 *Insurance premiums*
Premiums for insurance of works, 'all risks' insurance, third party insurance, where effected specifically for the project.

93 *Import duties*
Import duties, where not included in the cost of supply. Can also be used to segregate such costs, when they are recoverable.

94 *Exchange rate variance*
Variance between amounts paid, and amounts booked to a specific cost code, where fixed exchange rates are used for project costing purposes, in relation to imported equipment or supplies.

# Appendix C  Typical coordination procedure check list

The coordination procedure, discussed in Chapter 11 in the section headed 'Project organisation and definition', establishes the scope and detail of the various documents that will be exchanged between the several parties involved in the project and the manner in which those documents shall be circulated and stored. The use of a 'check list' should ensure that no significant aspects are overlooked.

**Section 1  Introduction**

    1:1   Object of document
    1:2   Scope of work
    1:3   Terms used

**Section 2  General policy**

    2:1   Relationship between parties
    2:2   Facilities and information from owner

**Section 3  Coordination with owner**

    3:1   Project description
    3:2   Project references and addresses
    3:3   Correspondence to and from owner
    3:4   Minutes of meetings with owner
    3:5   Contractor's progress reports

302 APPENDICES

3:6 Project programme
3:7 Approvals by owner
3:8 Change notice procedure
3:9 Code of accounts (cost code)
3:10 Project numbering system
3:11 Documentation issued to owner
3:12 Project information to be provided by owner

**Section 4 Coordination within contractor's organisation**

4:1 Project team and their responsibilities
4:2 Contractor's key personnel – titles and reporting line
4:3 Coordination with owner and other parties
4:4 Recording and distribution of documents
4:5 Project memos and instructions
4:6 Minutes of internal meetings
4:7 Progress reports for owner and contractor

**Section 5 Introduction to project**

5:1 Brief description of project
5:2 Basic contractual arrangements
5:3 Scope of contractor's services
5:4 Scope of contractor's supply
5:5 Scope of owner's supply and services

**Section 6 Engineering**

6:1 General
Design philosophy, standards, codes, units of measurement, spare parts, etc.
6:2 Process requirements and design
6:3 Project and package units
6:4 Piping
6:5 Heat transfer equipment, vessels, painting and insulation
6:6 Mechanical and rotating machinery
6:7 Instruments
6:8 Electrical

**Section 9 Drawings**

**Section 10 Documentation**

**Section 11 Financial and accounting**

**Section 12 Import Procedures**

**Section 13 Site arrangements**

# Appendix D    Index to a project specification

The 'project specification' describes the 'work' that the contractor will be required to do and the manner in which he has to do it. The 'conditions of contract' define the terms and conditions under which the contractor will carry out that 'work'. Hence, although the project specification is of prime importance and of continuing interest to all involved in the execution of the contract, it remains subject to the 'conditions of contract' and hence an annex to those conditions, all as set out below.

## INDEX

**Exhibit 1   Conditions of contract**

5.0 Construction
6.0 Advisory startup and training services
7.0 Technical support services

**Section 2 Technical information**

A *Process description*
   1.0 Description of basic product plant
   2.0 Process description, unit 100
   3.0 Process description, unit 200
   4.0 Process description, unit 300
   5.0 Process description, unit 400
   6.0 Steam factor and spares/standby policy
   7.0 Instrumentation
   8.0 Final storage of product
   9.0 Provision of packaging equipment
  10.0 Specialised equipment
  11.0 Future expansion
  12.0 Buildings
  13.0 Battery limits

B *Site information*
   1.0 Description of site
   2.0 Utilities
   3.0 General facilities

C *General design requirements*
   1.0 Standards
      1.1 Local standards and codes of practice
      1.2 American (ASA) standards and their related codes
      1.3 Company standards, codes and design requirements
   2.0 Units of measurement

**Exhibit 2 Information required in proposal**

   1.0 *Financial proposal*
      1.1 Financial quotation
      1.2 Target price
      1.3 Estimate of cost of construction

# Appendix E   Typical project manager's report

Part of a typical project manager's report to the owner. The report relates to Case 1, as discussed in Chapter 12 – Successful case histories

## Design engineering

1   *Process engineering*
Process design work for the contract is complete apart from back-up work related to additions and modifications to the Engineering Line Diagrams (ELDs).

The ELD for the firewater system is being reviewed and modifications to this diagram will be required. ELD symbols and abbreviations (ELD No. 1) has now been prepared and issued.

The preparation of the refinery operating manual is continuing.

2   *Civil design*
General arrangement drawings for the process compressor foundations have been issued to site, and this completes the issue of general arrangement drawings for the process area. The remaining compressor foundations and reinforcement details will be completed and issued in three weeks.

The drawing for the holding basin has not been issued, pending a decision regarding the use of seawater or fresh water for the fire fighting system. (Normally, the refinery fire system will be charged with fresh water, but should an appreciable fire break out, then seawater will be used, then later the system will be flushed out with fresh water.)

Work has not yet started on the grade pipe track in the offsite area, but this will be started soon, when piping details are received.

Work on the utility area foundations will continue during May, with the issue of further drawings.

Steelwork drawings for the process area have been completed, but some vendor's drawings for equipment supporting structures have not yet been received. These are being expedited.

A preliminary design for the diesel generator building has been prepared and issued for comment in-house.

Drawings for the steelwork for the workshop and for various pipe supports in the utilities area have been issued for comment.

Architectural general arrangement drawings for the buildings are now some 95 per cent complete, with the detail drawings being prepared. Providing local import tax does not change all doors and windows for these buildings will be exported from the UK, since investigation has shown that doors and windows available locally have also been imported from Europe and are more expensive than direct imports from the UK.

The strength of concrete poured at site has continued to improve during the last two months, as demonstrated by test cube crushing results. The improvement is attributed to close quality control at site and the use of a new batch of clinker at the local cement works.

3  *Piping design*
Work has continued on finalising piping studies and the general arrangement drawings, and in the preparation of the piping isometrics. Outstanding study and general arrangement draughting is limited to work in the utility area, holding basin area, and the firewater sprinkler systems in certain areas. Necessary information needed for this work to proceed is being expedited. A total of 500 'isometrics' have been issued to date, and this work is to programme.

The material take-off has been revised to incorporate the latest information. Additional minor materials have been requisitioned as necessary.

4  *Mechanical design*
Delays in the receipt of vendor's drawings are now being

reduced, and the drawings for the diesel generators and fire pumps have been received.

5    *Fabricated equipment design*
     Work is continuing in providing other groups with back-up technical information.

6    *Instrument design*
     Preliminary quotations (budget prices only) have been received for the main control and trip cubicles. Final quotations should be available next month. Most instruments and control valves are now on order and progress on instrumentation work is generally in accordance with programme.

7    *Electrical design*
     Power, layout and cabling drawings have been modified to suit the new position of the settler and the necessary amendment orders issued to cover these changes. Lighting and power layouts for the workshop, laboratory, utilities and LPG Area are still outstanding due to lack of information, as are the cable schedules and material take-offs for these same areas. As reported in the Civil Design section above, building layout work is progressing and the necessary information will be available very soon for the Electrical Design Group.

**Procurement**

Further replacements, spares and additional requirements for construction equipment have been placed on order during the last period.

Additional concrete mixers and dumpers have been procured to increase the capacity and flexibility for concrete manufacture and pouring on site.

A programme based on latest deliveries for equipment and drawings has been prepared at site and is currently being reviewed. When this programme has been finalised it will be possible to bring up to date the final estimate of the cost for the project, but this will depend largely on the quantity of pipework to be erected and the productivity and the mechanical erection.

**Site progress**

1    *Electricity*

Temporary installation complete except for the fabrication shop/stores building.

2 *Telephones*
Installation complete except for the fabrication shop/stores.

3 *Telex*
No success yet. A further letter has been sent to the owner for assistance in expediting this particular matter.

4 *Camp*
Complete, except for one 40 man unit now being completed. Amenity building is now in use, including restaurant.

5 *Pipeline*
a) Pipetrack being graded.
b) Distribution of supports in progress.
c) Excavation complete.
d) Still awaiting T-bar for the remainder of the supports.
e) Road crossing complete, except for barriers.

6 *Refinery drainage*
Work has commenced on the permanent septic tank located near the administration building.

7 *Water mains*
Filtration plant work still continues. There is some difficulty with the supply of materials.

8 *Culverts*
No work in progress. The drawings have still not been released for construction by the home office.

9 *Major civil foundations*
a) F-101 excavated, blinded, shuttering fixed, rebar fixed.
b) H-101, 102, 103, 104, 105 Base complete, columns still to pour, and H.D. bolts to fix.
c) P-101, A, B, V-101 excavated, blinded, shuttering fixed, rebar fixed.
d) V-105, 106, 107, 108 Base complete, columns still to pour.
e) V-204, 206, 208, P-206 A/B Base complete, but not backfilled.
f) P-301 A/B, P-302 A/B, V-305, 307, 308 Base complete, columns shuttered.

g) H-305, 307 A/B, V-306 Base complete, columns, shuttered.

h) H-301, V-301, 302, 303, 304 Base excavated, blinded, shuttering fixed, rebar fixed.

*Note*: It is imperative that all bases for concreting be released without any further delay to avoid complete disorganisation in the construction programme.

10 *Tankage*

a) Bases. Main tank from area complete. Intermediate tankage area 90 per cent complete.

b) Erection

T 1001 – 12.00% approx. complete
T 1002 – 31.00% approx. complete
T 1014 –  0.71% approx. complete
T 1015 –  0.71% approx. complete
T 1017 –  0.89% approx. complete
T 1018 –  8.00% approx. complete
T 1019 –  7.00% approx. complete
T 1020 –  9.00% approx. complete

Erection percentage complete: approx. 10% of total erection.

11 *Shipping*

Chartered ship with steel plates docked last week. Liaison between site and home office shipping departments now satisfactory. Home office shipping must avoid despatching two ships at the same time with large cargoes, as neither site nor port has the resources to handle two ships simultaneously. Better coordination with the shipping lines is necessary to enable arrivals at the port to be improved.

12 *Drawings*

Drawings for pipetracks, supports, etc., within refinery are urgently required on site.

13 *Welding school*

Progressing satisfactorily. First group of welders on loan to tank fabricator. Second group ready to commence welding on pipework. Third group still in training.

The report would also have sections on finance and other matters of interest, but these are not relevant in this context.

# Index

*Italic* numerals refer to figures